W9-BYP-906

THE WOMEN'S RIGHTS MOVEMENT

OPPOSING VIEWPOINTS®

Other Books in the American History Series:

The American Frontier
The American Revolution
The Bill of Rights
The Civil Rights Movement
The Civil War
The Cold War
The Creation of the Constitution
The Great Depression
Immigration
Isolationism
Puritanism
Reconstruction
Slavery

THE WOMEN'S RIGHTS MOVEMENT
OPPOSING VIEWPOINTS®

David L. Bender, *Publisher*
Bruno Leone, *Executive Editor*

William Dudley, *Series Editor*
John C. Chalberg, Ph.D., professor of history,
    Normandale Community College, *Consulting
    Editor*

Brenda Stalcup, *Book Editor*

Greenhaven Press, Inc.
San Diego, California

Cover photographs, clockwise from top: 1) World War II riveter at the Lockheed Aircraft Corporation (Library of Congress); 2) headquarters of the National Association Opposed to Woman Suffrage (Library of Congress); 3) suffragist demonstrating during the 1918 general election (Archive Photos); 4) 1976 Equal Rights Amendment march in Springfield, Illinois (UPI/Bettmann)

Library of Congress Cataloging-in-Publication Data

The women's rights movement : opposing viewpoints / Brenda
    Stalcup, book editor.
        p.   cm. — (American history series)
    Includes bibliographical references and index.
    ISBN 1-56510-367-X (lib. bdg. : alk. paper) —
ISBN 1-56510-366-1 (pbk. : alk. paper)
    1. Women's rights—United States—History. 2. Women—
United States—History. I. Stalcup, Brenda. II. Series: American
history series (San Diego, Calif.).
HQ1236.5.U6W685   1996
305.42'0973—dc20   95-51244
                                                       CIP

© 1996 by Greenhaven Press, Inc., PO Box 289009,
San Diego, CA 92198-9009

Printed in the U.S.A.

Every effort has been made to trace the owners of copyrighted material.

"America was born of revolt, flourished in dissent, became great through experimentation."

Henry Steele Commager

Contents

Foreword   9

Introduction   15

Chapter 1: Early Debates on Women's Rights

Chapter Preface   24

1. Women Should Have More Legal Rights   26
   Abigail Smith Adams

2. Women Do Not Need Additional Legal Rights   30
   John Adams

3. Women Should Not Take Part in Public Reform   34
   Catharine E. Beecher

4. Women Should Take Part in Public Reform   39
   Angelina Emily Grimké

5. Woman's Sphere Is Fulfilling   46
   Mrs. A.J. Graves

6. Woman's Sphere Is Restrictive   54
   Margaret Fuller

Chapter 2: Beginnings of a Movement

Chapter Preface   63

1. Men Have Not Purposely Subjugated Women   65
   Henry W. Bellows

2. Men Are Responsible for Women's Oppression   70
   William Lloyd Garrison

3. Dress Reform Is Vital to Women's Equality   75
   Gerrit Smith

4. Dress Reform Is Not Essential to Women's
   Equality   83
   Frances D. Gage

5. Divorce Laws Should Be Liberalized   88
   Elizabeth Cady Stanton

6. Divorce Laws Should Not Be Liberalized   98
   Antoinette Brown Blackwell

7. Feminists Should Not Object to the Fifteenth
   Amendment   108
   Wendell Phillips

8. The Fifteenth Amendment Should Include
   Women   114
   Parker Pillsbury

Chapter 3: The Era of the "New Woman"

Chapter Preface   120

1. Higher Education Harms Women   122
   Edward H. Clarke

2. Higher Education Does Not Harm Women   127
   Elizabeth Stuart Phelps

3. American Women Should Have the Right
   to Vote   132
   Julia Ward Howe

4. American Women Should Not Have the
   Right to Vote   140
   Emily P. Bissell

5. Family Size Should Not Be Limited   147
   Theodore Roosevelt

6. Women Should Have Access to Birth Control   152
   Margaret Sanger

Chapter 4: The Women's Liberation Movement

Chapter Preface   158

1. Women Should Be Housewives and Mothers   160
   Jennifer Colton

2. Women Should Work Outside the Home   165
   Betty Friedan

3. Abortion Should Be Legalized   170
   Marya Mannes

4. Abortion Should Not Be Legalized   176
   Robert F. Drinan

5. A Lesbian Perspective on Women's Liberation   183
   Radicalesbians

6. Feminists Do Not Have to Adopt a Lesbian
   Lifestyle   190
   Anne Koedt

7. The Equal Rights Amendment Should Be Passed   197
   Margaret M. Heckler

8. The Equal Rights Amendment Should Not
   Be Passed   202
   Phyllis Schlafly

Chapter 5: Historical Evaluations of the Suffrage Movement

Chapter Preface   210

1. Suffrage Was Not a Radical Reform   212
   William L. O'Neill

2. Suffrage Was a Radical Reform   228
   Ellen Carol DuBois

For Discussion   239
Chronology   242
Annotated Bibliography   248
Index   257

Foreword

Aboard the *Arbella* as it lurched across the cold, gray Atlantic, John Winthrop was as calm as the waters surrounding him were wild. With the confidence of a leader, Winthrop gathered his Puritan companions around him. It was time to offer a sermon. England lay behind them, and years of strife and persecution for their religious beliefs were over, he said. But the Puritan abandonment of England, he reminded his followers, did not mean that England was beyond redemption. Winthrop wanted his followers to remember England even as they were leaving it behind. Their goal should be to create a new England, one far removed from the authority of the Anglican church and King Charles I. In Winthrop's words, their settlement in the New World ought to be "a city upon a hill," a just society for corrupt England to emulate.

A Chance to Start Over

One June 8, 1630, John Winthrop and his company of refugees had their first glimpse of what they came to call New England. High on the surrounding hills stood a welcoming band of fir trees whose fragrance drifted to the *Arbella* on a morning breeze. To Winthrop, the "smell off the shore [was] like the smell of a garden." This new world would, in fact, often be compared to the Garden of Eden. Here, John Winthrop would have his opportunity to start life over again. So would his family and his shipmates. So would all those who came after them. These victims of conflict in old England hoped to find peace in New England.

Winthrop, for one, had experienced much conflict in his life. As a Puritan, he was opposed to Catholicism and Anglicanism, both of which, he believed, were burdened by distracting rituals and distant hierarchies. A parliamentarian by conviction, he despised Charles I, who had spurned Parliament and created a private army to do his bidding. Winthrop believed in individual responsibility and fought against the loss of religious and political freedom. A gentleman landowner, he feared the rising economic power of a merchant class that seemed to value only money. Once Winthrop stepped aboard the *Arbella*, he hoped, these conflicts would not be a part of his American future.

Yet his Puritan religion told Winthrop that human beings are fallen creatures and that perfection, whether communal or individual, is unachievable on this earth. Therefore, he faced a paradox: On the one hand, his religion demanded that he attempt to live a perfect life in an imperfect world. On the other hand, it told him that he was destined to fail.

Soon after Winthrop disembarked from the *Arbella*, he came face-to-face with this maddening dilemma. He found himself presiding not over a utopia but over a colony caught up in disputes as troubling as any he had confronted in his English past. John Winthrop, it seems, was not the only Puritan with a dream of a heaven on earth. But others in the community saw the dream differently. They wanted greater political and religious freedom than their leader was prepared to grant. Often, Winthrop was able to handle this conflict diplomatically. For example, he expanded, participation in elections and allowed the voters of Massachusetts Bay greater power.

But religious conflict was another matter because it was grounded in competing visions of the Puritan utopia. In Roger Williams and Anne Hutchinson, two of his fellow colonists, John Winthrop faced rivals unprepared to accept his definition of the perfect community. To Williams, perfection demanded that he separate himself from the Puritan institutions in his community and create an even "purer" church. Winthrop, however, disagreed and exiled Williams to Rhode Island. Hutchinson presumed that she could interpret God's will without a minister. Again, Winthrop did not agree. Hutchinson was tried on charges of heresy, convicted, and banished from Massachusetts.

John Winthrop's Massachusetts colony was the first but far from the last American attempt to build a unified, peaceful community that, in the end, only provoked a discord. This glimpse at its history reveals what Winthrop confronted: the unavoidable presence of conflict in American life.

American Assumptions

From America's origins in the early seventeenth century, Americans have often held several interrelated assumptions about their country. First, people believe that to be American is to be free. Second, because Americans did not have to free themselves from feudal lords or an entrenched aristocracy, America has been seen as a perpetual haven from the troubles and disputes that are found in the Old World.

John Winthrop lived his life as though these assumptions were true. But the opposing viewpoints presented in the American History Series should reveal that for many Americans, these assumptions were and are myths. Indeed, for numerous Americans, liberty has not always been guaranteed, and disputes have been an integral, sometimes welcome part of their life.

The American landscape has been torn apart again and again by a great variety of clashes—theological, ideological, political, economic, geographical, and social. But such a landscape is not necessarily a hopelessly divided country. If the editors hope to prove anything during the course of this series, it is not that the United States has been destroyed by conflict but rather that it has been enlivened, enriched, and even strengthened by Americans who have disagreed with one another.

Thomas Jefferson was one of the least confrontational of Americans, but he boldly and irrevocably enriched American life with his individualistic views. Like John Winthrop before him, he had a notion of an American Eden. Like Winthrop, he offered a vision of a harmonious society. And like Winthrop, he not only became enmeshed in conflict but eventually presided over a people beset by it. But unlike Winthrop, Jefferson believed this Eden was not located in a specific community but in each individual American. His Declaration of Independence from Great Britain could also be read as a declaration of independence for each individual in American society.

Jefferson's Ideal

Jefferson's ideal world was composed of "yeoman farmers," each of whom was roughly equal to the others in society's eyes, each of whom was free from the restrictions of both government and fellow citizens. Throughout his life, Jefferson offered a continuing challenge to Americans: Advance individualism and equality or see the death of the American experiment. Jefferson believed that the strength of this experiment depended upon a society of autonomous individuals and a society without great gaps between rich and poor. His challenge to his fellow Americans to create—and sustain—such a society has itself produced both economic and political conflict.

A society whose guiding document is the Declaration of Independence is a society assured of the freedom to dream—and to disagree. We know that Jefferson hated conflict, both personal and political. His tendency was to avoid confrontations of any sort, to squirrel himself away and write rather than to stand up and speak his mind. It is only through his written words that we can grasp Jefferson's utopian dream of a society of independent farmers, all pursuing their private dreams and all leading lives of middling prosperity.

Jefferson, this man of wealth and intellect, lived an essentially happy private life. But his public life was much more troublesome. From the first rumblings of the American Revolution in the 1760s to the North-South skirmishes of the 1820s that ultimately produced the Civil War, Jefferson was at or near the center of American political history. The issues were almost too many—and too crucial—for one lifetime: Jefferson had to choose between sup-

11

porting or rejecting the path of revolution. During and after the ensuing war, he was at the forefront of the battle for religious liberty. After endorsing the Constitution, he opposed the economic plans of Alexander Hamilton. At the end of the century, he fought the infamous Alien and Sedition Acts, which limited civil liberties. As president, he opposed the Federalist court, conspiracies to divide the union, and calls for a new war against England. Throughout his life, Thomas Jefferson, slaveholder, pondered the conflict between American freedom and American slavery. And from retirement at his Monticello retreat, he frowned at the rising spirit of commercialism he feared was dividing Americans and destroying his dream of American harmony.

No matter the issue, however, Thomas Jefferson invariably supported the rights of the individual. Worried as he was about the excesses of commercialism, he accepted them because his main concern was to live in a society where liberty and individualism could flourish. To Jefferson, Americans had to be free to worship as they desired. They also deserved to be free from an over-reaching government. To Jefferson, Americans should also be free to possess slaves.

Harmony, an Elusive Goal

Before reading the articles in this anthology, the editors ask readers to ponder the lives of John Winthrop and Thomas Jefferson. Each held a utopian vision, one based upon the demands of community and the other on the autonomy of the individual. Each dreamed of a country of perpetual new beginnings. Each found himself thrust into a position of leadership and found that conflict could not be avoided. Harmony, whether communal or individual, was a forever elusive goal.

The opposing visions of Winthrop and Jefferson have been at the heart of many differences among Americans from many backgrounds through the whole of American history. Moreover, their visions have provoked important responses that have helped shape American society, the American character, and many an American battle.

The editors of the American History Series have done extensive research to find representative opinions on the issues included in these volumes. They have found numerous outstanding opposing viewpoints from people of all times, classes, and genders in American history. From those, they have selected commentaries that best fit the nature and flavor of the period and topic under consideration. Every attempt was made to include the most important and relevant viewpoints in each chapter. Obviously, not every notable viewpoint could be included. Therefore, a selective, annotated bibliography has been provided at the end of each book to aid readers in seeking additional information.

The editors are confident that as this series reveals past conflicts, it will help revitalize the reader's views of the American present. In that spirit, the American History Series is dedicated to the proposition that American history is more complicated, more fascinating, and more troubling than John Winthrop or Thomas Jefferson ever dared to imagine.

John C. Chalberg
Consulting Editor

Introduction

"The women's rights movement raised questions not only about women's appropriate legal and political status as American citizens but also about the very definition of being female or male."

At 10 o'clock in the morning of January 10, 1917, twelve women silently marched to the iron gates of the White House. Holding banners decorated in purple, white, and gold, the women took position in front of the gates. They stood motionless throughout the cold winter day, not responding to the questions or jeers of passers-by. Their banners bore the slogans "Mr. President—What will you do for woman suffrage?" and "How long must women wait for liberty?"

The White House protesters were members of the Woman's Party, an organization that advocated a federal amendment granting women the right to vote. Two days prior to the protest, a delegation from the Woman's Party had met with President Woodrow Wilson, asking him to support women's suffrage. The meeting went badly: Wilson refused to take any public stance promoting the passage of a federal suffrage amendment and advised the suffragists to concentrate on swaying public opinion to their cause.

Wilson's response infuriated the members of the delegation. By 1917, American feminists had been trying to sway public opinion toward women's suffrage for almost seventy years. Some members of the Woman's Party were the second or third generation in their families to work for women's right to vote. In the last few years alone, the Woman's Party had organized huge suffrage parades in major U.S. cities, published pro-suffrage literature, instituted a billboard campaign, and held outdoor rallies. The organization's efforts had revived public interest in the federal suffrage amendment, which was first proposed in 1868: In 1913, the U.S. Congress had held debates on the amendment for the first time in twenty-six years. Thus far, however, Congress had voted against passage of the amendment. The Woman's Party had hoped that Wilson's public endorsement of women's suffrage would garner more public and Congressional support for the federal amendment. Many members of the Woman's Party, dismayed and frustrated over Wilson's refusal to back their cause, decided that a more drastic tactic was necessary to draw attention to women's suffrage.

Harriot Stanton Blatch—herself a second-generation feminist and the daughter of Elizabeth Cady Stanton, a prominent founder of the American women's rights movement—was one of several Woman's Party members who proposed a radical new strategy: picketing the White House. Blatch argued that suffragists should "stand beside the gateway where he [Wilson] must pass in and out, so that he can never fail to realize that there is a tremendous earnestness and insistence back of this measure." Alice Paul, the founder and leader of the Woman's Party, agreed, calling the picketers "a perpetual delegation" to the president and noting that "if a creditor stands before a man's house all day long, demanding payment of his bill, the man must either remove the creditor or pay the bill." The executive committee of the Woman's Party approved the plan, and on January 10th the organization commenced a silent vigil at the White House gates that would ultimately continue for a year and a half. Six days a week, from ten o'clock in the morning until five-thirty in the evening, the suffragists maintained their picket line.

Although the public was familiar with picketing from its use by labor unions, as historian Eleanor Flexner writes, "picketing the White House was novel" and therefore immediately attracted much attention and press coverage across the United States. According to historian Christine A. Lunardini, "thousands of women volunteered their services for picket line duty, ranging in time from one hour to days." The Woman's Party highlighted the diversity of supporters of the amendment by planning a series of special theme days, such as Teachers' Day, Wage Earners' Day, College Day, and days for picketers from individual states. Whether they were able to join the White House picket line or not, many suffragists supported the new strategy. "The work is certainly a distinct service to every woman in America," North Dakota suffragist Mary E. McCumber wrote in a letter to Alice Paul. "There are thousands of women scattered over the country who are watching your achievements with pride and gratitude." Other suffragists, however, were horrified by the picketing, which they considered an inappropriate and overly militant tactic. In particular, the National American Woman Suffrage Association (NAWSA)—an older and more conservative suffrage group that sought to obtain suffrage state-by-state rather than through a national amendment—expressed its disapproval of the picketers and the Woman's Party. On March 9, 1917, Anna Howard Shaw, the former president of NAWSA, declared, "No one can feel worse than I do over the foolishness of their picketing the White House." The leaders of NAWSA quickly distanced themselves from a strategy that they believed could only harm the cause of women's suffrage.

The general public's reaction to the White House picket line was similarly mixed. Some Americans were stirred by the tenacity and dedication of the suffragists who picketed regardless of rain and snow. As newspaper correspondent Gilson Gardner described:

> To see [the picketers] . . . holding their heavy banners, momentarily growing heavier—holding them against a wind that was half a gale—hour after hour, until their gloves were wet and their clothes soaked through . . . was a sight to impress even the jaded senses of one who has seen much.

On the other hand, many Americans who were opposed to women's suffrage cited the picketers' activities as proof that women were not fit to wield the vote. A January 11, 1917, editorial in the *New York Times*, for example, characterized the protesters as "hostile suffragists" and the picketing as "monstrous." Claiming that the militancy of the White House picketers was indicative of women's approach to politics, the editorial asserted:

> That the female mind is inferior to the male need not be assumed. That there is something about it essentially different, and that this difference is of a kind and degree that with votes for women would constitute a political danger is or ought to be plain to everybody.

The primary target of the picketing, President Wilson, himself displayed an equivocal response. Although Wilson frequently tipped his hat to the women as he went through the White House gates, he also rejected their leaders' requests for an official meeting. Despite the controversy created by the picketing, the demonstrators themselves were mainly treated with curiosity—and sometimes sympathy—by sightseeing crowds, the White House guards, and the police.

A Rise in Militancy

This courteous treatment ended shortly after the United States entered World War I on April 6, 1917. Unlike NAWSA, which declared its intention to support the war effort, the Woman's Party refused to commit itself to any cause except women's suffrage. Whereas NAWSA leaders hoped to prove women's patriotism and their fitness for the right to vote by mobilizing women for the war effort, the Woman's Party believed that such actions would hurt the suffrage movement. Expressing the feelings of most Woman's Party members, suffragist Doris Stevens argued:

> We must not let our voices be drowned by war trumpets or cannon. If we do, we shall find ourselves, when the war is over, with a peace that will only prolong our struggle, a democracy that will belie its name by leaving out half the people.

The Woman's Party therefore decided, regardless of the heightened tensions of a nation at war, to continue its daily White House demonstrations. In fact, the organization stepped up its attacks, carrying banners that decried "Kaiser Wilson" or quoted Wilson's own speeches about democracy. The public, once tolerant, increasingly felt that the picketers' actions were an embarrassment to the U.S. government and that they flaunted an appalling lack of patriotism. John Theurer, an indignant citizen, spoke for many Americans when he wrote:

> Now, millions of young men must leave for France and die for their country's honor. Is it right, is it justice to them, that at the same time females, who are no women are permitted to disgrace and insult the government and the manhood of this country?

Angry crowds began to tear the banners away and destroy them, sometimes physically assaulting demonstrators in the process.

On June 22, 1917, picketers Lucy Burns and Katherine Morey were arrested in front of the White House. The banner they carried that day bore a quote from President Wilson's April 2nd war message: "We shall fight for the things we have always held nearest our hearts—for democracy, for the right of those who submit to authority to have a voice in their own government." Over the next few months, many more White House demonstrators were arrested. At first all charges against the suffragists were dropped, but as the situation escalated a number of women were found guilty of obstructing sidewalk traffic and were sentenced to the Occuquan Workhouse in Virginia. During the fall and winter months of 1917, the imprisoned women demanded to be recognized as political prisoners—the first time U.S. citizens ever made such a request—and went on a hunger strike. Reports of forced feedings, unsanitary prison conditions, and guard brutality gave the prisoners the status of martyrs in the eyes of numerous Americans.

However, no other suffrage groups joined the Woman's Party in the picket lines or copied its civil disobedience tactics. Carrie Chapman Catt, the president of NAWSA, declined to protest the treatment of the imprisoned suffragists, and NAWSA continued to publicly disavow the picketers. In a November 13, 1917, article in the *New York Times*, Catt maintained that the methods of the Woman's Party were not effective:

> The pickets make the psychological mistake of injecting into this stage of the suffrage campaign tactics which are out of accord with it. Every reform, every change of idea in the world passes through three stages—agitation, argument, and surrender. We have passed through the first two stages and entered into the third. The mistake of the pickets is that they have no comprehensive idea of the movement and are trying to work this first stage in the third. We stand on the threshold of final

victory, and the only contribution these women make to it is to confuse the public mind.

Catt preferred less radical tactics. Throughout the war, Catt and other NAWSA members working quietly behind the scenes, lobbying politicians and building support for women's suffrage on a state-by-state level. In Washington, D.C., Catt frequently corresponded and met with President Wilson, cultivating an amiable working relationship. Catt promoted an image of NAWSA as a moderate, reasonable, and cooperative organization that represented the political desires of the majority of American women rather than those of a militant minority. Increasing numbers of politicians—including President Wilson—became willing to associate themselves with this moderate suffrage group and to concede to NAWSA's requests.

When the Nineteenth Amendment, which granted women the right to vote, was passed in August 1920, both NAWSA and the Woman's Party claimed primary responsibility for its success. According to NAWSA leaders, the suffragists' victory stemmed from the organization's perseverance and painstaking coalition-building. Members of the Woman's Party, on the other hand, asserted that they had won suffrage through their daring activism and the enormous publicity their protests had generated. Decades later, historians still disagree over which group of feminists was more crucial in obtaining passage of the Nineteenth Amendment. Some historians, such as William L. O'Neill, credit the suffrage victory to NAWSA's moderate campaign. In *Everyone Was Brave: A History of Feminism in America*, O'Neill argues that the Woman's Party's "principal contribution was to seriously embarrass an administration that had already been won over to woman suffrage by the patient, skillful efforts of Carrie Chapman Catt and the NAWSA." Other scholars of the women's rights movement contend that the Woman's Party, by shifting focus away from the state-by-state battle for suffrage and onto the passage of a federal amendment, was essential in rejuvenating the suffrage movement. Historian David Morgan writes in *Suffragists and Democrats* that the Woman's Party was "vital to the success of suffrage by galvanizing not politicians and parties, but suffragists." Yet other historians insist that both groups share equal credit and that women's suffrage could only have been achieved by a combination of moderate and militant strategies.

The Divisions Surrounding Women's Rights

The debates surrounding the final push for the suffrage amendment in the 1910s can serve as an illustration of the differing sides of the American women's rights movement throughout its history. Americans have responded to the majority of feminist issues in one of three ways: opposition to any change, support of moderate and gradual change, and demands for immediate, radical measures. Opponents of feminism generally base their arguments on conceptions of proper male and female roles that have existed far longer than the United States itself. They contend that these traditional roles are based on the inescapable and unalterable biological differences between men and women. In particular, they argue, women's childbearing and childrearing functions ensure women's fundamental difference from men and determine the pattern of women's lives. These opponents believe that women can best achieve personal fulfillment by devoting themselves to the private sphere of home and family, for which they are constitutionally suited, rather than attempting to take on ill-fitting male roles in the public sphere of work and politics. Furthermore, antifeminists assert, women provide contributions to society within the private world that are just as important as those men perform in the public world: Women raise the next generation of American citizens, teaching their children morals and values crucial for the stability of society.

Arguments against granting women the right to vote tended to echo these sentiments. Antisuffragists maintained that women's participation in the political process would adversely affect home life. Who would care for the children while mothers went to the polls to vote, antisuffragists asked, and who would tend to household duties? Arguing that women's suffrage would create dissension between married couples, Orestes A. Brownson, a noted author and editor, wrote in 1869:

> Extend now to women suffrage and eligibility; give them the political right to vote and to be voted for; render it feasible for them to enter the arena of political strife, to become canvassers in elections and candidates for office, and what remains of family union will soon be dissolved. The wife may espouse one political party, and the husband another. . . . Will political rivalry and the passions it never fails to engender increase the mutual affection of husband and wife for each other, and promote domestic union and peace, or will it not carry into the bosom of the family all the strife, discord, anger, and division of the political canvass?

Other opponents of suffrage insisted that women did not need to vote because their male relatives who did have the franchise would always cast their ballots with the women's best interests in mind. Women were fully capable, antisuffragists averred, of privately influencing the political opinions of their fathers, husbands, and sons. Likewise, as Abraham L. Kellogg contended in 1894, women could satisfy their desire to participate in the political process by raising their children to be good citizens:

> Let the hand which rocks the cradle teach the coming young men and women of America the Lord's Prayer and the Ten

Commandments, and you will do more for [women's] emancipation and for every right which you may possess in the whole realm of human rights, than you can do with both hands full of white ballots.

Women's suffrage, opponents believed, would benefit neither individual women nor society and would dangerously weaken traditional gender roles.

Supporters of feminism, whether moderate or radical in their inclinations, also share certain tenets. Feminists contend that the traditional belief in biologically determined gender roles has been used to justify placing women in a state of social and political inequality as compared to men. American women have been unfairly deprived of their constitutional rights and have been denied equal educational and occupational opportunities solely because of their sex, feminists assert. They argue that advances in women's rights would prove beneficial for individual women, family life, and society at large. In this respect, suffragists believed not only that enfranchisement was due to women as part of their rights as citizens but that women would also use the vote to improve society. Jane Addams, a renowned social worker, was one of many suffragists who maintained that women voters in particular would support public reform measures:

> Insanitary housing, poisonous sewage, contaminated water, infant mortality, the spread of contagion, adulterated food, impure milk, smoke-laden air, ill-ventilated factories, dangerous occupations, juvenile crime, unwholesome crowding, prostitution and drunkenness are the enemies which the modern cities must face and overcome would they survive. Logically, its electorate should be made up of those who . . . in the past have at least attempted to care for children, to clean houses, to prepare foods, to isolate the family from moral dangers.

Once women gained the right to vote, advocates insisted, they would be able to actively support laws that would protect children and promote family life.

Although they agree that women's rights should be expanded, American feminists have often divided between those who promote moderate reforms and gradual progress and those who favor radical reforms and rapid advancement. Moderate feminists maintain that the women's rights movement can harm itself if it presents too many challenges at once to the established concepts of women's roles. These feminists warn against radical measures or strategies that could create hostility toward the movement. Women's rights advocates should be pragmatic, the moderate faction argues, and should pursue only those reforms that the general public is prepared to accept. Radical feminists, however, believe that the women's rights movement should not accept compromise in its pursuit of equal rights. Women will never receive full equality if they only work for a few of their rights, the radical side contends. Rather than waiting for public acceptance of feminist goals, they assert, women's rights supporters should use whatever tactics are necessary to draw attention to and win sympathy for their cause.

This split between moderate and radical feminists occurred over the issue of suffrage at the very first women's rights convention, which was held in Seneca Falls, New York, in 1848. The five organizers of the convention had written a list of resolutions demanding certain rights for women. One of the organizers, Elizabeth Cady Stanton, had insisted—over the objections of the others—on including the resolution that "it is the duty of the women of this country to secure to themselves their sacred right to the elective franchise." This call for women's voting rights so upset Stanton's husband that he left town on the day of the convention to avoid the ridicule he thought would surely result. When the resolutions were introduced for consideration, the convention's participants quickly and unanimously approved the first eleven, but controversy broke out over the proposal for women's suffrage. Many expressed the concern that such an unprecedented demand would work against the less controversial proposals and would make the whole movement appear ridiculous. Frederick Douglass, a former slave and famous abolitionist, joined Stanton in persistent support of women's right to vote, and the two were able to sway enough convention members to pass the resolution by a small margin. It took several years, however, for the majority of feminists to back suffrage without hesitation.

Suffrage was only one of numerous issues debated by advocates and opponents of feminism. From colonial times to the late twentieth century, Americans have considered what the rights of women should be in such areas as property ownership, employment outside the home, equal wages, higher education, birth control, and abortion. The viewpoints contained in this volume offer an overview of the variety of debates that have surrounded the American women's rights movement throughout its long history. Although the selections in this book conclude with the 1970s, many of the topics they address remain controversial in the present day, as does the women's rights movement itself. Perhaps the primary reason that these issues continue to be hotly debated is that they raise questions not only about women's appropriate legal and political status as American citizens but also about the very definition of being female or male. In challenging age-old theories of proper male and female roles and behavior, the women's rights movement has had an impact not just on United States history but on women and men around the world. Whether feminism will continue to have an impact—and whether for good or for ill—remains to be seen.

CHAPTER 1

Early Debates on Women's Rights

Chapter Preface

The American Revolution was based on ideals of equality and individual liberties. The United States, the new nation born of the Revolution, experimented with an unprecedented expansion of citizens' political and legal rights as codified in the Constitution and the Bill of Rights. Yet, despite the country's enthusiasm for these revolutionary ideals, the political involvement and legal rights of certain groups remained restricted. In many cases, only property owners were allowed to vote; men who did not own property, the reasoning went, could not be self-sufficient and must therefore work for an employer who might influence their votes through bribes or threats. Similarly, black slaves were prohibited from voting in part because of the strong possibility that their masters would control their votes. Women were also considered to be ineligible for the vote since, legally bound to be obedient to their husbands, they would probably vote as their husbands dictated.

In fact, although the founders of the new republic instituted many legal innovations, for the most part American women remained governed by codes adapted from English common law. Under the common law doctrine of coverture, a married woman's legal identity and rights were covered by her husband. Without her husband's consent, she could not buy or sell property, sign contracts, sue in court, or even make a will. Any property she owned prior to her marriage fell under her husband's control, and in some instances he was legally allowed to sell this property without her consent. If a woman earned any income, her husband was within his rights to appropriate her wages. Her personal property, her household goods, even her clothing belonged to her husband. In theory, at least, single women retained these rights (although in practice their legal affairs were often managed by male relatives). However, single women and married women shared political restrictions: They were excluded from the right to vote and the right to sit on a jury.

Many jurists argued that coverture served to protect women. Husbands were required to support their wives financially and to assume responsibility for any debts their wives might incur or crimes they might commit. English jurist William Blackstone, whose 1765 *Commentaries on the Laws of England* greatly influenced American law well into the nineteenth century, wrote:

By marriage the husband and wife are one person in law; that is, the very being or legal existence of the woman is suspended during the marriage, or at least incorporated and consolidated into that of the husband; under whose wing, protection and cover, she performs everything.

Historian Nancy Woloch asserts that the majority of early American lawyers and jurists saw no need to revise the doctrine of coverture, which they considered to be "a balanced, time-tried system under which a married woman gave up her legal identity in exchange for support and protection."

On the other hand, some jurists maintained that coverture and other aspects of common law inflicted undue legal disabilities on women. In 1803, Virginia jurist St. George Tucker maintained that American women were subject to "taxation without representation; for they pay taxes without having the liberty of voting for representatives." Tucker concluded that "there is little reason for a compliment to our laws for their respect and favour to the female sex." An increasing number of women echoed Tucker's objection to coverture and other aspects of common law. For instance, the earliest organized campaign for women's rights was a twelve-year drive by New York women to win passage of the Married Woman's Property Act. Made law in 1848, the act nullified some coverture limitations by granting married women the right to own real and personal property.

The disparity between the ideals of the American Revolution and the actual rights of women was only one of several factors that prompted some women and men to question the proper status of women in society. As the antislavery movement grew, many of the women who became involved in that cause realized that they suffered under similar political, legal, and social constraints as those of the slaves. The Industrial Revolution caused an upheaval in traditional sex roles by separating the work world and the home. As historian Janet Wilson James contends, "corporations, swallowing up family enterprises . . . , drew the head of the family and his trade from home, leaving his wife . . . no longer his partner [in his livelihood] but an economic parasite." Simultaneously, the Industrial Revolution led to an increase in the number of women who worked outside the home. These changes in the political and social climate of the young nation sparked some of the earliest debates in America over the issue of women's rights.

25

"We . . . will not hold ourselves bound by any Laws in which we have no voice, or Representation."

Women Should Have More Legal Rights

Abigail Smith Adams (1744–1818)

The daughter of a distinguished Massachusetts minister, Abigail Smith Adams never received formal schooling outside the home. She married John Adams in 1764 and raised four children. From 1774 to 1784, a period when her husband was often in Pennsylvania or Europe on government business, Adams took over the management of the family farm and finances. Adams was keenly interested in political issues and advocated American independence in her voluminous correspondence. Many of Adams's letters to her husband during the Revolutionary War also contained vital information about the status of British troops in the Boston area.

The following viewpoint consists of excerpts from three letters in which Adams recommends that American lawmakers give greater consideration to the protection and expansion of the rights of women. The first letter, dated March 31, 1776, was written to her husband, who was then in Philadelphia attending the Second Continental Congress. If the congressional delegates should declare independence from England and form new laws, Adams argues, they should limit the legal authority that men have over women. Current English laws and customs do not provide women enough recourse against harsh treatment from men, Adams contends.

The second section of the viewpoint is taken from an April 27, 1776, letter Adams wrote to political essayist and playwright Mercy Otis Warren after receiving John Adams's reply to her rec-

From *The Adams Papers: Adams Family Correspondence*, vol. 1, edited by L.H. Butterfield (Cambridge, MA: Harvard Univ. Press, 1963), courtesy of the Massachusetts Historical Society, ©1963.

ommendation. Adams expresses her indignation with her husband's response and suggests that Warren might join her in presenting a petition on women's rights to the Continental Congress. Part III of this viewpoint is excerpted from Adams's May 7, 1776, letter to her husband, in which she stresses the hypocrisy of his vindicating the rights of men while denying such rights to women.

Adams and Warren never followed through on the proposal to petition the Continental Congress on the legal status of women. After the United States achieved independence from England, early U.S. law largely duplicated English law in matters concerning women.

I

I wish you would ever write me a Letter half as long as I write you; and tell me if you may where your Fleet are gone? What sort of Defence Virginia can make against our common Enemy? Whether it is so situated as to make an able Defence? Are not the Gentery Lords and the common people vassals, are they not like the uncivilized Natives Brittain represents us to be? I hope their Riffel Men who have shewen themselves very savage and even Blood thirsty; are not a specimen of the Generality of the people. . . .

I have sometimes been ready to think that the passion for Liberty cannot be Eaquelly Strong in the Breasts of those who have been accustomed to deprive their fellow Creatures of theirs. Of this I am certain that it is not founded upon that generous and christian principal of doing to others as we would that others should do unto us. . . .

I long to hear that you have declared an independancy—and by the way in the new Code of Laws which I suppose it will be necessary for you to make I desire you would Remember the Ladies, and be more generous and favourable to them than your ancestors. Do not put such unlimited power into the hands of the Husbands. Remember all Men would be tyrants if they could. If perticuliar care and attention is not paid to the Laidies we are determined to foment a Rebelion, and will not hold ourselves bound by any Laws in which we have no voice, or Representation.

That your Sex are Naturally Tyrannical is a Truth so thoroughly established as to admit of no dispute, but such of you as wish to be happy willingly give up the harsh title of Master for the more tender and endearing one of Friend. Why then, not put it out of the power of the vicious and the Lawless to use us with cruelty and indignity with impunity. Men of Sense in all Ages abhor those customs which treat us only as the vassals of your Sex. Regard us then as Beings placed by providence under your protection and in immitation of the Supreem Being make use of that power only for our happiness.

Abigail Smith Adams, an early supporter of women's rights, was the wife of the second U.S. president and the mother of the sixth.

II

His [John Adams's] Letters to me have been generally short, but he pleads in Excuse the critical state of affairs and the Multiplicity of avocations and says further that he has been very Busy, and writ near ten Sheets of paper, about some affairs which he does not chuse to Mention for fear of accident.

A Saucy Reply

He is very sausy to me in return for a List of Female Grievances which I transmitted to him. I think I will get you to join me in a petition to Congress. I thought it was very probable our wise Statesmen would erect a New Government and form a new code of Laws. I ventured to speak a word in behalf of our Sex, who are rather hardly dealt with by the Laws of England which gives such unlimitted power to the Husband to use his wife Ill.

I requested that our Legislators would consider our case and as all Men of Delicacy and Sentiment are averse to Excercising the power they possess, yet as there is a natural propensity in Humane Nature to domination, I thought the most generous plan was to put it out of the power of the Arbitary and tyranick to injure us with impunity by Establishing some Laws in our favour upon just and Liberal principals.

I believe I even threatned fomenting a Rebellion in case we were not considerd, and assured him we would not hold ourselves bound by any Laws in which we had neither a voice, nor representation.

In return he tells me he cannot but Laugh at My Extrodonary Code of Laws. That he had heard their Struggle had loosned the bands of Goverment, that children and apprentices were dissabedient, that Schools and Colledges were grown turbulant, that Indians slighted their Guardians, and Negroes grew insolent to their Masters. But my Letter was the first intimation that another Tribe more numerous and powerfull than all the rest were grown discontented. This is rather too coarse a complement, he adds, but that I am so sausy he wont blot it out.

So I have help'd the Sex abundantly, but I will tell him I have only been making trial of the Disintresstedness of his Virtue, and when weigh'd in the balance have found it wanting.

It would be bad policy to grant us greater power say they since under all the disadvantages we Labour we have the assendancy over their Hearts

And charm by accepting, by submitting sway.

III

I can not say that I think you very generous to the Ladies, for whilst you are proclaiming peace and good will to Men, Emancipating all Nations, you insist upon retaining an absolute power over Wives. But you must remember that Arbitary power is like most other things which are very hard, very liable to be broken—and notwithstanding all your wise Laws and Maxims we have it in our power not only to free ourselves but to subdue our Masters, and without voilence throw both your natural and legal authority at our feet—

"Charm by accepting, by submitting sway
Yet have our Humour most when we obey."

VIEWPOINT 2

"We know better than to repeal our Masculine systems."

Women Do Not Need Additional Legal Rights

John Adams (1735–1826)

John Adams was a Harvard-educated Massachusetts lawyer who became involved in colonial and revolutionary politics in the 1760s. He served as a delegate to the First Continental Congress in 1774 and the Second Continental Congress in 1775 and 1776, where he played a vital role in the drafting and passage of the Declaration of Independence. Adams subsequently spent several years during and after the Revolutionary War as a U.S. diplomat in France and Great Britain. Shortly after his return from Europe, Adams became the first vice president of the United States; in 1796 he was elected as the second U.S. president.

Part I of the following viewpoint contains excerpts from an April 14, 1776, letter that Adams wrote to Abigail Smith Adams, his wife, in reply to her letter advocating the expansion of women's legal and political rights. In his response, Adams argues that while men may have legal power over women, in practice women rule men. He writes that he "cannot but laugh" at the idea of women threatening to rebel if their demands for additional rights are not met.

The second part of the viewpoint is taken from Adams's May 26, 1776, letter to James Sullivan, a Massachusetts public official and Revolutionary political leader. In this letter, Adams responds to Sullivan's questions about the necessary qualifications for voting. Maintaining that general guidelines must be set to determine who is fit to vote, Adams argues that suffrage should be limited to men who hold property. Women should be excluded from the

From *The Adams Papers: Adams Family Correspondence*, vol. 1, edited by L.H. Butterfield (Cambridge, MA: Harvard Univ. Press, 1963), courtesy of the Massachusetts Historical Society, ©1963; and from *The Works of John Adams*, edited by Charles Adams (Boston: Little, Brown, 1854).

franchise, Adams asserts, not only because they are physically unfit for dealing with political concerns but also because they are dependent on men and would therefore tend to vote as their husbands directed.

I

You justly complain of my short Letters, but the critical State of Things and the Multiplicity of Avocations must plead my Excuse.—You ask where the Fleet is. The inclosed Papers will inform you. You ask what Sort of Defence Virginia can make. I believe they will make an able Defence. . . . The Gentry are very rich, and the common People very poor. This Inequality of Property, gives an Aristocratical Turn to all their Proceedings, and occasions a strong Aversion in their Patricians, to [Thomas Paine's pamphlet] Common Sense. But the Spirit of these Barons, is coming down, and it must submit. . . .

As to Declarations of Independency, be patient. Read our Privateering Laws, and our Commercial Laws. What signifies a Word.

As to your extraordinary Code of Laws, I cannot but laugh. We have been told that our Struggle has loosened the bands of Government every where. That Children and Apprentices were disobedient—that schools and Colledges were grown turbulent—that Indians slighted their Guardians and Negroes grew insolent to their Masters. But your Letter was the first Intimation that another Tribe more numerous and powerfull than all the rest were grown discontented.—This is rather too coarse a Compliment but you are so saucy, I wont blot it out.

Depend upon it, We know better than to repeal our Masculine systems. Altho they are in full Force, you know they are little more than Theory. We dare not exert our Power in its full Latitude. We are obliged to go fair, and softly, and in Practice you know We are the subjects. We have only the Name of Masters, and rather than give up this, which would compleatly subject Us to the Despotism of the Peticoat, I hope General Washington, and all our brave Heroes would fight. I am sure every good Politician would plot, as long as he would against Despotism, Empire, Monarchy, Aristocracy, Oligarchy, or Ochlocracy.—A fine Story indeed. I begin to think the Ministry as deep as they are wicked. After stirring up Tories, Landjobbers, Trimmers, Bigots, Canadians, Indians, Negroes, Hanoverians, Hessians, Russians, Irish Roman Catholicks, Scotch Renegadoes, at last they have stimulated the [women] to demand new Priviledges and threaten to rebell.

John Adams believed that voting rights should be restricted to male property owners.

II

It is certain, in theory, that the only moral foundation of government is, the consent of the people. But to what an extent shall we carry this principle? Shall we say that every individual of the community, old and young, male and female, as well as rich and poor, must consent, expressly, to every act of legislation? No, you will say, this is impossible. How, then, does the right arise in the majority to govern the minority, against their will? Whence arises the right of the men to govern the women, without their consent? Whence the right of the old to bind the young, without theirs?

But let us first suppose that the whole community, of every age, rank, sex, and condition, has a right to vote. This community is assembled. A motion is made, and carried by a majority of one voice. The minority will not agree to this. Whence arises the right of the majority to govern, and the obligation of the minority to obey?

From necessity, you will say, because there can be no other rule.

But why exclude women?

You will say, because their delicacy renders them unfit for practice and experience in the great businesses of life, and the hardy enterprises of war, as well as the arduous cares of state. Besides, their attention is so much engaged with the necessary nurture of their children, that nature has made them fittest for domestic cares. And children have not judgment or will of their own. True. But will not these reasons apply to others? Is it not equally true, that men in general, in every society, who are wholly destitute of property, are also too little acquainted with public affairs to form a right judgment, and too dependent upon other men to have a will of their own? If this is a fact, if you give to every man who has no property, a vote, will you not make a fine encouraging provision for corruption, by your fundamental law? Such is the frailty of the human heart, that very few men who have no property, have any judgment of their own. They talk and vote as they are directed by some man of property, who has attached their minds to his interest. . . .

Your idea that those laws which affect the lives and personal liberty of all, or which inflict corporal punishment, affect those who are not qualified to vote, as well as those who are, is just. But so they do women, as well as men; children, as well as adults. What reason should there be for excluding a man of twenty years eleven months and twenty-seven days old, from a vote, when you admit one who is twenty-one? The reason is, you must fix upon some period in life, when the understanding and will of men in general, is fit to be trusted by the public. Will not the same reason justify the state in fixing upon some certain quantity of property, as a qualification?

The same reasoning which will induce you to admit all men who have no property, to vote, with those who have, for those laws which affect the person, will prove that you ought to admit women and children; for, generally speaking, women and children have as good judgments, and as independent minds, as those men who are wholly destitute of property; these last being to all intents and purposes as much dependent upon others, who will please to feed, clothe, and employ them, as women are upon their husbands, or children on their parents. . . .

Society can be governed only by general rules. Government cannot accommodate itself to every particular case as it happens, nor to the circumstances of particular persons. It must establish general comprehensive regulations for cases and persons. The only question is, which general rule will accommodate most cases and most persons.

Depend upon it, Sir, it is dangerous to open so fruitful a source of controversy and altercation as would be opened by attempting to alter the qualifications of voters; there will be no end of it. New claims will arise; women will demand a vote; lads from twelve to twenty-one will think their rights not enough attended to; and every man who has not a farthing, will demand an equal voice with any other, in all acts of state. It tends to confound and destroy all distinctions, and prostrate all ranks to one common level.

VIEWPOINT 3

"It is neither appropriate nor wise, nor right, for a woman to petition for the relief of oppressed females."

Women Should Not Take Part in Public Reform

Catharine E. Beecher (1800–1878)

The campaign to abolish slavery in the United States was an important antecedent to the women's rights movement. Women took part in the 1833 formation of the American Anti-Slavery Society and often played an active role in the movement by circulating petitions, publishing articles and books, and delivering speeches. Many Americans, however, felt that these abolitionist activities were inappropriate for women. According to the mores of the time, it was improper—even scandalous—for women to publicly express their political opinions and to speak to mixed audiences of men and women. The debate over whether women should be involved in public reform concerns such as abolition would become one of the primary issues of the women's rights movement.

Catharine E. Beecher was among those who criticized the participation of women in political reform movements. A strong advocate of providing education for women, Beecher founded several women's schools, promoted teaching as a career for women, and introduced standardized instruction in domestic science. Although she was devoted to improving women's status as homemakers, Beecher disapproved of women's involvement in activities outside the domestic sphere. In the following excerpts from Beecher's *An Essay on Slavery and Abolitionism with Reference to the Duty of American Females*, she criticizes female reformers—particularly abolitionists—for overstepping the appropriate boundaries of feminine behavior. Women should be subordinate to men,

From *An Essay on Slavery and Abolitionism with Reference to the Duty of American Females* by Catharine E. Beecher (Philadelphia: n.p., 1837).

Beecher argues, and therefore should not endeavor to act like men by publicly participating in reform movements. However, Beecher contends, women can have some influence over political issues by privately and unassertively persuading men to take up their cause.

It has of late become quite fashionable in all benevolent efforts, to shower upon our sex an abundance of compliments, not only for what they have done, but also for what they can do; and so injudicious and so frequent, are these oblations, that while I feel an increasing respect for my countrywomen, that their good sense has not been decoyed by these appeals to their vanity and ambition, I cannot but apprehend that there is some need of inquiry as to the just bounds of female influence, and the times, places, and manner in which it can be appropriately exerted.

It is the grand feature of the Divine economy, that there should be different stations of superiority and subordination, and it is impossible to annihilate this beneficent and immutable law. On its first entrance into life, the child is a dependent on parental love, and of necessity takes a place of subordination and obedience. As he advances in life these new relations of superiority and subordination multiply. The teacher must be the superior in station, the pupil a subordinate. The master of a family the superior, the domestic a subordinate—the ruler a superior, the subject a subordinate. Nor do these relations at all depend upon superiority either in intellectual or moral worth. . . . In this arrangement of the duties of life, Heaven has appointed to one sex the superior, and to the other the subordinate station, and this without any reference to the character or conduct of either. It is therefore as much for the dignity as it is for the interest of females, in all respects to conform to the duties of this relation. And it is as much a duty as it is for the child to fulfil similar relations to parents, or subjects to rulers. But while woman holds a subordinate relation in society to the other sex, it is not because it was designed that her duties or her influence should be any the less important, or all-pervading. But it was designed that the mode of gaining influence and of exercising power should be altogether different and peculiar.

The Power Lawful to Women

It is Christianity that has given to woman her true place in society. And it is the peculiar trait of Christianity alone that can sustain her therein. "Peace on earth and good will to men" is the character of all the rights and privileges, the influence, and the power of woman. A man may act on society by the collision of intellect, in public debate; he may urge his measures by a sense of shame, by fear and by personal interest; he may coerce by the combination of public sentiment; he may drive by physical force, and he does not outstep the boundaries of his sphere. But all the power, and all the conquests that are lawful to woman, are those only which appeal to the kindly, generous, peaceful and benevolent principles.

Unnatural Conduct

In 1837, the General Association of Massachusetts Congregational Churches issued a pastoral letter designed to be read by ministers to their congregations. The third section of the pastoral letter, from which the following excerpt is taken, criticizes women who give public speeches or otherwise participate in public reform measures.

We appreciate the unostentatious prayers and efforts of woman in advancing the cause of religion at home and abroad; in Sabbath-schools; in leading religious inquirers to the pastors for instruction; and in all such associated effort as becomes the modesty of her sex; and earnestly hope that she may abound more and more in these labors of piety and love.

But when she assumes the place and tone of man as a public reformer, our care and protection of her seem unnecessary; we put ourselves in self-defence against her; she yields the power which God has given her for protection, and her character becomes unnatural. . . . We cannot, therefore, but regret the mistaken conduct of those who encourage females to bear an obtrusive and ostentatious part in measure of reform, and countenance any of that sex who so far forget themselves as to itinerate in the character of public lecturers and teachers.—We especially deplore the intimate acquaintance and promiscuous conversation of females with regard to things "which ought not to be named"; by which that modesty and delicacy which is the charm of domestic life, and which constitutes the true influence of woman in society, is consumed, and the way opened, as we apprehend, for degeneracy and ruin.

Woman is to win everything by peace and love; by making herself so much respected, esteemed and loved, that to yield to her opinions and to gratify her wishes, will be the free-will offering of the heart. But this is to be all accomplished in the domestic and social circle. There let every woman become so cultivated and refined in intellect, that her taste and judgment will be respected; so benevolent in feeling and action; that her motives will be reverenced;—so unassuming and unambitious, that collision and competition will be banished;—so "gentle and easy to be entreated," as that every heart will repose in her presence; then, the fathers, the husbands, and the sons, will find an influence thrown around them, to which they will yield not only willingly but proudly. A man is never ashamed to own such influences, but feels dignified and ennobled in acknowledging them. But the moment woman begins to feel the promptings of ambition, or the thirst for power, her aegis of defence is gone. All the sacred protection of religion, all the generous promptings of chivalry, all the poetry of romantic gallantry, depend upon woman's retaining her place as dependent and defenceless, and making no claims, and maintaining no right but what are the gifts of honour, rectitude and love.

A woman may seek the aid of co-operation and combination among her own sex, to assist her in her appropriate offices of piety, charity, maternal and domestic duty; but whatever, in any measure, throws a woman into the attitude of a combatant, either for herself or others—whatever binds her in a party conflict—whatever obliges her in any way to exert coercive influences, throws her out of her appropriate sphere. If these general principles are correct, they are entirely opposed to the plan of arraying females in any Abolition movement; because it enlists them in an effort to coerce the South by the public sentiment of the North; because it brings them forward as partisans in a conflict that has been begun and carried forward by measures that are any thing rather than peaceful in their tendencies; because it draws them forth from their appropriate retirement, to expose themselves to the ungoverned violence of mobs, and to sneers and ridicule in public places; because it leads them into the arena of political collision, not as peaceful mediators to hush the opposing elements, but as combatants to cheer up and carry forward the measures of strife.

If it is asked, "May not woman appropriately come forward as a suppliant for a portion of her sex who are bound in cruel bondage?" It is replied, that, the rectitude and propriety of any such measure, depend entirely on its probable results. If petitions from females will operate to exasperate; if they will be deemed obtrusive, indecorous, and unwise, by those to whom they are addressed; if they will increase, rather than diminish the evil which it is wished to remove; if they will be the opening wedge, that will tend eventually to bring females as petitioners and partisans into every political measure that may tend to injure and oppress their sex, in various parts of the nation, and under the various public measures that may hereafter be enforced, then it is neither appropriate nor wise, nor right, for a woman to petition for the relief of oppressed females.

The case of Queen Esther [biblical queen who interceded on her people's behalf] is one often appealed to as a precedent. When a woman is placed in similar circumstances, where death to herself and all her nation is one alternative, and there is nothing worse to fear, but something to hope as the other alternative, then she may safely follow such an example. But when a woman is asked to join an Abolition Society, or to put her name to a petition to congress, for the purpose of contributing her measure of influence to keep up agitation in congress, to promote the excitement of the North against the iniquities of the South, to coerce the South by fear, shame, anger, and a sense of odium to do what she has determined not to do, the case of Queen Esther is not at all to be regarded as a suitable example for imitation.

In this country, petitions to congress, in reference to the official duties of legislators, seem, IN ALL CASES, to fall entirely without the sphere of female duty. Men are the proper persons to make appeals to the rulers whom they appoint, and if their female friends, by arguments and persuasions, can induce them to petition, all the good that can be done by such measures will be secured. But if females cannot influence their nearest friends, to urge forward a public measure in this way, they surely are out of their place, in attempting to do it themselves.

Viewpoint 4

"The right of petition is the only political right that women have: why not let them exercise it whenever they are aggrieved?"

Women Should Take Part in Public Reform

Angelina Emily Grimké (1805–1879)

Angelina Emily Grimké was born into an upper-class slave-holder family in South Carolina. In 1827, Grimké became a Quaker; two years later, she moved to Philadelphia and joined the Female Anti-Slavery Society, participating in antislavery peti-tion drives and writing abolitionist tracts. In 1837, Grimké and her older sister, Sarah, began a speaking tour of New England, becoming two of the first American women to present public lec-tures in front of audiences of both men and women.

The Grimkés' tour attracted enormous attention because public speeches by women—especially before mixed audiences and on controversial political issues such as slavery—were prohibited by the customs of the day. Catharine Beecher was among the Grimkés' critics. In 1837, she published *An Essay on Slavery and Abolitionism*, addressed to Angelina Grimké, that admonished women who participated in public reform movements. Grimké replied in a series of letters that were collected in 1838 under the title *Letters to Catherine E. Beecher*. Examining Beecher's argu-ments point by point, Grimké contends that they are not upheld by biblical teachings on the role of women. Christian women have the same right and duty to publicly proclaim truth as do men, she asserts. In addition, Grimké defends women's use of the petition in public reform causes, noting that it is the only political right available to women and the only form of representation they have under the law.

From *Letters to Catherine E. Beecher, in Reply to "An Essay on Slavery and Abolitionism,"* *Addressed to A.E. Grimké* by Angelina Emily Grimké (Boston: Isaac Knapp, 1838).

BROOKLINE, Mass. *8th month*, 28*th*, 1837.

DEAR FRIEND: I come now to that part of thy book, which is, of all others, the most important to the women of this country; thy 'general views in relation to the place woman is appointed to fill by the dispensations of heaven.' I shall quote paragraphs from thy book, offer my objections to them, and then throw before thee my own views.

Thou sayest, 'Heaven has appointed to one sex the *superior*, and to the other the *subordinate* station, and this without any reference to the character or conduct of either.' This is an assertion without proof. Thou further sayest, that 'it was designed that the mode of gaining influence and exercising power should be *altogether different and peculiar*.' Does the Bible teach this? 'Peace on earth, and good will to men, is the character of all the rights and privileges, the influence and the power of *woman*.' Indeed! Did our Holy Redeemer preach the doctrines of *peace to our sex* only? 'A *man* may act on Society by the collision of intellect, in public debate; *he* may urge his measures by a sense of shame, by fear and by personal interest; *he* may coerce by the combination of public sentiment; *he* may drive by physical force, and *he* does *not* overstep the boundaries of his sphere.' Did Jesus, then, give a different rule of action to men and women? Did he tell his disciples, when he sent them out to preach the gospel, that man might appeal to the fear, and shame, and interest of those he addressed, and coerce by public sentiment, and drive by physical force? 'But (that) all the power and all the conquests that are lawful to *woman* are those only which appeal to the kindly, generous, peaceful and benevolent principles?' If so, I should come to a very different conclusion from the one at which thou hast arrived: I should suppose that *woman was the superior*, and *man the subordinate being*, inasmuch as moral power is immeasurably superior to 'physical force.'

Christianity and Women's Role

'Woman is to win every thing by peace and love; by making *herself* so much respected, &c. that to yield to *her* opinions, and to gratify *her* wishes, will be the free-will offering of the heart.' This principle may do as the rule of action to the fashionable belle, whose idol is *herself*; whose every attitude and smile are designed to win the admiration of others to *herself*; and who enjoys, with exquisite delight, the double-refined incense of flattery which is offered to *her* vanity, by yielding to *her* opinions, and gratifying *her* wishes, because they are *hers*. But to the humble Christian, who feels that it is *truth* which she seeks to recommend to others, *truth* which she wants them to esteem and love, and not herself, this subtle principle must be rejected with holy indignation. Suppose she could win thousands to her opinions; and govern them by her wishes, how much nearer would they be to Jesus Christ, if she presents no higher motive, and points to no higher leader?

'But this is all to be accomplished in the domestic circle.' Indeed! 'Who made thee a ruler and a judge over all?' I read in the Bible, that Miriam, and Deborah, and Huldah, were called to fill *public stations* in Church and State. I find Anna, the prophetess, speaking in the temple 'unto all them that looked for redemption in Jerusalem.' During his [Christ's] ministry on earth, I see women following him from town to town, in the most public manner; I hear the woman of Samaria, on her return to the city, telling the *men* to come and see a man who had told her all things that ever she did. I see them even standing on Mount Calvary, around his cross, in the most exposed situation; but He never *rebuked* them; He never told them it was unbecoming *their sphere in life* to mingle in the crowds which followed his footsteps. Then, again, I see the cloven tongues of fire resting on each of the heads of the one hundred and twenty disciples, some of whom were *women*; yea, I hear *them preaching* on the day of Pentecost to the multitudes who witnessed the outpouring of the spirit on that glorious occasion; for, unless *women* as well as men received the Holy Ghost, and *prophesied*, what did Peter mean by telling them, 'This is *that* which was spoken by the prophet Joel: And it shall come to pass in the last days, said *God*, I will pour out my spirit upon *all* flesh: and your sons and your *daughters shall prophesy.* . . . And on my servants and on my *handmaidens*, I will pour out in those days of my spirit; and *they shall prophesy.'.* . . .

Thou sayest, 'the moment woman begins to feel the promptings of ambition, or the thirst for power, her aegis of defence is gone.' Can man, then, retain his aegis when he indulges these guilty passions? Is it woman only who suffers this loss?

'All the generous promptings of chivalry, all the poetry of romantic gallantry, depend upon woman's retaining her place as *dependent* and *defenceless*, and making no claims, and maintaining no rights, but what are the gifts of honor, rectitude and love.'

I cannot refrain from pronouncing this sentiment as beneath the dignity of any woman who names the name of Christ. No woman, who understands her dignity as a moral, intellectual, and accountable being, cares aught for any attention or any protection, vouchsafed by 'the promptings of chivalry, and the poetry of romantic gallantry.' Such a one loathes such littleness, and turns with disgust from all such silly insipidities. Her noble nature is insulted by such paltry, sickening adulation, and she will not stoop to drink the foul waters of so turbid a stream. If all this sinful foolery is to be withdrawn from our sex, with all my heart I say, *the sooner the better.* Yea, I say more, no woman who lives up to the true glory of her womanhood, will ever be treated with such *practical contempt.* Every man, when in the presence of true moral greatness, 'will find an influence thrown around him,' which will utterly forbid the exercise of 'the poetry of romantic gallantry.'

What dost thou mean by woman's retaining her place as defenceless and dependent? Did our Heavenly Father furnish man with any offensive or defensive weapons? Was *he* created any less defenceless than *she* was? Are they not equally defenceless, equally dependent on Him? What did Jesus say to his disciples, when he commissioned them to preach the gospel?—'Behold, I send you forth as sheep in the midst of wolves; be ye wise as serpents, and *harmless as doves.'* What more could he have said to women?

Again, she must 'make no claims, and maintain no rights, but what are the gifts of honor, rectitude and love.' From whom does woman receive her *rights*? From God, or from man? What dost thou mean by saying, her rights are the *gifts* of honor, rectitude and love? One would really suppose that man, as her lord and master, was the gracious giver of her rights, and that these rights were bestowed upon her by 'the promptings of chivalry, and the poetry of romantic gallantry,'—out of the abundance of his honor, rectitude and love. Now, if I understand the real state of the case, woman's rights are not the gifts of man—no! nor the *gifts* of God. His gifts to her may be recalled at his good pleasure—but her *rights* are an integral part of her moral being; they cannot be withdrawn; they must live with her forever. Her rights lie at the foundation of all her duties; and, so long as the divine commands are binding upon her, so long must her rights continue.

'A woman may seek the aid of co-operation and combination among her own sex, to assist her in her appropriate offices of piety, charity,' &c. *Appropriate* offices! Ah! here is the great difficulty. What are they? Who can point them out? Who has ever attempted to draw a line of separation between the duties of men and women, as *moral* beings, without committing the grossest inconsistencies on the one hand, or running into the most arrant absurdities on the other?

'Whatever, in any measure, throws a woman into the attitude of a combatant, either for herself or others—whatever binds her in a party conflict—whatever obliges her in any way to exert coercive influences, throws her out of her appropriate sphere.' If, by a *combatant*, thou meanest one who 'drives by *physical force,'* then I say, *man* has no more right to appear as such a combatant than woman; for all the pacific precepts of the gospel were given to *him*, as well as to her. If, by a *party conflict*, thou meanest a struggle for power, either civil or ecclesiastical, a thirst for the praise and the honor of man, why, then I would ask, is this the proper sphere of *any* moral, accountable being, man or woman? If, by *coercive influences*, thou meanest the use of force or of fear, such as slaveholders and warriors employ, then, I repeat, that *man* has no more right to exert these than *woman*. All such influences are repudiated by the precepts and examples of Christ, and his apostles; so that, after all, this appropriate sphere of woman is *just as appropriate to man*. These 'general principles are correct,' if thou wilt only permit them to be of *general application*.

The Right to Petition

Thou sayest that the propriety of woman's coming forward as a suppliant for a portion of her sex who are bound in cruel bondage, depends entirely on its *probable results*. I thought the disciples of Jesus were to walk by *faith, not* by sight. Did Abraham reason as to the *probable results* of his offering up Isaac? No! or he could not have raised his hand against the life of his son; because in Isaac, he had been told, his seed should be called,—that seed in whom all the nations of the earth were to be blessed. O! when shall we learn that God is wiser than man—that his ways are higher than our ways, his thoughts than our thoughts—and that 'obedience is better than sacrifice, and to hearken than the fat of rams'? If we are always to *reason* on the *probable results* of performing our duty, I wonder what our Master meant by telling his disciples, that they must become like *little children*. I used to think he designed to inculcate the necessity of walking by faith, in childlike simplicity, docility and humility. But if we are to *reason* as to the *probable results* of obeying the injunctions to plead for the widow and the fatherless, and to deliver the spoiled out of the hand of the oppressor, &c., then I do not know what he meant to teach.

According to what thou sayest, the women of this country are not to be governed by principles of duty, but by the effect their petitions produce on the members of Congress, and by the opinions of these men. If they deem them 'obtrusive, indecorous, and unwise,' they must not be sent. If *thou* canst consent to exchange the precepts of the Bible for the opinions of *such a body of men* as now sit on the destinies of this nation, I cannot. What is this but *obeying man* rather than God, and seeking the *praise of man* rather than of God? As to our petitions increasing the evils of slavery, this is merely an opinion, the correctness or incorrectness of which remains to be proved. When I hear Senator [William Campbell] Preston of South Carolina, saying, that 'he regarded the concerted movement upon the District of Columbia as an attempt to storm the gates of the citadel—as throwing the bridge over the moat'—and declaring that 'the South must resist the danger in its inception, or it would *soon become irresistible*'—I feel confident that petitions will effect the work of emancipation, *thy*

43

opinion to the contrary notwithstanding. And when I hear Francis W. Pickens, from the same State, saying in a speech delivered in Congress—'Mr. Speaker, we cannot mistake all these things. The truth is, the moral power of the world is against us. It is idle to disguise it. We must, sooner or later, meet the great issue that is to be made on this subject. Deeply connected with this, is the movement to be made on the District of Columbia. If the power be asserted in Congress to interfere here, or any approach be made toward that end, *it will give a shock to our institutions* and the country, the consequences of which no man can foretell. Sir, as well might you grapple with iron grasp into the very heart and vitals of South Carolina, as to touch this subject here.' When I

Ridiculing Women Is a Sin

Many historians believe that Maria Stewart, a free black from New England, was the first American-born woman to deliver public speeches. Stewart lectured primarily on abolition, but in an address on September 21, 1833, she defended the right of black women to speak publicly.

What if I am a woman; is not the God of ancient times the God of these modern days? Did he not raise up Deborah, to be a mother, and a judge in Israel? Did not queen Esther save the lives of the Jews? And Mary Magdalene first declare the resurrection of Christ from the dead? Come, said the woman of Samaria, and see a man that hath told me all things that ever I did, is not this the Christ? St. Paul declared that it was a shame for a woman to speak in public, yet our great High Priest and Advocate did not condemn the woman for a more notorious offence than this; neither will he condemn this worthless worm. . . . Did St. Paul but know of our wrongs and deprivations, I presume he would make no objections to our pleading in public for our rights. Again; holy women ministered unto Christ and the apostles; and women of refinement in all ages, more or less, have had a voice in moral, religious and political subjects. Again; why the Almighty hath imparted unto me the power of speaking thus, I cannot tell. . . .

If such women as are here described have once existed, be no longer astonished then, my brethren and friends, that God at this eventful period should raise up your own females to strive, by their example both in public and private, to assist those who are endeavoring to stop the strong current of prejudice that flows so profusely against us at present. No longer ridicule their efforts, it will be counted for sin. . . .

What if such women as are here described should rise among our sable race? And it is not impossible. For it is not the color of the skin that makes the man or the woman, but the principle formed in the soul. Brilliant wit will shine, come from whence it will; and genius and talent will not hide the brightness of its lustre.

hear these things from the lips of keen-eyed politicians of the South, northern apologies for not interfering with the subject of slavery, 'lest it should increase, rather than diminish the evils it is wished to remove' affect me little.

Another objection to woman's petitions is, that they may 'tend to bring females, as petitioners and partisans, into every political measure that may tend to injure and oppress their sex.' As to their ever becoming partisans, i.e. sacrificing principles to power or interest, I reprobate this under all circumstances, and in *both* sexes. But I trust my sisters may always be permitted to *petition* for a redress of grievances. Why not? The right of petition is the only political right that women have: why not let them exercise it whenever they are aggrieved? Our fathers waged a bloody conflict with England, because *they* were taxed without being represented. This is just what unmarried women of property now are. *They* were not willing to be governed by laws which *they* had no voice in making; but this is the way in which women are governed in this Republic. If, then, *we* are taxed without being represented, and governed by laws *we* have no voice in framing, then, surely, we ought to be permitted at least to remonstrate against 'every political measure that may tend to injure and oppress our sex in various parts of the nation, and under the various public measures that may hereafter be enforced.' Why not? Art thou afraid to trust the women of this country with discretionary power as to petitioning? Is there not sound principle and common sense enough among them, to regulate the exercise of this right? I believe they will always use it wisely. I am not afraid to trust my sisters—not I.

Thou sayest, 'In this country, petitions to Congress, in reference to official duties of legislators, seem, IN ALL CASES, to fall entirely without the sphere of female duty. Men are the proper persons to make appeals to the rulers whom they appoint,' &c. Here I entirely dissent from thee. The fact that women are denied the right of voting for members of Congress, is but a poor reason why they should also be deprived of the right of petition. If their numbers are counted to swell the number of Representatives in our State and National Legislatures, the *very least* that can be done is to give them the right of petition in all cases whatsoever; and without any abridgement. If not, they are mere slaves, known only through their masters. . . .

For the present, [I] subscribe myself,

Thy Friend, A. E. GRIMKÉ.

VIEWPOINT 5

"Home is [woman's] appropriate and appointed sphere of action."

Woman's Sphere Is Fulfilling

Mrs. A.J. Graves (dates unknown)

Throughout much of early American history, men and women were thought of as inhabiting different spheres. According to this philosophy, men spent most of their time and energy outside the home: They worked, transacted financial affairs, participated in political matters, and concerned themselves with the world at large. Women, however, were expected to devote themselves to the domestic sphere—not only performing household chores but also imparting morals and virtues to their children and making home a peaceful sanctuary for their husbands. Many Americans believed that this distinct separation and balancing of gender roles was essential to the harmonious functioning of society.

The following viewpoint is taken from Mrs. A.J. Graves's 1841 book *Woman in America*. Graves expresses concern that many American families are neglecting to cultivate their home life and are becoming too involved in outside activities. Women in particular should concentrate on home and family matters as dictated by biblical scripture, she argues. Regardless of what a woman's specific talents or interests may be, Graves avers, she can find the greatest fulfillment of those capabilities only in the domestic sphere.

From *Woman in America* by Mrs. A.J. Graves (New York: Harper & Bros., 1841).

Next to the obligations which woman owes directly to her God, are those arising from her relation to the family institution. That *home* is her appropriate and appointed sphere of action there cannot be a shadow of doubt; for the dictates of nature are plain and imperative on this subject, and the injunctions given in Scripture no less explicit. Upon this point there is nothing equivocal or doubtful; no passage admitting of an interpretation varying with the judgments or inclinations of those who read. . . . "Let your women keep silence in the churches"—be "keepers at home"—taught "to guide the house.". . . And as no female of the present day can be so presumptuous as to suppose herself included in the miraculous *exceptions* mentioned in Scripture, these apostolic injunctions are doubtless to be considered as binding upon all: and if different views have been advocated, and a different practice has in many instances prevailed, the writer of these pages cannot but look upon such views and such practices as in direct violation of the apostle's commands, and as insidiously sapping the very foundations of the family institution.

The family institution is of God's own appointment, and He has ordered it for the best and wisest purposes. In His own Word we find that the spiritual welfare of the family is a paramount object in establishing the marriage relation. It was not for man's benefit alone that a helpmate was given him, and that he was to be the husband of one wife; for the holy prophet declares the revealed will of God when he says, "And did He not make *one*? yet had He the residue of the Spirit. And wherefore *one*? *That He might seek a godly seed.*" The Scriptures are full of express as well as incidental instruction on this point. We read there that the spiritual interests of children are specially committed to the care of parents, and that there is a blessing promised, or a curse denounced, according to their faithfulness or unfaithfulness in this charge. . . . It is not in our power, we know, to give new hearts to our children; yet towards the attainment of this blessing God has assigned us a work to perform, which He has graciously promised to perfect for us. As reasonably might we expect a harvest from the field we have left untilled and unsown, as to look for the fruits of righteousness in our sons and daughters, if we leave them to grow up from youth to maturity without religious instruction. Some pious parents rely upon their prayers for the conversion of their children; but in this we are called upon to labour as well as to pray. Fervent prayer, we may hope, will be answered with a blessing; but, though it is declared that it availeth *much*, it is nowhere said that it availeth *everything*. . . .

Seeing, then, that the family institution is of Divine appointment, and the Holy Scriptures enjoin upon fathers to be faithful as teachers and rulers in causing their households to "keep the way of the Lord"; at the same time requiring of mothers that they be "keepers at home," that by the influence of their presence, example and instruction they may most effectually promote the welfare of their families, should not all Christian parents honour and cherish this institution far above whatever man has sought out or devised? And they should maintain a jealous watchfulness over the religious movements of the times, lest they be carried away by the spirit of the age contrary to the spirit of the Gospel. The present state of the world, with its stirring appeals, its strong excitements, its public teachings of every kind, and its public occupations and diversions, powerfully tends to depreciate and weaken individual mind and character, and the sacred bonds and responsibilities connected with the domestic relations. By taking a brief survey, therefore, of the state of society, in some of its most prominent characteristics, as it now exists, we shall be the better enabled to judge how far, in following its spirit, even Christian women have deviated from the strict line of duty in regard to their domestic responsibilities.

The Effects of Organized Associations

One of the most striking characteristics of the times is the universality of organized associations, and the high-wrought excitement so frequently produced by them. In these associations, where great numbers assemble together, whatever may be the object intended to be effected, there is a predominating influence which rules all minds, and communicates, as if by contagion, from one to another. When thus uniting in masses, men unconsciously give up their individual opinions, feelings, and judgments, and yield to the voice and the will of those around them. The power of sympathy, so potent in the human breast, makes the nerves of all thrill in unison, every heart throb with the same emotions, and every understanding submit to the same convictions, whether of truth or error, as though one spirit, and heart, and mind animated the whole. . . .

In such union there is a might which has accomplished widespread desolation and ruin, and glorious achievements too, so strikingly manifesting the power of man that he has been ready to deem himself as God in wisdom and greatness. When man is alone, he can form a just estimate of his strength and his weakness; of what God has enabled him to do, and what is denied to human agency. But when he combines his strength with that of others, and sees mighty results, he is tempted to think himself omnipotent. . . .

As a necessary consequence of this all-pervading spirit of association, there is at the present day a striking deficiency of individual and of private action. Our present schemes for human improvement are of a nature to weaken personal effort, to draw mankind from their homes, and to repress the high and holy influences flowing from our social instincts. The education of our youth must be carried on in *masses,* and hence the crowded schoolroom is deemed the most fitting place for the acquisition of knowledge, and the excitement of competition more favourable to its attainment than the love of it for its own sake, based on the instinctive *desire to know,* so early and so powerfully exhibited in childhood. . . .

The Two Spheres

Primarily known for his pro-slavery writings, Thomas R. Dew was a law professor at the College of William and Mary in Williamsburg, Virginia. In his May 1835 article "Dissertation on the Characteristic Differences between the Sexes, and on the Position and Influence of Woman in Society," Dew argues that women are not physically suited for an active life.

The relative position of the sexes in the social and political world, may certainly be looked upon as the result of organization. The greater physical strength of man, enables him to occupy the foreground in the picture. He leaves the domestic scenes; he plunges into the turmoil and bustle of an active, selfish world; in his journey through life, he has to encounter innumerable difficulties, hardships and labors which constantly beset him. His mind must be nerved against them. Hence courage and boldness are his attributes. It is his province, undismayed, to stand against the rude shocks of the world; to meet with a lion's heart, the dangers which threaten him. He is the shield of woman, destined by nature to guard and protect her. Her inferior strength and sedentary habits confine her within the domestic circle; she is kept aloof from the bustle and storm of active life; she is not familiarized to the out of door dangers and hardships of a cold and scuffling world: timidity and modesty are her attributes. . . . Grace, modesty and loveliness are the charms which constitute her power. By these, she creates the magic spell that subdues to her will the more mighty physical powers by which she is surrounded. Her attributes are rather of a passive than active character.

The duty of charity is performed by societies instead of individuals, and thus it fails of its most beneficent effect, both as it regards the giver and the receiver. Neither men nor women think, feel, or act for themselves, and from this it is that we see so few instances of individual greatness, either moral or intellectual. . . .
Men may be personally more free, but their minds they have

surrendered to be controlled by others, by the mass, by the omnipotence of public opinion. "Patient thought," which alone made a Newton, is given up for the ephemeral instruction of the public lecturer; and knowledge must be gained with steam-power rapidity, for we cannot wait the slow results of self-education. Hence the superficial character of our current literature: reviews, magazines, and fictitious narratives; picture-books of all kinds, and scenic illustrations for all ages; but how few works of real enduring worth, leading men to think deeply, and think for themselves. We seek to be released as much as possible from the labour of thought, and require our authors to illustrate and explain the truths they would teach as though they were writing for children.

Another distinctive feature of the age, in all its great movements, whether political or moral, is an impatience for quick returns to our labours, and a constant studying to enlist the passions of the masses, to hurry onward whatever is undertaken. Instead of addressing the reason, and endeavouring to enlighten the judgment by a sober exhibition of truth, some point is seized upon which will best arouse the feelings. . . . Too impatient to wait for the gradual but enduring growth of principle, we call to our aid the more active and impetuous elements of man's nature, that we may realize more sudden and visible results, though these results may be but of momentary duration, quickly forced into maturity, and as rapidly declining into decay. It is not in the pursuit of riches only that men are making so much haste; but the same bustling, hurrying spirit has entered into undertakings whose high ends can only be attained by those who move calmly and steadily forward—their souls filled with a love for all that is great and good, too deep for noisy utterance, and their spirits nerved for every difficulty by the strength of well-considered and abiding principles. . . .

Woman's Proper Sphere

We would not undervalue the good, nor should we overlook the evils either necessarily or incidentally connected with this spirit of association; and we allude to it only for the purpose of showing its effects upon the character and usefulness of woman. Our chief aim throughout these pages is to prove that her domestic duties have a paramount claim over everything else upon her attention—that *home* is her appropriate sphere of action; and that whenever she neglects these duties, or goes out of this sphere of action to mingle in any of the great public movements of the day, she is deserting the station which God and nature have assigned to her. She can operate far more efficiently in promoting the great interests of humanity by supervising her own household than in any other way. Home, if we may so speak, is the cradle of the human race; and it is here the human character is fashioned either for good or for evil. It is the "nursery of the future man and of the undying spirit"; and woman is the nurse and the educator. Over infancy she has almost unlimited sway; and in maturer years she may powerfully counteract the evil influences of the world by the talisman of her strong, enduring love, by her devotedness to those intrusted to her charge, and by those lessons of virtue and of wisdom which are not of the world.

The Magic Power of Women

Jonathan F. Stearns was a Presbyterian minister in Newburyport, Massachusetts. In the following excerpt from his July 30, 1837, sermon entitled "Female Influence," Stearns contends that women who step outside of their proper station lose their influence over men's opinions.

I am confident no virtuous and delicate female, who rightly appreciates the design of her being, and desires to sustain her own influence and that of her sex, and fulfil the high destiny for which she is formed, would desire to abate one jot or tittle from the seeming restrictions imposed upon her conduct. . . . Let her lay aside delicacy, and her influence over our sex is gone.

And for what object should she make such sacrifices? That she may do good more extensively? Then she sadly mistakes her vocation. But why then? That she may see her name blazoned on the rolls of fame, and hear the shouts of delighted assemblies, applauding her eloquence? That she may place her own sex on a fancied equality with men, obtain the satisfaction of calling herself *independent*, and occupy a station in life which she can never adorn? For this would she sacrifice the almost magic power, which, in her own proper sphere, she now wields over the destinies of the world? Surely *such privileges*, obtained at *such cost*, are unworthy of a wise and virtuous woman's ambition.

And is not this a sphere wide enough and exalted enough to satisfy her every wish? Whatever may be her gifts or acquirements, here is ample scope for their highest and noblest exercise. If her bosom burns with ardent piety, here she will find hearts to be kindled into devotion, and souls to be saved. Is she a patriot? It is here she can best serve her country, by training up good citizens, just, humane, and enlightened legislators. Has she a highly-cultivated intellect? Let her employ it, then, in leading those young, inquiring minds, which look up to her for guidance, along the pleasant paths of knowledge. Does her spirit burn within her to promote the prosperity of Zion? From this sacred retreat she may send forth a messenger of salvation to preach repentance to a fallen world; . . . to bear the glad tidings of the Gospel to the un-tutored savage, or to the benighted heathen of other climes. Oh! that the mind of woman were enlightened fully to discern the extent and the importance of her domestic duties—to appreciate her true position in society; for then she would be in no danger of wandering from her proper sphere, or of mistaking the design of her being.

That woman should regard home as her appropriate domain is not only the dictate of religion, but of enlightened human reason. Well-ordered families are the chief security for the permanent peace and prosperity of the state, and such families must be trained up by enlightened female influence acting within its legitimate sphere. Again, there is a tendency in human nature to extremes, in all the changes through which society is passing, from one age to another; and the wisdom of God has devised certain influences to counteract these excesses. The domestic institution, which may be rendered so potential through the properly-directed influence of woman, contains within it a counter-balancing power to regulate and control the passions which give too great an impetus to the social machine. If man's duties lie abroad, woman's duties are within the quiet seclusion of home. If his greatness and power are most strikingly exhibited in associ-ated action upon associated masses, her true greatness and her highest efficiency consist in individual efforts upon individual be-ings. The religion and the politics of man have their widest sphere in the world without; but the religious zeal and the patriotism of woman are most beneficially and powerfully exerted upon the members of her household. It is in her home that her strength lies; it is here that the gentle influence, which is the secret of her might, is most successfully employed; and this she loses as soon as she descends from her calm height into the world's arena. . . .

In this age of excitement, it is specially incumbent upon woman to exert her utmost influence, to maintain unimpaired the sacred-ness and the power of the family institution. "The causes of exter-nal excitement," says a late writer, "are increasing, and along with them the current seems to set from, rather than to, the do-mestic circle; and parental influences are in danger of being over-whelmed. There are more things out of doors, and fewer things within doors. The right of father, and mother, and home is in dan-ger of becoming obsolete amid the thousand things that are crowding on the minds, and awakening the wonder, and the en-terprise and ambition of the vigorous and the young. It cannot justly excite our astonishment, then, to find the value of home de-preciated, its influences weakened, and its restraints less re-garded. Sons often seem to look upon the parental abode as the place of mere boarding and lodging; and the opportunities for parental inspection, and the culture of the social feelings which chasten and sweeten life, become circumscribed to the few fleeting moments of a hurried repast. And thus becomes formed a taste for everything abroad and for but little at home. . . .

"Do we behold the family establishment in danger of waning before the excitements of the age? its restraints in danger of being diminished? its hallowed institutions in danger of being overwhelmed? Then there is the louder call upon the fidelity of all who can exert the smallest counteracting influence?"

Such is the language of this writer, and such his appeal to those who stand upon the watchtowers of Zion, to give timely notice of the approach of every danger. But may not the same appeal be made with equal force to the religious women of our country? for it is to them chiefly that we must look for aid in elevating the family institution to that high and commanding position in society which will cause it to be honoured and valued as God designed it should be. . . . In this Eden woman has been placed as a help meet for man; and a work has been given her to do, and pleasures have been given her to be enjoyed, sufficient to retain her a willing resident within its bounds.

Amid the prevailing neglect of household duty, there are, we rejoice to see, some indications of the approach of a brighter day. The awakened interest on the subject of maternal responsibility, which has given rise to our numerous Maternal Associations, will, we trust, be speedily followed by the best and happiest results. And if it has been deemed necessary so far to follow the tendencies of the age as to bring in the spirit of association and of combined action, we still fervently hope that mothers will remember that, though associations may accomplish great things, yet it is only by the individual influence of each one upon her own household that the great end of these associations can be accomplished. . . . We would fain hope that these associations are the harbingers of better things to come; that the time is not distant when every American mother shall duly appreciate her domestic responsibilities; and when our homes shall be made attractive by the pure and satisfying enjoyments which religion, intellect, and the social affections have gathered around them. Then, when our husbands and our sons go forth into the busy and turbulent world, we may feel secure that they will walk unhurt amid its snares and temptations. Their hearts will be at home, where their treasure is; and they will rejoice to return to its sanctuary of rest, there to refresh their wearied spirits, and renew their strength for the toils and conflicts of life.

"We would have every path laid open to woman as freely as to man."

Woman's Sphere Is Restrictive

Margaret Fuller (1810–1850)

Margaret Fuller received an education that was exceptional for a woman of her time: Her father ensured that she studied classical and modern languages, philosophy, and literature from a young age. In the early 1840s, Fuller edited the quarterly transcendentalist journal the *Dial* and held a series of lectures and discussion groups for women. In 1844, she joined the staff of the *New York Tribune* as a literary editor and later became a foreign correspondent in Europe. Fuller's book *Woman in the Nineteenth Century*, from which the following viewpoint is excerpted, was published in 1845.

Comparing the legal and social status of women to that of slaves, Fuller argues that women are constrained by their lack of equal rights. She takes issue with those who believe that women can find fulfillment in the domestic sphere, noting that, at best, this arrangement relegates women to household drudgery and denies them the freedom to develop their talents. At worst, she maintains, it leaves women susceptible to and defenseless against abuse by men. Moreover, Fuller contends, this social division prevents women from protecting their own best interests by representing themselves legally and politically.

From *Woman in the Nineteenth Century* by Margaret Fuller (New York: Greeley & McElrath, 1845).

Though the national independence be blurred by the servility of individuals, though freedom and equality have been proclaimed only to leave room for a monstrous display of slave-dealing and slave-keeping; though the free American so often feels himself free, like the Roman, only to pamper his appetites and his indolence through the misery of his fellow beings, still it is not in vain, that the verbal statement has been made, "All men are born free and equal." There it stands, a golden certainty wherewith to encourage the good, to shame the bad. The new world may be called clearly to perceive that it incurs the utmost penalty, if it reject or oppress the sorrowful brother. And, if men are deaf, the angels hear. But men cannot be deaf. It is inevitable that an external freedom, an independence of the encroachments of other men, such as has been achieved for the nation, should be so also for every member of it. That which has once been clearly conceived in the intelligence cannot fail sooner or later to be acted out. . . .

We have waited here long in the dust; we are tired and hungry, but the triumphal procession must appear at last.

Of all its banners, none has been more steadily upheld, and under none have more valor and willingness for real sacrifices been shown, than that of the champions of the enslaved African. And this band it is, which, partly from a natural following out of principles, partly because many women have been prominent in that cause, makes, just now, the warmest appeal in behalf of woman.

Considering Woman's Condition

Though there has been a growing liberality on this subject, yet society at large is not so prepared for the demands of this party, but that they are and will be for some time, coldly regarded as the Jacobins of their day.

"Is it not enough," cries the irritated trader, "that you have done all you could to break up the national union, and thus destroy the prosperity of our country, but now you must be trying to break up family union, to take my wife away from the cradle and the kitchen hearth to vote at polls, and preach from a pulpit? Of course, if she does such things, she cannot attend to those of her own sphere. She is happy enough as she is. She has more leisure than I have, every means of improvement, every indulgence."

"Have you asked her whether she was satisfied with these *indulgences?*"

"No, but I know she is. She is too amiable to wish what would make me unhappy, and too judicious to wish to step beyond the sphere of her sex. I will never consent to have our peace disturbed by any such discussions."

"'Consent—you?' it is not consent from you that is in question, it is assent from your wife."

"Am not I the head of my house?"

"You are not the head of your wife. God has given her a mind of her own."

"I am the head and she the heart."

"God grant you play true to one another then. I suppose I am to be grateful that you did not say she was only the hand. If the head represses no natural pulse of the heart, there can be no question as to your giving your consent. Both will be of one accord, and there needs but to present any question to get a full and true answer. There is no need of precaution, of indulgence, or consent. But our doubt is whether the heart does consent with the head, or only obeys its decrees with a passiveness that precludes the exercise of its natural powers, or a repugnance that turns sweet qualities to bitter, or a doubt that lays waste the fair occasions of life. It is to ascertain the truth, that we propose some liberating measures."

Thus vaguely are these questions proposed and discussed at present. But their being proposed at all implies much thought and suggests more. Many women are considering within themselves, what they need that they have not, and what they can have, if they find they need it. Many men are considering whether women are capable of being and having more than they are and have, *and*, whether, if so, it will be best to consent to improvement in their condition. . . .

The numerous party, whose opinions are already labelled and adjusted too much to their mind to admit of any new light, strive, by lectures on some model-woman of bride-like beauty and gentleness, by writing and lending little treatises, intended to mark out with precision the limits of woman's sphere, and woman's mission, to prevent other than the rightful shepherd from climbing the wall, or the flock from using any chance to go astray.

Without enrolling ourselves at once on either side, let us look upon the subject from the best point of view which to-day offers. No better, it is to be feared, than a high house-top. A high hill-top, or at least a cathedral spire, would be desirable.

It may well be an Anti-Slavery party that pleads for woman, if we consider merely that she does not hold property on equal terms with men; so that, if a husband dies without making a will, the wife, instead of taking at once his place as head of the family, inherits only a part of his fortune, often brought him by herself, as if she were a child, or ward only, not an equal partner.

We will not speak of the innumerable instances in which profligate and idle men live upon the earnings of industrious wives; or if the wives leave them, and take with them the children, to perform the double duty of mother and father, follow from place to place, and threaten to rob them of the children, if deprived of the rights of a husband, as they call them, planting themselves in their poor lodgings, frightening them into paying tribute by taking from them the children, running into debt at the expense of these otherwise so overtasked helots. Such instances count up by scores within my own memory. I have seen the husband who had stained himself by a long course of low vice, till his wife was wearied from her heroic forgiveness, by finding that his treachery made it useless, and that if she would provide bread for herself and her children, she must be separate from his ill fame. I have known this man come to instal himself in the chamber of a woman who loathed him and say she should never take food without his company. I have known these men steal their children whom they knew they had no means to maintain, take them into dissolute company, expose them to bodily danger, to frighten the poor woman, to whom, it seems, the fact that she alone had borne the pangs of their birth, and nourished their infancy, does not give an equal right to them. I do believe that this mode of kidnapping, and it is frequent enough in all classes of society, will be by the next age viewed as it is by Heaven now, and that the man

Margaret Fuller conducted both her professional and her private life in ways that were considered unconventional for women of her era.

who avails himself of the shelter of men's laws to steal from a mother her own children, or arrogate any superior right in them, save that of superior virtue, will bear the stigma he deserves, in common with him who steals grown men from their mother land, their hopes, and their homes.

I said, we will not speak of this now, yet I have spoken, for the subject makes me feel too much. I could give instances that would startle the most vulgar and callous, but I will not, for the public opinion of their own sex is already against such men, and where cases of extreme tyranny are made known, there is private action in the wife's favor. But she ought not to need this, nor, I think, can she long. Men must soon see that as, on their own ground, woman is the weaker party, she ought to have legal protection, which would make such oppression impossible. But I would not deal with "atrocious instances" except in the way of illustration, neither demand from men a partial redress in some one matter, but go to the root of the whole. If principles could be established, particulars would adjust themselves aright. Ascertain the true destiny of woman, give her legitimate hopes, and a standard within herself; marriage and all other relations would by degrees be harmonized with these.

Men Cannot Represent Women

But to return to the historical progress of this matter. Knowing that there exists in the minds of men a tone of feeling towards women as towards slaves, such as is expressed in the common phrase, "Tell that to women and children," that the infinite soul can only work through them in already ascertained limits; that the gift of reason, man's highest prerogative, is allotted to them in much lower degree; that they must be kept from mischief and melancholy by being constantly engaged in active labor, which is to be furnished and directed by those better able to think, &c. &c.; we need not multiply instances, for who can review the experience of last week without recalling words which imply, whether in jest or earnest, these views or views like these; knowing this, can we wonder that many reformers think that measures are not likely to be taken in behalf of women, unless their wishes could be publicly represented by women?

That can never be necessary, cry the other side. All men are privately influenced by women; each has his wife, sister, or female friends, and is too much biased by these relations to fail of representing their interests, and, if this is not enough, let them propose and enforce their wishes with the pen. The beauty of home would be destroyed, the delicacy of the sex be violated, the dignity of halls of legislation degraded by an attempt to introduce them there. Such duties are inconsistent with those of a mother; and then we have ludicrous pictures of ladies in hysterics at the polls, and senate chambers filled with cradles.

But if, in reply, we admit as truth that woman seems destined by nature rather for the inner circle, we must add that the arrangements of civilized life have not been, as yet, such as to secure it to her. Her circle, if the duller, is not the quieter. If kept from "excitement," she is not from drudgery. Not only the Indian squaw carries the burdens of the camp, but the favorites of Louis the Fourteenth accompany him in his journeys, and the washerwoman stands at her tub and carries home her work at all seasons, and in all states of health. Those who think the physical circumstances of woman would make a part in the affairs of national government unsuitable, are by no means those who think it impossible for the negresses to endure field work, even during pregnancy or the sempstresses to go through their killing labors.

As to the use of the pen, there was quite as much opposition to woman's possessing herself of that help to free agency, as there is now to her seizing on the rostrum or the desk; and she is likely to draw, from a permission to plead her cause that way, opposite inferences to what might be wished by those who now grant it.

As to the possibility of her filling with grace and dignity, any such position, we should think those who had seen the great actresses, and heard the Quaker preachers of modern times, would not doubt, that woman can express publicly the fulness of thought and creation, without losing any of the peculiar beauty of her sex. What can pollute and tarnish is to act thus from any motive except that something needs to be said or done. Women could take part in the processions, the songs, the dances of old religion; no one fancied their delicacy was impaired by appearing in public for such a cause.

As to her home, she is not likely to leave it more than she now does for balls, theatres, meetings for promoting missions, revival meetings, and others to which she flies, in hope of an animation for her existence, commensurate with what she sees enjoyed by men. Governors of ladies' fairs are no less engrossed by such a change, than the Governor of the state by his; presidents of Washingtonian societies no less away from home than presidents of conventions. If men look straitly to it, they will find that, unless their lives are domestic, those of the women will not be. A house is no home unless it contain food and fire for the mind as well as for the body. The female Greek, of our day, is as much in the street as the male to cry, What news? We doubt not it was the same in Athens of old. The women, shut out from the market place, made up for it at the religious festivals. For human beings are not so constituted that they can live without expansion. If they do not get it one way, they must another, or perish.

59

As to men's representing women fairly at present, while we hear from men who owe to their wives not only all that is comfortable or graceful, but all that is wise in the arrangement of their lives, the frequent remark, "You cannot reason with a woman," when from those of delicacy, nobleness, and poetic culture, the contemptuous phrase "women and children," and that in no light sally of the hour, but in works intended to give a permanent statement of the best experiences, when not one man, in the million, shall I say? no, not in the hundred million, can rise above the belief that woman was made *for man*, when such traits as these are daily forced upon the attention, can we feel that man will always do justice to the interests of woman? Can we think that he takes a sufficiently discerning and religious view of her office and destiny, *ever* to do her justice, except when prompted by sentiment, accidentally or transiently, that is, for the sentiment will vary according to the relations in which he is placed. The lover, the poet, the artist, are likely to view her nobly. The father and the philosopher have some chance of liberality; the man of the world, the legislator for expediency, none.

Freedom for Women

Under these circumstances, without attaching importance, in themselves, to the changes demanded by the champions of woman, we hail them as signs of the times. We would have every arbitrary barrier thrown down. We would have every path laid open to woman as freely as to man. Were this done and a slight temporary fermentation allowed to subside, we should see crystallizations more pure and of more various beauty. We believe the divine energy would pervade nature to a degree unknown in the history of former ages, and that no discordant collision, but a ravishing harmony of the spheres would ensue.

Yet, then and only then, will mankind be ripe for this, when inward and outward freedom for woman as much as for man shall be acknowledged as a right, not yielded as a concession. As the friend of the negro assumes that one man cannot by right, hold another in bondage, so should the friend of woman assume that man cannot, by right, lay even well-meant restrictions on woman. If the negro be a soul, if the woman be a soul, appareled in flesh, to one Master only are they accountable. There is but one law for souls, and if there is to be an interpreter of it, he must come not as man, or son of man, but as son of God.

Were thought and feeling once so far elevated that man should esteem himself the brother and friend, but nowise the lord and tutor of woman, were he really bound with her in equal worship, arrangements as to function and employment would be of no consequence. What woman needs is not as a woman to act or rule, but as a nature to grow, as an intellect to discern, as soul to live freely and unimpeded, to unfold such powers as were given her when we left our common home. If fewer talents were given her, yet if allowed the free and full employment of these, so that she may render back to the giver his own with usury she will not complain; nay I dare to say she will bless and rejoice in her earthly birth-place, her earthly lot. Let us consider what obstructions impede this good era, and what signs give reason to hope that it draws near. . . .

It is not the transient breath of poetic incense that women want; each can receive that from a lover. It is not life-long sway; it needs but to become a coquette, a shrew, or a good cook, to be sure of that. It is not money, nor notoriety, nor the badges of authority that men have appropriated to themselves. If demands, made in their behalf, lay stress on any of these particulars, those who make them have not searched deeply into the need. It is for that which at once includes these and precludes them; which would not be forbidden power, lest there be temptation to steal and misuse it; which would not have the mind perverted by flattery from a worthiness of esteem. It is for that which is the birthright of every being capable to receive it,—the freedom, the religious, the intelligent freedom of the universe, to use its means; to learn its secret as far as nature has enabled them, with God alone for their guide and their judge.

CHAPTER 2

Beginnings of a Movement

Chapter Preface

The seeds of the American women's rights movement were actually planted in England during the June 1840 World Anti-Slavery Convention. Several American women—including the prominent abolitionist Lucretia Mott—had traveled to London as delegates to the convention, where their presence created an uproar. The male delegates spent the entire first day of the convention debating whether to allow the women to take part in the proceedings. Some men supported the women's right to serve as members of the convention, but the majority agreed that women were, as one delegate argued, "constitutionally unfit for public or business meetings." Instead, the women were banned from participating in the convention and were seated behind a curtain.

It was at this convention that Lucretia Mott and a young newlywed, Elizabeth Cady Stanton, first met. Indignant over their treatment, Mott and Stanton spent hours discussing the question of women's equality and resolved to form a society advocating women's rights. Eight years passed before they were able to implement their plan, but in July 1848 Mott, Stanton, and three other women organized the first women's rights convention in Seneca Falls, New York. More than three hundred women and men attended the convention, debating such concerns as legal discrimination against women, social attitudes about women's proper role, and—most controversial of all—women's right to vote.

The Seneca Falls convention was condemned in newspapers and from church pulpits nationwide; one editorial declared the convention "the most shocking and unnatural incident ever recorded in the history of humanity." At the same time, however, reports of the convention stimulated interest in women's rights issues elsewhere. Only two weeks after Seneca Falls, a second women's rights convention was held in Rochester, New York. Many more regional and national conventions followed as the movement gained support. Among the women who became involved in the cause in the early 1850s were Susan B. Anthony and Lucy Stone. Both Anthony and Stone quickly took on highly visible roles as lecturers and political organizers. In particular, Stanton and Anthony developed a strong working partnership in which Stanton formulated feminist theories and composed speeches that Anthony would then promulgate as she canvassed the country, lecturing, and establishing women's rights organizations.

In the early days of the movement, feminists focused on a broad spectrum of issues. Besides suffrage, they debated and worked for causes such as married women's property rights, liberalized divorce laws, equal pay for working women, dress reform, and expansion of educational opportunities. They discussed social attitudes toward housework, women's health issues, and the double standard of morality for men and women. Although the movement was still modest in size, it steadily gained momentum until the outbreak of the Civil War in 1861. Busy with the war effort, the leaders of the women's movement decided to discontinue their conventions until the war's end and concentrate all their energies into relief societies, fundraising, abolitionist activities, and nursing. Many feminists, especially Stanton, considered the hiatus of the movement a strategic move: They reasoned that women would prove themselves worthy of the vote by their patriotic endeavors during the war.

After the Civil War, however, feminists were rudely awakened when they discovered that the proposed Fourteenth Amendment protected the right of black men to vote while specifically excluding women. The feminist leaders hurriedly remobilized the movement, circulating petitions that protested the amendment's wording and establishing the American Equal Rights Association to demand suffrage "irrespective of race, color, or sex." Despite several years of effort, the women's rights leaders ultimately were unable to change the wording of either the Fourteenth or the Fifteenth Amendment, both of which were designed to guarantee suffrage only for black men.

Furthermore, the battle over the amendments led to a significant break in the women's rights movement. Some believed that the two amendments should not be passed at all unless altered to include women. Others objected to the wording of the amendments but refused to try to block their passage, arguing that the former slaves were in more urgent need of suffrage than were women. After heated debate between the two factions at the May 1869 meeting of the American Equal Rights Association, the women's rights movement split in half. Stanton and Anthony founded the more radical organization, the National Woman Suffrage Association. This group refused to support the Fifteenth Amendment, advocated a national constitutional amendment for women's suffrage, and addressed other women's rights issues besides suffrage (including extremely controversial ones such as divorce reform). Lucy Stone and her followers formed the more mainstream American Woman Suffrage Association, which supported the Fifteenth Amendment, made suffrage its only cause, and worked for suffrage solely on a local and state level.

Meanwhile, in the midst of feminists' disappointment over their exclusion from the postwar amendments and their bitterness over the movement's division, one victory occurred. On December 10, 1869, the Wyoming Territory gave women the right to vote.

VIEWPOINT 1

"If the female sex is injured in its present position, it is an injury growing out of universal mistake . . . in which the sexes have conspired."

Men Have Not Purposely Subjugated Women

Henry W. Bellows (1814–1882)

The pastor of the Church of All Souls in New York City, Henry W. Bellows authored several books on theology and medicine and was the editor of the Unitarian newspaper *Christian Inquirer*. Bellows initially opposed the women's rights movement and criticized women for taking part in public debates at the women's rights conventions. By the early 1850s, however, he actively supported the movement and promoted many of its goals.

The following viewpoint is excerpted from Bellows's *Christian Inquirer* article covering the Second National Woman's Rights Convention, which was held on October 15 and 16, 1851, in Worcester, Massachusetts. Admitting to his former disapproval of the movement, Bellows argues that most men who object to women's rights do so not from a desire to oppress women but because the proposed reforms conflict with established social customs and behavior. He contends that the traditional division of male and female roles was devised both by men and women and was intended to benefit women rather than to subjugate them. Although this societal arrangement may now be outdated and unfair to women, Bellows concludes, women should not hold men responsible for their grievances.

From "The Woman's Rights Convention in Worcester" by Henry W. Bellows, in *History of Woman Suffrage*, vol. 1, edited by Elizabeth Cady Stanton, Susan B. Anthony, and Matilda Joslyn Gage (New York: Fowler & Wells, 1881).

We have read the report of the proceedings of this [Woman's Rights] Convention [at Worcester, Massachusetts] with lively interest and general satisfaction. We confess ourselves to be much surprised at the prevailing good sense, propriety, and moral elevation of the meeting. No candid reader can deny the existence of singular ability, honest and pure aims, eloquent and forcible advocacy, and a startling power in the reports and speeches of this Convention. For good, or for evil, it seems to us to be the most important meeting since that held in the cabin of the *Mayflower*. That meeting recognized the social and political equality of one-half the human race; this asserts the social and political equality of the other half, and of the whole. Imagine the difference which it would have made in our Declaration of Independence, to have inserted "and women" in the first clause of the self-evident truths it asserts: "that all men *and women* are created equal." This Convention declares this to be the true interpretation of the Declaration, and at any rate, designs to amend the popular reading of the instrument to this effect. Nor is it a theoretical change which is aimed at. No more practical or tremendous revolution was ever sought in society, than that which this Woman's Rights Convention inaugurates. To emancipate half the human race from its present position of dependence on the other half; to abolish every distinction between the sexes that can be abolished, or which is maintained by statute or conventional usage; to throw open all the employments of society with equal freedom to men and women; to allow no difference whatsoever, in the eye of the law, in their duties or their rights, this, we submit, is a reform, surpassing, in pregnancy of purpose and potential results, any other now upon the platform, if it do not outweigh Magna Charta and our Declaration themselves.

We very well recollect the scorn with which the annual procession of the first Abolitionists was greeted in Boston, some thirty years ago. The children had no conception of the "Bobolition Society," but as of a set of persons making themselves ridiculous for the amusement of the public; but that "Bobolition Society" has shaken the Union to its center, and filled the world with sympathy and concern. The Woman's Rights Convention is in like manner a thing for honest scorn to point its finger at; but a few years may prove that we pointed the finger, not at an illuminated balloon, but at the rising sun.

We have no hesitation in acknowledging ourselves to be among those who have regarded this movement with decided distrust and distaste. If we have been more free than others to express this disgust, we have perhaps rendered some service, by representing a common sentiment with which this reform has to contend. We would be among the first to acknowledge that our objections have not grown out of any deliberate consideration of the principles involved in the question. They have been founded on instinctive aversion, on an habitual respect for public sentiment, on an irresistible feeling of the ludicrousness of the proposed reform in its details. Certainly social instinct has its proper place in the judgments we pass on the manners of both sexes. What is offensive to good taste—meaning by good taste, the taste of the most educated and refined people—has the burden of proof resting upon it when it claims respect and attention. But we should be the last to assert that questions of right and rights have no appeal from the bar of conventional taste to that of reason.

No Intentional Injustice by Men

And however it may have been at the outset, we think the Woman's Rights question has now made good its title to be heard in the superior court. The principles involved in this great question we can not now discuss; but we have a few thoughts upon the attitude of the reformer toward society, which we would respectfully commend to attention. If the female sex is injured in its present position, it is an injury growing out of universal mistake; an honest error, in which the sexes have conspired, without intentional injustice on one side, or feeling of wrong on the other. Indeed, we could not admit that there had been thus far any wrong or mistake at all, except in details. Mankind have hitherto found the natural functions of the two sexes marking out different spheres for them. Thus far, as we think, the circumstances of the world have compelled a marked division of labor, and a marked difference of culture and political position between the sexes.

The facts of superior bodily strength on the masculine side, and of maternity on the feminine side, small as they are now made to appear, are very great and decisive facts in themselves, and have necessarily governed the organization of society. It is between the sexes, as between the races, the strongest rules; and it has hitherto been supposed to be of service to the common interest of society, that this rule should be legalized and embodied in the social customs of every community. As a fact, woman, by her bodily weakness and her maternal office, was from the first, a comparatively private and domestic creature; her education, from circumstances, was totally different, her interests were different, the sources of her happiness different from man's, and as a fact, all these things, though with important modifications, have continued to be so to this day. The fact has seemed to the world a final one. It has been thought that in her present position, she was in her best position relative to man, which her nature or organization admitted of. That she is man's inferior in respect to all offices and duties requiring great bodily powers, or great moral courage, or great intellectual effort, has been almost universally supposed,—honestly thought too, and without the least disposition to deny her equality, on this account, in the scale of humanity.

We Are Both in Fault

At the Fourth National Woman's Rights Convention in October 1853, debate broke out over language in the Seneca Falls Declaration of Sentiments that blamed men for women's oppression. During the debate, feminist Ernestine Rose argued that both men and women were accountable for maintaining women's subjugated position in society, although she stressed that men bore the greater responsibility.

I heartily agree that [men and women] are both in fault; and yet we are none in fault. I also said, that woman, on account of the position in which she has been placed, by being dependent upon man, by being made to look up to man, is the first to cast out her sister. I know it and deplore it; hence I wish to give her her rights, to secure her dependence upon herself. In regard to that sentiment in the Declaration, our friend [Asa Mahan] said that woman created it. Is woman really the creator of the sentiment? . . .

Man utters the sentiment, and woman echoes it. As I said before—for I have seen and felt it deeply—she even appears to be quite flattered with her cruel tyrant, for such he has been made to be—she is quite flattered with the destroyer of woman's character—aye, worse than that, the destroyer of woman's self-respect and peace of mind—and when she meets him, she is flattered with his attentions. Why should she not be? He is admitted into Legislative halls, and to all places where men "most do congregate;" why, then, should she not admit him to her parlor?

For in respect to moral sensibility, affections, manners, tastes, and the passive virtues, woman has long been honestly felt to be the superior of man. The political disfranchisement of women, and their seclusion from publicity, have grown out of sincere convictions that their nature and happiness demanded from man an exemption from the cares, and a protection from the perils of the out-of-door world. Mankind, in both its parts, may have been utterly mistaken in this judgment; but it has been nearly universal, and thoroughly sincere,—based thus far, we think, upon staring facts and compulsory circumstances.

In starting a radical reform upon this subject, it is expedient that it should be put, not on the basis of old grievances, but upon the ground of new light, of recent and fresh experiences, of change of circumstances. It may be that the relative position of the sexes is so changed by an advancing civilization, that the time has come for questioning the conclusion of the world respecting woman's sphere. All surprise at opposition to this notion, all sense of injury, all complaint of past injustice, ought to cease. Woman's part has been the part which her actual state made necessary. If another and a better future is opening, let us see it and rejoice in it as a new gift of Providence.

And we are not without suspicion that the time for some great change has arrived. At any rate, we confess our surprise at the weight of the reasoning brought forward by the recent Convention, and shall endeavor henceforth to keep our masculine mind,—full, doubtless, of conventional prejudices,—open to the light which is shed upon the theme.

Men's Respect for Women

Meanwhile, we must beg the women who are pressing this reform, to consider that the conservatism of instinct and taste, though not infallible, is respectable and worth attention. The opposition they will receive is founded on prejudices that are not selfish, but merely masculine. It springs from no desire to keep women down, but from a desire to keep them up; from a feeling, mistaken it may be, that their strength, and their dignity, and their happiness, lie in their seclusion from the rivalries, strifes, and public duties of life. The strength and depth of the respect and love for woman, as woman, which characterize this age, can not be overstated. But woman insists upon being respected, as a kindred intellect, a free competitor, and a political equal. And we have suspicions that she may surprise the conservative world by making her pretensions good. Only meanwhile let her respect the affectionate and sincere prejudices, if they be prejudices, which adhere to the other view, a view made honorable, if not proved true, by the experiences of all the ages of the past. We hope to give the whole subject more attention in future. Indeed it will force attention. It may be the solution of many social problems, long waiting an answer, is delayed by the neglect to take woman's case into fuller consideration. The success of the present reform would give an entirely new problem to political and social philosophers! At present we endeavor to hold ourselves in a candid suspense.

VIEWPOINT 2

"[Women] are the victims in this land . . . to the tyrannical power and godless ambition of man."

Men Are Responsible for Women's Oppression

William Lloyd Garrison (1805–1879)

William Lloyd Garrison was a leading abolitionist and social reformer. He founded the American Anti-Slavery Society in 1833 and published an abolitionist periodical, the *Liberator*, from 1831 to 1865. Garrison was also an early and adamant supporter of women's rights. When members of the 1840 World Anti-Slavery Convention in London voted to exclude female delegates from participating in the proceedings, Garrison protested this decision by joining the women in their segregated seating and refusing to publicly address the assembly. From the 1850s on, he attended and took part in a number of the women's rights conventions.

The Fourth National Woman's Rights Convention was held in Cleveland, Ohio, from October 6 to October 8, 1853. During the convention, controversy arose over whether the delegates should formally adopt the Seneca Falls Declaration of Sentiments. Asa Mahan, the president of Oberlin College, began the debate by objecting to wording in the declaration that charged that men were responsible for women's subjugation. Women themselves, he claimed, were to blame for their condition. Among the speakers who answered Mahan was Ernestine Rose, a feminist and one of the convention's organizers. She took the middle ground, stating that women and men both were at fault.

When the floor was yielded to Garrison, he delivered the following speech. Expressing his disagreement with both Mahan

From William Lloyd Garrison's 1853 speech to the Fourth National Woman's Rights Convention, Cleveland, Ohio, as reprinted in *History of Woman Suffrage*, vol. 1, edited by Elizabeth Cady Stanton, Susan B. Anthony, and Matilda Joslyn Gage (New York: Fowler & Wells, 1881).

and Rose, Garrison insists that men knowingly and purposefully oppress women, just as slaveowners oppress slaves. In fact, he argues, until men understand and accept their responsibility for women's inequality, little progress will be made in bettering the status of women. The irrational reaction that most men have to the idea of women's rights betrays their conscious desire to suppress women, Garrison contends.

It was this morning objected to the Declaration of Sentiments, that it implied that man was the only transgressor, that he had been guilty of injustice and usurpation, and the suggestion was also made, that woman should not be criminated, in this only, but regarded rather as one who had erred through ignorance; and our eloquent friend, Mrs. [Ernestine] Rose, who stood on this platform and pleaded with such marked ability, as she always does plead in any cause she undertakes to speak upon, told us her creed. She told us she did not blame anybody, really, and did not hold any man to be criminal, or any individual to be responsible for public sentiment, as regards the difference of criminality of man and woman.

For my own part, I am not prepared to respect that philosophy. I believe in sin, therefore in a sinner; in theft, therefore in a thief; in slavery, therefore in a slaveholder; in wrong, therefore in a wrong-doer; and unless the men of this nation are made by woman to see that they have been guilty of usurpation, and cruel usurpation, I believe very little progress will be made. To say all this has been done without thinking, with calculation, without design, by mere accident, by a want of light; can anybody believe this who is familiar with all the facts in the case? Certainly, for one, I hope ever to lean to the charitable side, and will try to do so. I, too, believe things are done through misconception and misapprehension, which are injurious, yes, which are immoral and unchristian; but only to a limited extent. There is such a thing as intelligent wickedness, a design on the part of those who have the light to quench it, and to do the wrong to gratify their own propensities, and to further their own interests. So, then, I believe, that as man has monopolized for generations all the rights which belong to woman, it has not been accidental, not through ignorance on his part; but I believe that man has done this through calculation, actuated by a spirit of pride, a desire for domination which has made him degrade woman in her own eyes, and thereby tend to make her a mere vassal.

Men Are Knowing Transgressors

It seems to me, therefore, that we are to deal with the consciences of men. It is idle to say that the guilt is common, that the women are as deeply involved in this matter as the men. Never can it be said that the victims are as much to be blamed as the victimizer; that the slaves are to be as much blamed as the slaveholders and slave-drivers; that the women who have no rights, are to be as much blamed as the men who have played the part of robbers and tyrants. We must deal with conscience. The men of this nation, and the men of all nations, have no just respect for woman. They have tyrannized over her deliberately, they have not sinned through ignorance, but theirs is not the knowledge that saves. Who can say truly, that in all things he acts up to the light he enjoys, that he does not do something which he knows is not the very thing, or the best thing he ought to do? How few there are among mankind who are able to say this with regard to themselves. Is not the light all around us? Does not this nation know how great its guilt is in enslaving one-sixth of its people? Do not the men of this nation know ever since the landing of the pilgrims, that they are wrong in making subject one-half of the people? Rely upon it, it has not been a mistake on their part. It has been sin. It has been guilt; and they manifest their guilt to a demonstration, in the manner in which they receive this movement. Those who do wrong ignorantly, do not willingly continue in it, when they find they are in the wrong. Ignorance is not an evidence of guilt certainly. It is only an evidence of a want of light. They who are only ignorant, will never rage, and rave, and threaten, and foam, when the light comes; but being interested and walking in the light, will always present a manly front, and be willing to be taught, and be willing to be told they are in the wrong.

Take the case of slavery: How has the anti-slavery cause been received? Not argumentatively, not by reason, not by entering the free arena of fair discussion and comparing notes; the arguments have been rotten eggs, and brickbats and calumny, and in the southern portion of the country, a spirit of murder, and threats to cut out the tongues of those who spoke against them. What has this indicated on the part of the nation? What but conscious guilt? Not ignorance, not that they had not the light. They had the light and rejected it.

How has this Woman's Rights movement been treated in this country, on the right hand and on the left? This nation ridicules and derides this movement, and spits upon it, as fit only to be cast out and trampled underfoot. This is not ignorance. They know all about the truth. It is the natural outbreak of tyranny. It is because the tyrants and usurpers are alarmed. They have been and are called to judgment, and they dread the examination and

An Absolute Tyranny

Modeled on the Declaration of Independence, the Declaration of Sentiments was written between July 14 and 18, 1848, by the organizers of the first Woman's Rights Convention at Seneca Falls, New York.

The history of mankind is a history of repeated injuries and usurpations on the part of man toward woman, having in direct object the establishment of an absolute tyranny over her. To prove this, let facts be submitted to a candid world.

He has never permitted her to exercise her inalienable right to the elective franchise.

He has compelled her to submit to laws, in the formation of which she had no voice. . . .

He has made her, if married, in the eye of the law, civilly dead.

He has taken from her all right in property, even to the wages she earns. . . .

He has so framed the laws of divorce, as to what shall be the proper causes of divorce, and in case of separation, to whom the guardianship of the children shall be given, as to be wholly regardless of the happiness of women—the law, in all cases, going upon a false supposition of the supremacy of man, and giving all power into his hands. . . .

He closes against her all the avenues to wealth and distinction, which he considers most honorable to himself. As a teacher of theology, medicine, or law, she is not known.

He has denied her the facilities for obtaining a thorough education—all colleges being closed against her.

He allows her in Church as well as State, but a subordinate position, claiming Apostolic authority for her exclusion from the ministry, and, with some exceptions, from any public participation in the affairs of the Church.

He has created a false public sentiment by giving to the world a different code of morals for men and women, by which moral delinquencies which exclude women from society, are not only tolerated, but deemed of little account in man. . . .

He has endeavored, in every way that he could, to destroy her confidence in her own powers, to lessen her self-respect, and to make her willing to lead a dependent and abject life.

exposure of their position and character.

Women of America! you have something to blame yourselves for in this matter, something to account for to God and the world. Granted. But then you are the victims in this land, as the women of all lands are, to the tyrannical power and godless ambition of man; and we must show who are responsible in this matter. We must test everybody here. Every one of us must give an account of himself to God. It is an individual testing of character. Mark the man or the woman who derides this movement, who turns his or her back upon it; who is disposed to let misrule keep on, and you will find you have a sure indication of character. You will find that such persons are destitute of principles; for if you can convict a man of being wanting in principle anywhere, it will be everywhere. He who loves the right for its own sake, loves the right everywhere. He who is a man of principle, is a man of principle always. Let me see the man who is willing to have any one of God's rational creatures sacrificed to promote anything, aside form the well-being of that creature himself, and I will show you an unprincipled man.

It is so in this movement. Nobody argues against it, nobody pretends to have an argument. Your platform is free everywhere, wherever these Conventions are held. Yet no man comes forward in a decent, respectable manner, to show you that you are wrong in the charges you bring against the law-makers of the land. There is no argument against it. The thing is self-evident. I should not know how to begin to frame an argument. That which is self-evident is greater than argument, and beyond logic. It testifies of itself. You and I, as human beings, claim to have rights, but I never think of going into an argument with anybody, to prove that I ought to have rights. I have the argument and logic here, it is in my own breast and consciousness; and the logic of the schools becomes contemptible beside these. The more you try to argue, the worse you are off. It is not the place for metaphysics, it is the place for affirmation. Woman is the counterpart of man; she has the same divine image, having the same natural and inalienable rights as man. To state the proposition is enough; it contains the argument, and nobody can gainsay it, in an honorable way.

The Guilt of Individuals

I rose simply to say, that though I should deprecate making our platform a theological arena, yet believing that men are guilty of intentional wrong, in keeping woman subject, I believe in having them criminated. You talk of injustice, then there is an unjust man somewhere. Even Mrs. Rose could talk of the guilt of society. Society! I know nothing of society. I know the guilt of individuals. Society is an abstract term: it is made up of individuals, and the responsibility rests with individuals. So then, if we are to call men to repentance, there is such a thing as wrong-doing intelligently, sinning against God and man, with light enough to convict us, and to condemn us before God and the world. Let this cause then be pressed upon the hearts and consciences, against those who hold unjust rights in their possession.

VIEWPOINT 3

"Strive as you will to elevate woman, nevertheless the disabilities and degradation of this dress . . . will make your striving vain."

Dress Reform Is Vital to Women's Equality

Gerrit Smith (1797–1874)

In the mid-1800s, women's fashions required the use of tight ribbed corsets, several petticoats, and floor-length hoop skirts. According to some advocates of women's rights, these outfits restricted women's movements and activities and even caused physical ailments. A number of early feminists adopted a style of dress called bloomers, which consisted of loose trousers worn underneath a knee-length skirt. Although bloomers were named for Amelia Bloomer, who popularized the outfit, they were actually designed in 1850 by Elizabeth Smith Miller, after her father, Gerrit Smith, encouraged her to develop a healthier dress design.

Well-known for his work in the abolitionist movement, Gerrit Smith was a wealthy landowner, a philanthropist, and a social reformer. He supported the aims of the women's rights movement and took particular interest in the issue of dress reform. However, bloomers were the subject of intense ridicule by the general public and eventually most women reformers—even Smith's cousin, leading feminist Elizabeth Cady Stanton—gave up wearing the outfit.

On December 1, 1855, Smith wrote an open letter to Stanton on the issue of dress reform. Women will never obtain political or social equality without reforming their mode of dress, Smith argues. Not only do popular fashions make women fragile and

From an 1855 letter of Gerrit Smith, as reprinted in *History of Woman Suffrage*, vol. 1, edited by Elizabeth Cady Stanton, Susan B. Anthony, and Matilda Joslyn Gage (New York: Fowler & Wells, 1881).

helpless, he contends, but men will continue to believe women are physically inferior as long as women voluntarily cripple themselves with their clothing. In particular, Smith condemns members of the women's rights movement for demanding their rights from men while they themselves persist in wearing an oppressive style of dress.

Elizabeth C. Stanton, *my dear friend*,

The "Woman's Rights Movement" has deeply interested your generous heart, and you have ever been ready to serve it with your vigorous understanding. It is, therefore, at the risk of appearing somewhat unkind and uncivil, that I give my honest answer to your question. You would know why I have so little faith in this movement. I reply, that it is not in the proper hands; and that the proper hands are not yet to be found. The present age, although in advance of any former age, is, nevertheless, very far from being sufficiently under the sway of reason to take up the cause of woman, and carry it forward to success. A much stronger and much more widely diffused common sense than has characterized any of the generations, must play its mightiest artillery upon the stupendous piles of nonsense, which tradition and chivalry and a misinterpreted and superstitious Christianity have reared in the way of this cause, ere woman can have the prospect of the recognition of her rights and of her confessed equality with man.

The object of the "Woman's Rights Movement" is nothing less than to recover the rights of woman—nothing less than to achieve her independence. She is now the dependent of man; and, instead of rights, she has but privileges—the mere concessions (always revocable and always uncertain) of the other sex to her sex. I say nothing against this object. It is as proper as it is great; and until it is realized, woman can not be half herself, nor can man be half himself. I rejoice in this object; and my sorrow is, that they, who are intent upon it, are not capable of adjusting themselves to it—not high-souled enough to consent to those changes and sacrifices in themselves, in their positions and relations, essential to the attainment of this vital object.

Women Are Crippled by Their Dress

What if a nation in the heart of Europe were to adopt, and uniformly adhere to, the practice of cutting off one of the hands of all their new-born children? It would from this cause be reduced to poverty, to helpless dependence upon the charity of surrounding nations, and to just such a measure of privileges as they might see fit to allow it, in exchange for its forfeited rights. Very great, indeed, would be the folly of this strange nation. But a still greater folly would it be guilty of, should it, notwithstanding this voluntary mutilation, claim all the wealth, and all the rights, and all the respect, and all the independence which it enjoyed before it entered upon this systematic mutilation.

Amelia Bloomer published this illustration of herself in the September 1851 issue of her newspaper, the Lily.

Now, this twofold folly of this one-hand nation illustrates the similar twofold folly of some women. Voluntarily wearing, in common with their sex, a dress which imprisons and cripples them, they, nevertheless, follow up this absurdity with the greater one of coveting and demanding a social position no less full of admitted rights, and a relation to the other sex no less full of independence, than such position and relation would naturally and necessarily have been, had they scorned a dress which leaves them less than half their personal power of self-subsistence and usefulness. I admit that the mass of women are not chargeable with this latter absurdity of cherishing aspirations and urging claims so wholly and so glaringly at war with this voluntary imprisonment and this self-degradation. They are content in their helplessness and poverty and destitution of rights. Nay, they are so deeply deluded as to believe that all this belongs to their natural and unavoidable lot. But the handful of women of whom I am here complaining—the woman's rights women—persevere just as blindly and stubbornly as do other women, in wearing a dress that both marks and makes their impotence, and yet, O amazing inconsistency! they are ashamed of their dependence, and remonstrate against its injustice. They claim that the fullest measure of rights and independence and dignity shall be accorded to them, and yet they refuse to place themselves in circumstances corresponding with their claim. They demand as much for themselves as is acknowledged to be due to men, and yet they refuse to pay the necessary, the never-to-be-avoided price of what they demand—the price which men have to pay for it.

I admit that the dress of woman is not the primal cause of her helplessness and degradation. That cause is to be found in the false doctrines and sentiments of which the dress is the outgrowth and symbol. On the other hand, however, these doctrines and sentiments would never have become the huge bundle they now are, and they would probably have all languished, and perhaps all expired, but for the dress. For, as in many other instances, so in this, and emphatically so in this, the cause is made more efficient by the reflex influence of the effect. Let woman give up the irrational modes of clothing her person, and these doctrines and sentiments would be deprived of their most vital aliment by being deprived of their most natural expression. In no other practical forms of folly to which they might betake themselves, could they operate so vigorously and be so invigorated by their operation.

Were woman to throw off the dress, which, in the eye of chivalry and gallantry, is so well adapted to womanly gracefulness and womanly helplessness, and to put on a dress that would leave her free to work her own way through the world, I see not but that chivalry and gallantry would nearly or quite die out. No longer would she present herself to man, now in the bewitching character of a plaything, a doll, an idol, and now in the degraded character of his servant. But he would confess her transmutation into his equal; and, therefore, all occasion for the display of chivalry and gallantry toward her on the one hand, and tyranny on the other, would have passed away. Only let woman attire her person fitly for the whole battle of life—that great and often rough battle, which she is as much bound to fight as man is, and the common sense expressed in the change will put to flight all the nonsensical fancies about her superiority to man, and all the nonsensical fancies about her inferiority to him. No more will then be heard of her being made of a finer material than man is made of; and, on the contrary, no more will then be heard of her being but the complement of man, and of its taking both a man and a woman (the woman, of course, but a small part of it) to make up a unit. No more will it then be said that there is sex in mind—an original sexual difference in intellect. What a pity that so many of our noblest women make this foolish admission! It is made by the great majority of the women who plead the cause of woman.

I am amazed that the intelligent women engaged in the "Woman's Rights Movement," see not the relation between their dress and the oppressive evils which they are striving to throw off. I am amazed that they do not see that their dress is indispensable to keep in countenance the policy and purposes out of which those evils grow. I hazard nothing in saying, that the relation between the dress and degradation of an American woman, is as vital as between the cramped foot and degradation of a Chinese woman; as vital as between the uses of the inmate of the harem and the apparel and training provided for her. Moreover, I hazard nothing in saying, that an American woman will never have made her most effectual, nor, indeed, any serviceable protest against the treatment of her sex in China, or by the lords of the harem, so long as she consents to have her own person clothed in ways so repugnant to reason and religion, and grateful only to a vitiated taste, be it in her own or in the other sex.

Women Must Reform Themselves First

Women are holding their meetings; and with great ability do they urge their claim to the rights of property and suffrage. But, as in the case of the colored man, the great needed change is in himself, so, also, in the case of woman, the great needed change is in herself. Of what comparative avail would be her exercise of the right of suffrage, if she is still to remain the victim of her present false notions of herself and of her relations to the other sex?— false notions so emphatically represented and perpetuated by her dress? Moreover, to concede to her the rights of property would be to benefit her comparatively little, unless she shall resolve to break out from her clothes-prison, and to undertake right earnestly, as right earnestly as a man, to get property. Solomon says: "The destruction of the poor is their poverty." The adage that knowledge is power, is often repeated; and there are, indeed, many instances to verify it. Nevertheless, as a general proposition, it is a thousandfold more emphatically true that property is power. Knowledge helps to get property, but property is the power. That the slaves are a helpless prey, is chiefly because they are so poor and their masters so rich. The masses almost everywhere are well-nigh powerless, because almost everywhere they are poor. How long will they consent to be poor? Just so long as they shall consent to be robbed of their God-given right to the soil. That women are helpless is no wonder, so long as women are paupers.

The Physical Effects of Women's Fashions

Physician Mary F. Thomas was one of the first women to earn a medical degree from an American university. Her editorial advocating the health benefits of dress reform was published in the August 1852 edition of the Lily.

In order that we may have sound minds in sound bodies, our dress must be such as to allow the full expansion of the chest, and the most perfect muscular development of the whole body. . . .
Is it any wonder that the female constitution is becoming proverbially deteriorated, when we consider the enervating effects of the long, tight bodice, and the heavy skirts suspended from the hips.
A short time ago a lady, evidently suffering severely the penalty of the slave of fashion, said, on my remonstrating on her course, that she *"could not* change; for *she had worn stiff whale-bones so long that she could not support her body in an upright position without them."* And this is by no means an isolated case.
Thousands of women are in the same wretched situation. . . .
This state of things calls loudly for a reformation in the form of dress; and all women . . . are in *duty bound* to investigate the subject, and fashion their dress according to the dictates of *reason* and *common sense.*

As long as woman shall be silly enough to learn her lessons in the schools of gallantry and chivalry, so long will it be the height of her ambition to be a graceful and amiable burden upon the other sex. But as soon as she shall consent to place herself under the instructions of reason and common sense, and to discard, as wholly imaginary, those differences between the nature of man and the nature of woman, out of which have grown innumerable nonsensical doctrines and notions, and all sorts of namby pamby sentiments, so soon will she find that, to no greater extent than men are dependent on each other, are women to foster the idea of their dependence on men. Then, and not till then, will women learn that, to be useful and happy, and to accomplish the high purposes of their being, they must, no less emphatically than men, stand upon their own feet, and work with their own hands, and bear the burdens of life with their own strength, and brave its storms with their own resoluteness.

The next "Woman's Rights Convention" will, I take it for granted, differ but little from its predecessors. It will abound in righteous demands and noble sentiments, but not in the evidence that they who enunciate these demands and sentiments are prepared to put themselves in harmony with what they conceive and demand. In a word, for the lack of such preparation and of the deep earnestness, which alone can prompt to such preparation, it will be, as has been every other Woman's Rights Convention, a failure. Could I see it made up of women whose dress would indicate their translation from cowardice to courage; from slavery to freedom; from the kingdom of fancy and fashion and foolery to the kingdom of reason and righteousness, then would I hope for the elevation of woman, aye, and of man too, as perhaps I have never yet hoped. What should be the parts and particulars of such dress, I am incapable of saying. Whilst the "Bloomer dress" is unspeakably better than the common dress, it nevertheless affords not half that freedom of the person which woman is entitled and bound to enjoy. I add, on this point, that however much the dresses of the sexes should resemble each other, decency and virtue and other considerations require that they should be obviously distinguishable from each other.

I am not unaware that such views as I have expressed in this letter will be regarded as serving to break down the characteristic delicacy of woman. I frankly admit that I would have it broken down; and that I would have the artificial and conventional, the nonsensical and pernicious thing give place to the natural delicacy which would be common to both sexes. As the delicacy, which is made peculiar to one of the sexes, is unnatural, and, therefore, false, this, which would be common to both, would be natural, and, therefore, true. I would have no characteristic delicacy of woman, and no characteristic coarseness of man. On the contrary, believing man and woman to have the same nature, and to be therefore under obligation to have the same character, I would subject them to a common standard of morals and manners. The delicacy of man should be no less shrinking than that of woman, and the bravery of woman should be one with the bravery of man. Then would there be a public sentiment very unlike that which now requires the sexes to differ in character, and which, therefore, holds them amenable to different codes—codes that, in their partiality to man, allow him to commit high crimes, and that, in their cruelty to woman, make the bare suspicion of such crimes on her part the justification of her hopeless degradation and ruin. . . .

But if woman is of the same nature and same dignity with man, and if as much and as varied labor is needed to supply her wants as to supply the wants of man, and if for her to be, as she so emphatically is, poor and destitute and dependent, is as fatal to her happiness and usefulness and to the fulfillment of the high purposes of her existence, as the like circumstances would be to the honor and welfare of man, why then put her in a dress which compels her to be a pauper—a pauper, whether in ribbons or rags? Why, I ask, put her in a dress suited only to those occasional and brief moods, in which man regards her as his darling, his idol, and his angel; or to that general state of his mind in which he looks upon her as his servant, and with feelings certainly much nearer contempt than adoration. Strive as you will to elevate woman, nevertheless the disabilities and degradation of this dress, together with that large group of false views of the uses of her being and of her relations to man, symbolized and perpetuated, as I have already said, by this dress, will make your striving vain.

Woman must first fight against herself—against personal and mental habits so deep-rooted and controlling, and so seemingly inseparable from herself, as to be mistaken for her very nature. And when she has succeeded there, an easy victory will follow. But where shall be the battle-ground for this indispensable self-conquest? She will laugh at my answer when I tell her, that her dress, aye, her dress, must be that battle-ground. What! no wider, no sublimer field than this to reap her glories in! My further answer is, that if she shall reap them anywhere, she must first reap them there. I add, that her triumph there will be her triumph everywhere; and that her failure there will be her failure everywhere.

VIEWPOINT 4

"Let us own ourselves, our earnings, our genius; . . . then will each woman adjust her dress to her relations in life."

Dress Reform Is Not Essential to Women's Equality

Frances D. Gage (1808–1884)

Many early feminists advocated women's dress reform and began to wear bloomers, which were more comfortable and allowed greater freedom of movement than hoop skirts and corsets. However, at a time when most American women would not even reveal their ankles, the bloomer outfit—with its trousers and short skirt—was considered shockingly indecent. Women who wore bloomers were ridiculed and harassed in the streets, lampooned by newspaper cartoonists, and denounced from pulpits for wearing "men's clothing." By the mid-1850s, most feminists believed that the attempt to make bloomers publicly acceptable had failed; very few continued to wear the style.

Frances D. Gage was an author, newspaper editor, and lecturer on such reform causes as women's equality, temperance, and the abolition of slavery. The following viewpoint is taken from Gage's December 24, 1855, letter to the abolitionist newspaper *North Star*, in which she responded to Gerrit Smith's criticism of the abandonment of dress reform. Although Gage admits that she finds current women's fashions to be physically hampering, she argues that feminists can strive for women's rights in hoop skirts just as well as in bloomers. Other issues, such as gaining economic and political equality, are far more important to women than reforming clothing styles, Gage concludes.

From an 1855 letter of Frances D. Gage, as reprinted in *History of Woman Suffrage*, vol. 1, edited by Elizabeth Cady Stanton, Susan B. Anthony, and Matilda Joslyn Gage (New York: Fowler & Wells, 1881).

Dear Sir:

In your issue of December 1st, 1855, I find a letter from Hon. Gerrit Smith to Elizabeth C. Stanton, in reference to the Woman's Rights Movement, showing cause, through labored columns, why it has proved a failure.

This article, though addressed to Mrs. Stanton, is an attack upon every one engaged in the cause. For he boldly asserts that the movement "is not in proper hands, and that the proper hands are not yet to be found." I will not deny the assertion, but must still claim the privilege of working in a movement that involves not only my own interest, but the interests of my sex, and through us the interests of a whole humanity. And though I may be but a John the Baptist, unworthy to unloose the latchet of the shoes of those who are to come in *short skirts* to redeem the world, I still prefer that humble position to being Peter to deny my Master, or a Gerrit Smith to assert that truth *can* fail.

Dress Reform Will Follow Equal Rights

I do not propose to enter into a full criticism of Mr. Smith's long letter. He has made the whole battle-ground of the Woman's Rights Movement her dress. Nothing brighter, nothing nobler than a few inches of calico or brocade added to or taken from her skirts, is to decide this great and glorious question—to give her freedom or to continue her a slave. This argument, had it come from one of the less influence than Gerrit Smith, would have been simply ridiculous. But coming from *him*, the almost oracle of a large portion of our reformers, it becomes worthy of an answer from every earnest woman in our cause. I will not say one word in defense of our present mode of dress. Not I; but bad as it is, and cumbersome and annoying, I still feel that we can wear it, and yet be lovers of liberty, speaking out our deep feeling, portraying our accumulated wrongs, saving ourselves for a time yet from that antagonism which we must inevitably meet when we don the semi-male attire. We *must own ourselves under the law first*, own our bodies, our earnings, our genius, and our consciences; then we will turn to the lesser matter of what shall be the garniture of the body. Was the old Roman less a man in his cumbrous toga, than Washington in his tights? Was Christ less a Christ in His vesture, woven without a seam, than He would have been in the suit of a Broadway dandy?

"Moreover, to concede to her rights of property, would be to benefit her comparatively little, unless she shall resolve to break out of her clothes-prison, and to undertake right earnestly, as earnestly as a man, to get property." So says Gerrit Smith. And he imputes the want of earnestness to her clothes. It is a new doctrine that high and holy purposes go from without inward, that the garments of men or women govern and control their aspirations. But do not women *now* work right earnestly? Do not the German women and our market women labor right earnestly? Do not the wives of our farmers and mechanics toil? Is not the work of the *mothers* in our land as important as that of the father? "Labor is the foundation of wealth." The reason that our women are "paupers," is not that they do not labor "right earnestly," but that the law gives their earnings into the hands of manhood. Mr. Smith says, "That women are helpless, is no wonder, so long as they are paupers"; he might add, no wonder that the slaves of the cotton plantation are helpless, so long as they are paupers. What reduces both the woman and the slave to this condition? The law which gives the husband and the master entire control of the person and earnings of each; the law that robs each of the rights and liberties that every "free white male citizen" takes to himself as God-given. Truth falling from the lips of a Lucretia Mott in long skirts is none the less truth, than if uttered by a Lucy Stone in

---

Unsexed Women

On September 7, 1853, the New York Herald published an editorial criticizing attendees of the New York City Woman's Rights Convention for wearing bloomers.

The assemblage of rampant women which convened at the [Broadway] Tabernacle yesterday was an interesting phase in the comic history of the nineteenth century.

We saw, in broad daylight, in a public hall in the city of New York, a gathering of unsexed women—unsexed in mind all of them, and many in habiliments—publicly propounding the doctrine that they should be allowed to step out of their appropriate sphere, and mingle in the busy walks of every-day life, to the neglect of those duties which both human and divine law have assigned to them. . . .

It is almost needless for us to say that these women are entirely devoid of personal attractions. They are generally thin maiden ladies, or women who perhaps have been disappointed in their endeavors to appropriate the breeches and the rights of their unlucky lords. . . . They violate the rules of decency and taste by attiring themselves in eccentric habiliments, which hang loosely and inelegantly upon their forms, making that which we have been educated to respect, to love, and to admire, only an object of aversion and disgust. A few of these unfortunate women have awoke from their momentary trance, and quickly returned to the dress of decent society; but we saw yesterday many disciples of the Bloomer school at the Tabernacle.

short dress, or a Helen Maria Weber in pants and swallowtail coat. And I can not yet think so meanly of manly justice, as to believe it will yield simply to a change of garments. Let us assert our right to be free. Let us get out of our prison-house of law. Let us own ourselves, our earnings, our genius; let us have power to control as well as to earn and to own; then will each woman adjust her dress to her relations in life.

Progress

Mr. Smith speaks of reforms as failures; what can he mean? "The Temperance Reform still drags." I have been in New York thirty-seven days; have given thirty-three lectures; have been at taverns, hotels, private houses, and depots; rode in stages, country wagons, omnibuses, carriages, and railroad cars; met the masses of people daily, and yet have not seen one drunken man, scarce an evidence that there was such a thing as intemperance in the Empire State. If the whole body has been diseased from childhood and a cure be attempted, shall we cry out against the physician that his effort is a failure, because the malady does not wholly disappear at once? Oh, no! let us rather cheer than discourage, while we see symptoms of amendment, hoping and trusting that each day will give renewed strength for the morrow, till the cure shall be made perfect. The accumulated ills of centuries can not be removed in a day or a year. Shall we talk of the Anti-Slavery Cause as a "failure," while our whole great nation is shaking as if an Etna were boiling below? When did the North ever stand, as now, defiant of slavery? Anti-slavery may be said to be written upon the "chariots and the bells of the horses." Our National Congress is nothing more or less than a great Anti-slavery Convention. Not a bill, no matter how small or how great its importance, but hinges upon the question of slavery. The Anti-Slavery Cause is no failure, RIGHT CAN NOT FAIL.

"The next Woman's Rights Convention will be, as has every other Woman's Rights Convention, a failure, notwithstanding it will abound in righteous demands and noble sentiments." So thinks Mr. Smith. Has any Woman's Rights Convention been a failure? No movement so radical, striking so boldly at the foundation of all social and political order, has ever come before the people, or ever so rapidly and widely diffused its doctrine. The reports of our conventions have traveled wherever newspapers are read, causing discussion for and against, and these discussions have elicited truth, and aroused public thought to the evils growing out of woman's position. New trades and callings are opening to us; in every town and village may be found advocates for the equality of privilege under the law, for every thinking, reasoning human soul. Shall we talk of failure, because forty, twenty, or seven years have not perfected all things? When intemperance shall have passed away, and the four million chattel slaves shall sing songs of freedom; when woman shall be recognized as man's equal, socially, legally, and politically, there will yet be reforms and reformers, and men who will despair and look upon one branch of the reform as the great *battle-ground*, and talk of the failure of the eternal law of progress. Still there will be stout hearts and willing hands to work on, honestly believing that truth and right are sustained by no single point, and their watchword will be "onward!" We can not fail, for our cause is just.

VIEWPOINT 5

"The best interests of the individual, the family, the State, the nation, cry out against these legalized marriages of force and endurance."

Divorce Laws Should Be Liberalized

Elizabeth Cady Stanton (1815–1902)

The daughter of a judge, Elizabeth Cady Stanton received special permission to attend a boys' school, where she obtained a classical education. She also studied law with her father but was unable to become a lawyer because women were not admitted to the bar. Throughout her life, Stanton retained her interest in the law, and she applied her legal knowledge to the movement for women's rights, especially to marriage and divorce reform. One of the most prominent feminists of her day, Stanton organized the first women's rights convention at Seneca Falls, wrote numerous articles and speeches, and participated in several equal rights organizations.

On May 10, 1860, at the Tenth National Woman's Rights Convention in New York City, Stanton delivered the following speech advocating the liberalization of New York's state laws on divorce. Stanton argues that women should be able to divorce husbands who are physically abusive, alcoholic, or fraudulent. Current laws that bind women in unhappy and loveless marriages require them to sacrifice their lives for the purported good of society, Stanton contends. The good of society would be better served, she asserts, if women were equal partners in marriage, retaining the right to control their property and person and having the ability to sue for divorce if necessary to protect their rights and well-being.

From Elizabeth Cady Stanton's address of May 10, 1860, to the Tenth National Woman's Rights Convention, New York, 10–11 May 1860, as recorded in the convention's proceedings.

1. Resolved, That, in the language (slightly varied) of John Milton, "Those who marry intend as little to conspire their own ruin, as those who swear allegiance, and as a whole people is to *an ill government*, so is one man or woman *to an ill marriage*. If a whole people, against any authority, covenant or statute, may, by the sovereign edict of charity, save not only their lives, but honest liberties, from unworthy bondage, as well may a married party, against any private covenant, which he or she never entered, *to his or her mischief*, be redeemed from unsupportable disturbances, to honest peace, and just contentment."

2. Resolved, That all men are created equal, and all women, in their natural rights, are the equals of men; and endowed by their Creator with the same inalienable right to the pursuit of happiness.

3. Resolved, That any constitution, compact or covenant between human beings, that failed to produce or promote human happiness, could not, in the nature of things, be of any force or authority;—and it would be not only a right, but a duty, to abolish it.

4. Resolved, That though marriage be in itself divinely founded, and is fortified as an institution by innumerable analogies in the whole kingdom of universal nature, still, a true marriage is only known by its results; and, like the fountain, if pure, will reveal only pure manifestations. Nor need it ever be said, "What God hath joined together, let not man put asunder" [Matthew 19:6; Mark 10:9], for man could not put it asunder; nor can he any more unite what God and nature have not joined together.

5. Resolved, That of all insulting mockeries of heavenly truth and holy law, none can be greater than that physical *impotency* is cause sufficient for divorce, while no amount of mental or moral or spiritual *imbecility* is ever to be pleaded in support of such a demand.

6. Resolved, That such a law was worthy of those dark periods when marriage was held by the greatest doctors and priests of the Church to be a *work of the flesh only*, and almost, if not altogether, a defilement; denied wholly to the clergy, and a second time, forbidden to all.

7. Resolved, That an unfortunate or ill-assorted marriage is ever a calamity, but not ever, perhaps never, a crime;—and when society or government, by its laws or customs, compels its continuance, always to the grief of one of the parties, and the actual loss and damage of both, it usurps an authority never delegated to man, nor exercised by God himself.

8. Resolved, That observation and experience daily show how incompetent are men, as individuals, or as governments, to select partners in business, teachers for their children, ministers of their religion, or makers, adjudicators or administrators of their laws;

and as the same weakness and blindness must attend in the selection of matrimonial partners, the dictates of humanity and common sense alike show that the latter and most important contract should no more be perpetual than either or all of the former.

9. Resolved, That children born in these unhappy and unhallowed connections are, in the most solemn sense, of *unlawful birth*,—the fruit of lust, but not of love;—and so not of God, divinely descended, but from beneath, whence proceed all manner of evil and uncleanness.

10. Resolved, That next to the calamity of such a birth to the child, is the misfortune of being trained in the atmosphere of a household where love is not the law, but where discord and bitterness abound; stamping their demoniac features on the moral nature, with all their odious peculiarities;—thus continuing the race in a weakness and depravity that must be a sure precursor of its ruin, as a just penalty of long-violated law.

Human Rights Are Above All Laws

Mrs. President—In our common law, in our whole system of jurisprudence, we find man's highest idea of right. The object of law is to secure justice. But inasmuch as fallible man is the maker and administrator of law, we must look for many and gross blunders in the application of its general principles to individual cases.

The science of theology, of civil, political, moral and social life, all teach the common idea, that man ever has been, and ever must be, sacrificed to the highest good of society; the one to the many—the poor to the rich—the weak to the powerful—and all to the institutions of his own creation. Look, what thunderbolts of power man has forged in the ages for his own destruction!—at the organizations to enslave himself! And through those times of darkness, those generations of superstition, behold all along the relics of his power and skill, that stand like mile-stones, here and there, to show how far back man was great and glorious! Who can stand in those vast cathedrals of the old world, as the deep-toned organ reverberates from arch to arch, and not feel the grandeur of immortality? Here is the incarnated thought of man, beneath whose stately dome the man himself now bows in fear and doubt, knows not himself, and knows not God,—a mere slave to symbols,—and with holy water signs the Cross, whilst he who died thereon declared man God.

I repudiate this popular idea. I place man above all governments, all institutions—ecclesiastical and civil—all constitutions and laws. It is a mistaken idea, that the same law that oppresses the individual, can promote the highest good of society. The best interests of a community never can require the sacrifice of one innocent being—of one sacred right. In the settlement, then, of any question, we must simply consider the highest good of the individual. It is the inalienable right of all to be happy. It is the highest duty of all to seek those conditions in life, those surroundings, which may develop what is noblest and best, remembering that the lessons of these passing hours are not for time alone, but for the ages of eternity. They tell us, in that future home—the heavenly paradise—that the human family shall be sifted out, and the good and pure shall dwell together in peace. If that be the heavenly order, is it not our duty to render earth as near like heaven as we may?

Elizabeth Cady Stanton and her daughter, Harriot, in 1856. Stanton's appeal for reformed divorce laws shocked many women's rights advocates.

For years, there has been before the Legislature of this State [New York] a variety of bills, asking for divorce in cases of drunkenness, insanity, desertion, cruel and brutal treatment, endangering life. My attention was called to this question very early in life, by the sufferings of a friend of my girlhood, a victim of one of those unfortunate unions, called marriage. What my great love for that young girl, and my holy intuitions, then decided to be right, has not been changed by years of experience, observation and reason. I have pondered well these things in my heart, and ever felt the deepest interest in all that has been written and said upon the subject, and the most profound respect and loving sympathy for those heroic women, who, in the face of law and public sentiment, have dared to sunder the unholy ties of a joyless, loveless union.

If marriage is a human institution, about which man may legislate, it seems but just that he should treat this branch of his legislation with the same common sense that he applies to all others. If it is a mere legal contract, then should it be subject to the restraints and privileges of all other contracts. A contract, to be valid in law, must be formed between parties of mature age, with an honest intention in said parties to do what they agree. The least concealment, fraud, or intention to deceive, if proved, annuls the contract. A boy cannot contract for an acre of land, or a horse, until he is twenty-one, but he may contract for a wife at fourteen. If a man sell a horse, and the purchaser find in him great incompatibility of temper—a disposition to stand still, when the owner is in haste to go—the sale is null and void, the man and his horse part company. But in marriage, no matter how much fraud and deception are practiced, nor how cruelly one or both parties have been misled; no matter how young, inexperienced or thoughtless the parties, nor how unequal their condition and position in life, the contract cannot be annulled. Think of a husband telling a young and trusting girl, but one short month his wife, that he married her for her money; that those letters, so precious to her, that she had read and re-read, and kissed and cherished, were written by another; that their splendid home, of which, on their wedding day, her father gave to him the deed, is already in the hands of his creditors; that she must give up the elegance and luxury that now surround her, unless she can draw fresh supplies of money to meet their wants! When she told the story of her wrongs to me,—the abuse to which she was subject, and the dread in which she lived,—I impulsively urged her to fly from such a monster and villain, as she would before the hot breath of a ferocious beast of the wilderness. And she did fly; and it was well with her. Many times since, as I have felt her throbbing heart against my own, she has said, "Oh, but for your love and sympathy, your encouragement, I should never have escaped from that bondage. Before I could, of myself, have found courage to break those chains, my heart would have broken in the effort."

Unholy Unions

Marriage, as it now exists, must seem to all of you a mere human institution. Look through the universe of matter and mind,—all God's arrangements are perfect, harmonious and complete! There is no discord, friction, or failure in his eternal plans. Immutability, perfection, beauty, are stamped on all his laws. Love is the vital essence that pervades and permeates, from the centre to the circumference, the graduating circles of all thought and action. Love is the talisman of human weal and woe,—the *open sesame* to every human soul. Where two beings are drawn together, by the natural laws of likeness and affinity, union and happiness are the result. Such marriages might be Divine. But how is it now? You all know our marriage is, in many cases, a mere outward tie, impelled by custom, policy, interest, necessity; founded not even in friendship, to say nothing of love; with every possible inequality of condition and development. In these heterogeneous unions, we find youth and old age, beauty and deformity, refinement and vulgarity, virtue and vice, the educated and the ignorant, angels of grace and goodness, with devils of malice and malignity: and the sum of all this is human wretchedness and despair; cold fathers, sad mothers, and hapless children, who shiver at the hearthstone, where the fires of love have all gone out. The wide world, and the stranger's unsympathizing gaze, are not more to be dreaded for young hearts than homes like these. Now, who shall say that it is right to take two beings, so unlike, and anchor them right side by side fast bound—to stay all time, until God shall summon one away?

Do wise, Christian legislators need any arguments to convince them that the sacredness of the family relation should be protected at all hazards? The family, that great conservator of national virtue and strength, how can you hope to build it up in the midst of violence, debauchery and excess? Can there be any thing sacred at that family altar, where the chief priest who ministers makes sacrifice of human beings, of the weak and the innocent? where the incense offered up is not to the God of justice and mercy, but to those heathen divinities, who best may represent the lost man in all his grossness and deformity? Call that sacred, where woman, the mother of the race,—of a Jesus of Nazareth,— unconscious of the true dignity of her nature, of her high and holy destiny, consents to live in legalized prostitution!—her whole soul revolting at such gross association!—her flesh shivering at the cold contamination of that embrace,—held there by no tie but the iron chain of the law, and a false and most unnatural public sentiment? Call that sacred, where innocent children, trembling with fear, fly to the corners and dark places of the house, to hide themselves from the wrath of drunken, brutal fathers, but, forgetting their past sufferings, rush out again at their mother's frantic screams, "Help, oh help"? Behold the agonies of those young hearts, as they see the only being on earth they love, dragged about the room by the hair of the head, kicked and pounded, and left half dead and bleeding on the floor! Call that sacred, where fathers like these have the power and legal right to hand down their natures to other beings,—to curse other generations with such moral deformity and death?

Men and brethren, look into your asylums for the blind, the deaf and dumb, the idiot, the imbecile, the deformed, the insane; go out into the by-lanes and dens of this vast metropolis, and contemplate that reeking mass of depravity; pause before the terrible revelations made by statistics of the rapid increase of all this moral and physical impotency, and learn how fearful a thing it is to violate the immutable laws of the beneficent Ruler of the universe; and there behold the terrible retributions of your violence on woman! Learn how false and cruel are those institutions, which, with a coarse materialism, set aside those holy instincts of the woman to bear no children but those of love! In the best condition of marriage, as we now have it, to woman comes all the penalties and sacrifices. A man, in the full tide of business or pleasure, can marry and not change his life one iota; he can be husband, father, and every thing beside: but in marriage, woman gives up all. Home is her sphere, her realm. Well, be it so. If here you will make us all supreme, take to yourselves the universe beside; explore the North Pole; and, in your airy car, all space; in your Northern homes and cloud-capt towers, go feast on walrus flesh and air, and lay you down to sleep your six months' night away, and leave us to make these laws that govern the inner sanctuary of our own homes, and faithful satellites we will ever be to the dinner-pot, the cradle, and the old arm-chair.

A Life-Long Penalty

Fathers, do you say, let your daughters pay a life-long penalty for one unfortunate step? How could they, on the threshold of life, full of joy and hope, believing all things to be as they seemed on the surface, judge of the dark windings of the human soul? How could they foresee that the young man, to-day so noble, so generous, would in a few short years be transformed into a cowardly, mean tyrant, or a foul-mouthed, bloated drunkard? What father could rest at his home by night, knowing that his lovely daughter was at the mercy of a strong man drunk with wine and passion, and that, do what he might, he was backed up by law and public sentiment? The best interests of the individual, the family, the State, the nation, cry out against these legalized marriages of force and endurance. There can be no heaven without love, and nothing is sacred in the family and home, but just so far as it is built up and anchored in love. Our newspapers teem with startling accounts of husbands and wives having shot or poisoned each other, or committed suicide, choosing death rather than the indissoluble tie; and, still worse, the living death of faithless wives and daughters, from the first families in this State, dragged from the privacy of home into the public prints and courts, with all the painful details of sad, false lives. What say you to facts like these? Now, do you believe, men and women, that all these wretched matches are made in heaven? that all these sad, miserable people are bound together by God? . . . Our lawmakers have dug a pit, and the innocent have fallen into it; and now will you coolly cover them over with statute laws . . . and tell them to stay there, and pay the life-long penalty of having fallen in? [The Roman emperor] Nero was thought the chief of tyrants, because he made laws and hung them up so high that his subjects could not read them, and then punished them for every act of disobedience. What better are our Republican legislators? The mass of the women of this nation know nothing about the laws, yet all their specially barbarous legislation is for woman. Where have they made any provision for her to learn the laws? Where is the Law School for our daughters?—where the law office, the bar, or the bench, now urging them to take part in the jurisprudence of the nation? But, say you, does not separation cover all these difficulties? No one objects to separation when the parties are so disposed. Now, to separation there are two very serious objections. First, so long as you insist on marriage as a Divine institution, as an indissoluble tie, so long as you maintain your present laws against divorce, you make separation, even, so odious, that the most noble, virtuous and sensitive men and women choose a life of concealed misery, rather than a partial, disgraceful release. Sec-

---

A Marriage Protest

Lucy Stone and Henry Blackwell, both active supporters of the cause of women's rights, were married on May 1, 1855. The following protest against unequal marriage laws was read during their wedding ceremony.

While acknowledging our mutual affection by publicly assuming the relationship of husband and wife, yet in justice to ourselves and a great principle, we deem it a duty to declare that this act on our part implies no sanction of, nor promise of voluntary obedience to such of the present laws of marriage, as refuse to recognize the wife as an independent, rational being, while they confer upon the husband an injurious and unnatural superiority, investing him with legal powers which no honorable man would exercise, and which no man should possess. . . .

We believe that personal independence and equal human rights can never be forfeited, except for crime; that marriage should be an equal and permanent partnership, and so recognized by law; that until it is so recognized, married partners should provide against the radical injustice of present laws, by every means in their power. . . .

Thus reverencing law, we enter our protest against rules and customs which are unworthy of the name, since they violate justice, the essence of law.

ondly, those who, in their impetuosity and despair, do, in spite of public sentiment, separate, find themselves in their new position beset with many temptations to lead a false, unreal life. This isolation bears especially hard on woman. Marriage is not all of life to man. His resources for amusement and occupation are boundless. He has the whole world for his home. His business, his politics, his club, his friendships with either sex, can help to fill up the void made by an unfortunate union or separation. But to woman, marriage is all and every thing; her sole object in life,—that for which she is educated,—the subject of all her sleeping and her waking dreams. Now, if a noble, generous girl of eighteen marries, and is unfortunate, because the cruelty of her husband compels separation, in her dreary isolation, would you drive her to a nunnery; and shall she be a nun indeed? Her solitude is nothing less, as, in the present undeveloped condition of woman, it is only through our fathers, brothers, husbands, sons, that we feel the pulsations of the great outer world.

One unhappy, discordant man or woman in a neighborhood, may mar the happiness of all the rest. You cannot shut up discord, any more than you can small-pox. There can be no morality, where there is a settled discontent. A very wise father once remarked, that in the government of his children, he forbade as few things as possible; a wise legislation would do the same. It is folly to make laws on subjects beyond human prerogative, knowing that in the very nature of things they must be set aside. To make laws that man cannot and will not obey, serves to bring all law into contempt. It is very important in a republic, that the people should respect the laws, for if we throw them to the winds, what becomes of civil government? What do our present divorce laws amount to? Those who wish to evade them have only to go into another State to accomplish what they desire. If any of our citizens cannot secure their inalienable rights in New York State, they may in Connecticut and Indiana. Why is it that all agreements, covenants, partnerships, are left wholly at the discretion of the parties, except the contract, which of all others is considered most holy and important, both for the individual and the race? This question of divorce, they tell us, is hedged about with difficulties; that it cannot be approached with the ordinary rules of logic and common sense. It is too holy, too sacred to be discussed, and few seem disposed to touch it. From man's stand-point, this may be all true,—as to him they say belong reason, and the power of ratiocination. Fortunately, I belong to that class endowed with mere intuitions,—a kind of moral instinct, by which we feel out right and wrong. In presenting to you, therefore, my views of divorce, you will of course give to them the weight only of the woman's intuitions. But inasmuch as that is all God saw fit to give us, it is evident we need nothing more. Hence, what we do perceive of truth must be as reliable as what man grinds out by the longer process of reason, authority, and speculation. . . .

A New Kind of Marriage

There is one kind of marriage that has not been tried, and that is, a contract made by equal parties to live an equal life, with equal restraints and privileges on either side. Thus far, we have had the man marriage, and nothing more. From the beginning, man has had the sole and whole regulation of the matter. He has spoken in Scripture, he has spoken in law. As an individual, he has decided the time and cause for putting away a wife, and as a judge and legislator, he still holds the entire control. In all history, sacred and profane, the woman is regarded and spoken of simply as the toy of man,—made for his special use,—to meet his most gross and sensuous desires. She is taken or put away, given or received, bought or sold, just as the interest of the parties might dictate. But the woman has been no more recognized in all these transactions, through all the different periods and conditions of the race, than if she had had no part nor lot in the whole matter. The right of woman to put away a husband, be he ever so impure, is never hinted at in sacred history. Even Jesus himself failed to recognize the sacred rights of the holy mothers of the race. We cannot take our gauge of womanhood from the past, but from the solemn convictions of our own souls, in the higher development of the race. No parchments, however venerable with the mould of ages, no human institutions, can bound the immortal wants of the royal sons and daughters of the great I Am,—rightful heirs of the joys of time, and joint heirs of the glories of eternity.

If in marriage either party claims the right to stand supreme, to woman, the mother of the race, belongs the sceptre and the crown. Her life is one long sacrifice for man. You tell us that among all womankind there are no Moses, Christs, or Pauls,—no Michael Angelos, Beethovens, or Shakespeares—no Columbuses or Galileos,—no [John] Lockes or [Francis] Bacons. Behold those mighty minds attuned to music and the arts, so great, so grand, so comprehensive,—these are our great works of which we boast! Which, think you, stands first, the man, or what he does? By just so far as Galileo is greater than his thought, is the mother far above the man. Into you, oh sons of earth, go all of us that is great and grand. In you centre our very life-thoughts, our hopes, our intensest love. For you we gladly pour out our heart's blood and die. Willingly do we drink the cup in the holy sacrament of marriage, in the same faith that the Son of Mary died on Calvary,— knowing that from our suffering comes forth a new and more glorious resurrection of thought and life.

"Marriage must be as permanent and indissoluble as the relation of parent and child."

Divorce Laws Should Not Be Liberalized

Antoinette Brown Blackwell (1825–1921)

Antoinette Brown Blackwell graduated from Oberlin College in 1847 and from Oberlin's theological seminary in 1850. In 1853 she was ordained as a minister of the First Congregational Church in South Butler, New York, thereby becoming the first American woman ordained in a mainstream denomination. Blackwell was a frequent lecturer on women's rights and other reform causes and the author of several books, including *The Sexes Throughout Nature.*

Blackwell attended the Tenth National Woman's Rights Convention in New York City and was in the audience on May 10, 1860, when Elizabeth Cady Stanton called for the liberalization of New York's divorce laws. After Stanton's appeal, Blackwell took the floor and delivered the following speech to the members of the convention. Marriage, Blackwell argues, is a sacred and lifelong union that should be upheld by the laws of the state. Although Blackwell concedes that married women should be able to legally protect themselves and their children from abusive husbands, she contends that these wives should not leave their husbands but instead should try to reform them. Unhappy marriages can be avoided not by liberalizing divorce laws, Blackwell avers, but by encouraging women to marry at an older age and to maintain other interests outside of the home.

From Antoinette Brown Blackwell's address of May 10, 1860, to the Tenth National Woman's Rights Convention, New York, 10–11 May 1860, as recorded in the convention's proceedings.

Mrs. President,—Ours has always been a free platform. We have believed in the fullest freedom of thought and in the free expression of individual opinion. I propose to speak upon the subject discussed by our friend, Mrs. Stanton. It is often said that there are two sides to every question; but there are three sides, many sides, to every question. Let Mrs. Stanton take hers; . . . I only ask the privilege of stating mine. I have embodied my thought, hastily, in a series of resolutions, and my remarks following them will be very brief.

1. Resolved, That marriage is the voluntary alliance of two persons of opposite sexes into one family, and that such an alliance, with its possible incidents of children, its common interests, etc., must be, from the nature of things, as permanent as the life of the parties.

2. Resolved, That if human law attempts to regulate marriage at all, it should aim to regulate it according to the fundamental principles of marriage; and that as the institution is inherently as continuous as the life of the parties, so all laws should look to its control and preservation as such.

3. Resolved, That as a parent can never annul his obligations towards even a profligate child, because of the inseparable relationship of the parties, so the married partner cannot annul his obligations towards the other, while both live, no matter how profligate that other's conduct may be, because of their still closer and alike permanent relationship; and, therefore, that all divorce is naturally and morally impossible, even though we should succeed in annulling all legalities.

4. Resolved, That gross fraud and want of good faith in one of the parties contracting this alliance, such as would invalidate any other voluntary relation, are the only causes which can invalidate this, and this, too, solely upon the ground that the relation never virtually existed, and that there are, therefore, no resulting moral obligations.

5. Resolved, however, That both men and women have a first and inviolable right to themselves, physically, mentally and morally, and that it can never be the duty of either to surrender his personal freedom in any direction to his own hurt.

6. Resolved, That the great duty of every human being is to secure his own highest moral development, and that he cannot owe to society, or to an individual, any obligation which shall be degrading to himself.

7. Resolved, That self-devotion to the good of another, and especially to the good of the sinful and guilty, like all disinterestedness, must redound to the highest good of its author, and that the

husband or wife who thus seeks the best interest of the other, is obedient to the highest law of benevolence.

8. Resolved, That this is a very different thing from the culpable weakness which allows itself to be immolated by the selfishness of another, to the hurt of both; and that the miserable practice, now so common among wives, of allowing themselves, their children and family interests, to be sacrificed to a degraded husband and father, is most reprehensible.

9. Resolved, That human law is imperatively obligated to give either party ample protection to himself, to their offspring, and to all other family interests, against wrong, injustice, and usurpation on the part of the other; and that, if it be necessary to this, it should grant a legal separation; and yet, that even such separation cannot invalidate any real marriage obligation.

10. Resolved, That every married person is imperatively obligated to do his utmost thus to protect himself and all family interests against injustice and wrong, let it arise from what source it may.

11. Resolved, That every woman is morally obligated to maintain her equality in human rights in all her relations in life, and that if she consents to her own subjugation, either in the family, Church or State, she is as guilty as the slave is in consenting to be a slave.

12. Resolved, That a perfect union cannot be expected to exist until we first have perfect units, and that every marriage of finite beings must be gradually perfected through the growth and assimilation of the parties.

13. Resolved, That the permanence and indissolubility of marriage tend more directly than any thing else towards this result.

Maintaining Independence in Marriage

I believe that all the laws which God has established are sacred and inviolable; that his laws are the best which exist; that they are all founded on the natures or relation of things, and that he has no laws which are not as eternal as the natures and relations to which he has given existence. I believe, therefore, that the highest laws of our being are those which we find written within our being; that the first moral laws which we are to obey are the laws which God's own finger has traced upon our own souls. Therefore, our first duty is to ourselves, and we may never, under any circumstances, yield this to any other. I say, we are first responsible for ourselves to ourselves, and to the God who has laid the obligation upon us to make ourselves the best, the grandest we may. Marriage grows out of the relations of parties. The law of our development comes wholly from within; but the relation of marriage supposes two persons as being united to each other,

Marriage Laws Affect Both Sexes Equally

Wendell Phillips, a well-known orator and social reformer, joined the debate over divorce law reform at the Tenth National Woman's Rights Convention. In this excerpt from his speech, Phillips contends that the women's rights movement should not be concerned with the subject of marriage and divorce.

This Convention is no Marriage Convention,—if it were, the subject would be in order; but this Convention, if I understand it, assembles to discuss the laws that rest unequally upon women, not those that rest equally upon men and women. It is the laws that make distinctions between the sexes. Now, whether a man and a woman are married for a year or a life is a question which affects the man just as much as the woman. At the end of a month, the man is without a wife exactly as much as the woman is without a husband. The question whether, having entered into a contract, you shall be bound to an unworthy partner, affects the man as much as the woman. Certainly, there are cases where men are bound to women carcasses as well as where women are bound to men carcasses. We have nothing to do with a question which affects both sexes equally. Therefore, it seems to me we have nothing to do with the theory of Marriage, which is the basis . . . of Divorce.

and from this relation originates the law. Mrs. Stanton calls marriage a "tie." No, marriage is a *relation*; and, once formed, that relation continues as long as the parties continue with the natures which they now essentially have. Let, then, the two parties deliberately, voluntarily consent to enter into this relation. It is one which, from its very nature, must be permanent. Its interests are permanent. Can the mother ever destroy the relation which exists between herself and her child? Can the father annul the relation which exists between himself and his child? Then, can the father and mother annul the relation which exists between themselves, the parents of the child? It cannot be. The interests of marriage are such that they cannot be destroyed, and the only question must be, "Has there been a marriage in this case or not?" If there has, then the social law, the obligations out-growing from the relation, must be life-long.

But I assert that every woman, in the present state of society, is bound to maintain her own independence and her own integrity of character; to assert herself, earnestly and firmly, as the equal of man, who is only her peer. This is her first right, her first duty; and if she lives in a country where the law supposes that she is to be subjected to her husband, and she consents to this subjection, I do insist that she consents to degradation; that this is sin, and it is impossible to make it other than sin. True, in this State [New York], and in nearly all the States, the idea of marriage is that of subjection, in all respects, of the wife to the husband—personal subjection, subjection in the rights over their children, and over their property; but this is a false relation. Marriage is a union of equals—equal interests being involved, equal duties at stake; and if any woman has been married to a man who chooses to take advantage of the laws as they now stand, who chooses to subject her, ignobly, to his will, against her own, to take from her the earnings which belong to the family, and to take from her the children which belong to the family, I hold that that woman, if she cannot, by her influence, change this state of things, is solemnly obligated to go to some State where she can be legally divorced; and then she would be as solemnly bound to return again, and, standing for herself and her children, regard herself, in the sight of God, as being bound still to the father of those children, to work for his best interests, while she still maintains her own sovereignty. Of course, she must be governed by the circumstances of the case. She may be obliged, for the protection of the family, to live on one continent while her husband is on the other; but she is never to forget that in the sight of God and her own soul, she is his wife, and that she owes to him the wife's loyalty; that to work for his redemption is her highest social obligation, and that to teach her children to do the same is her first motherly duty. Legal divorce may be necessary for personal and family protection; if so, let every woman obtain it. This, God helping me, is what I would certainly do; for under no circumstances will I ever give my consent to be subjected to the will of another, in any relation, for God has bidden me not to do it. But the idea of most women is, that they must be timid, weak, helpless, and full of ignoble submission. Only last week, a lady who has just been divorced from her husband said to me—"I used to be required to go into the field and do the hardest laborer's work, when I was not able to do it, and my husband would declare, that if I would not thus labor, I should not be allowed to eat, and I was obliged to submit." I say, the fault was as much with the woman as with the man; she should *never* have submitted.

Our trouble is not with marriage as a relation between two; it is all individual. We have few men or women fit to be married. They neither fully respect themselves and their own rights and duties, nor yet those of another. They have no idea how noble, how godlike is the relation which ought to exist between the husband and wife.

A Permanent Contract

Tell me, is marriage to be merely a contract—something entered into for a time, and then broken again—or is the true marriage permanent? One resolution read by Mrs. Stanton said that, as men are incompetent to select partners in business, teachers for their children, ministers of their religion, or makers, adjudicators or administrators of their laws, and as the same weakness and blindness must attend in the selection of matrimonial partners, the latter and most important contract should no more be perpetual than either or all of the former. I do not believe that, rightly understood, she quite holds to that position herself. Marriage must be either permanent, or capable of being any time dissolved. Which ground shall we take? I insist, that from the nature of things, marriage must be as permanent and indissoluble as the relation of parent and child. If so, let us legislate towards the right. Though evils must sometimes result, we are still to seek the highest law of the relation.

Self-devotion is always sublimely beautiful, but the law has no right to require either a woman to be sacrificed to any man, or a man to be sacrificed to any woman, or either to the good of society; but if either chooses to devote himself to the good of the other, no matter how low that other may have fallen, no matter how degraded he may be, let the willing partner strive to lift him up, not by going down and sitting side by side with him—that is wrong—but by steadily trying to win him back to the right; keeping his own sovereignty, but trying to redeem the fallen as long as life shall endure. I do not wish to go to the other state of being, and state what shall be our duty there, but I do say, that where there is sin and suffering in this universe of ours, we may none of us sit still until we have overcome that sin and suffering. Then, if my husband were wretched and degraded in this life, I believe God would give me strength to work for him while life lasted. I would do that for the lowest drunkard in the street, and certainly I would do as much for my husband. I believe that the greatest boon of existence is the privilege of working for those who are oppressed and fallen; and those who have oppressed their own natures are those who need the most help. My great hope is, that I may be able to lift them upwards. The great responsibility that has been laid upon me is the responsibility never to sit down and sing to myself psalms of happiness and content while any body suffers. Then, if I find a wretched man in the gutter, and feel that as a human sister, I must go and lift him up, and that I can never enjoy peace or rest until I have thus redeemed him and brought him out of his sins, shall I, if the man whom I solemnly swore to love, to associate with in all the interests of home and its holiest relations—shall I, if he falls into sin, turn him off, and go on enjoying life, while he is sunk in wretchedness and sin? I will not do it. To me, there is a higher idea of life. If, as an intelligent human being, I promised to co-work with him in all the higher interests of life, and if he prove false, I will not turn from him, but I must seek first to regenerate him, the nearest and dearest to me, as I would work, secondly, to save my children, who are next, and then my brothers, my sisters, and the whole human family.

Mrs. Stanton asks, "Would you send a young girl into a nunnery, when she has made a mistake?" Does Mrs. Stanton not know that nunneries belong to a past age, that people who had nothing to do might go there, and try to expiate their own sins? I would teach the young girl a higher way. I do not say to her, "If you have foolishly united yourself to another"—(not "if you have been tied by law"; for, remember, it was not the law that tied her; she said, "I will do it," and the law said, "So let it be!")—"sunder the bond"; but I say to her, that her duty is to reflect, "Now that I see my mistake, I will commence being true to myself; I will become a true unit, strong and noble in myself; and if I can never make our union a true one, I will work toward that good result, I will live for this great work—for truth and all its interests." Let me tell you, if she is not great enough to do this, she is not great enough to enter into any union!

Liberalizing Divorce Threatens the Family

Look at those who believe in thus easily dissolving the marriage obligation! In very many cases, they cannot be truly married, or truly happy in this relation, because there is something incompatible with it in their own natures. It is not always so; but when one feels that it is a relation easily to be dissolved, of course, incompatibility at once seems to arise in the other, and every difficulty that occurs, instead of being overlooked, as it ought to be, in a spirit of forgiveness, is magnified, and the evil naturally increased. We purchase a house, the deed is put into our hands, and we take possession. We feel at once that it is really very convenient. It suits us, and we are surprised that we like it so much better than we supposed. The secret is, that it is our house, and until we are ready to part with it, we make ourselves content with it as it is. We go to live in some country town. At first, we do not like it; it is not like the home we came from; but soon we begin to be reconciled, and feel that, as Dr. [Oliver Wendell] Holmes said of Boston, our town is the hub of the universe. So, when we are content to allow our relations to remain as they are, we adapt ourselves to them, and they adapt themselves to us, and we constantly, unconsciously (because God made us so) work towards the perfecting of all the interest arising from those relations. But the moment we wish to sell a house, or remove from a town, how many defects we discover! The place has not the same appearance to us at all; we wish we could get out of it; we feel all the time more and more dissatisfied. So, let any married person take the idea that he may dissolve this relation, and enter into a new one, and how many faults he may discover that otherwise never would have been noticed! The marriage will become intolerable. The theory will work that result; it is in the nature of things, and that to me is every thing. Of course, I would not have man or woman sacrificed—by no means. First of all, let every human being maintain his own position as a self-protecting human being. At all hazards, let him never sin, or consent to be sacrificed to the hurt of himself or of another; and when he has taken this stand, let him act in harmony with it. Would I say to any woman, "You are bound, because you are legally married to one who is debased to the level of the brute, to be the mother of his children?" I say to her, "No! while the law of God continues, you are bound never to make one whom you do not honor and respect, as well as love, the father of any child of yours. It is your first and highest duty to be true to yourself, true to posterity, and true to society." Thus, let each decide for himself and for herself what is right. But, I repeat, either marriage is in its very nature a relation which, once formed, never can be dissolved, and either the essential obligations growing out of it exist for ever, or the relation may at any time be dissolved, and at any time those obligations be annulled. And what are those obligations? Two persons, if I understand marriage, covenant to work together, to uphold each other in all excellence, and to mutually blend their lives and interests into a common harmony. I believe that God has so made man and woman, that it is not good for them to be alone, that they each need a co-worker. There is no work on God's footstool which man can do alone and do well, and there is no work which woman can do alone and do well. We need that the two should stand side by side every where. All over the world, we need this coöperation of the two classes,—not because they are alike, but because they are unlike,—in trying to make the whole world better. Then we need something more than these class workers. Two persons need to stand side by side, to stay up each other's hands, to take an interest in each other's welfare, to build up a family, to cluster about it all the beauties and excellencies of home life; in short, to be to each other what only one man and one woman can be to each other in all God's earth. No grown up human being ought to rush blindly into this most intimate, most important, most enduring of human relations; and will you let a young man, at the age of fourteen, contract marriage, or a young maiden either? If the law undertakes to regulate the matter at all, let it regulate it upon principles of common sense. But this is a matter which must be very much regulated by public opinion, by our teachers. What do you, the guides of our youth, say? You say to the young girl, "You ought to expect to be married before you

No Divorce

Elizabeth Oakes Smith's New York Tribune *articles on women's rights and marriage were compiled in the book* Woman and Her Needs *in 1851. Smith supported equal rights for women and reforms in marriage laws—measures that she believed would make divorce unnecessary.*

Let our legislators, or let public opinion, forbid premature marriages, but admit of no divorce. In a right relation crime could not take place; in a false one, entered into in the maturity of judgment, let it be one of the contingencies from which there is no appeal. Let it not be entered into from pecuniary motives by our sex—allow woman the rights of property, open to her the avenues to wealth, permit her not only to hold property, but to enter into commerce, or into the professions, if she is fit for them. In that case she should assuredly take the stand that her fathers took, that taxation without representation is oppressive; and then, from the nature of things, society would grow more harmonious, marriage would be sacred, and divorce pass from the statute-book.

are twenty, or about that time; you should intend to be; and from the time you are fifteen, it should be made your one life purpose; and in all human probability, you may expect to spend the next ten or twenty years in the nursery, and at forty or fifty, you will be an old woman, your life will be well-nigh worn out." I stand here to say that this is all false. Let the young girl be instructed that, above her personal interests, her home, and social life, she is to have a great life purpose, as broad as the rights and interests of humanity. I say, let every young girl feel this, as much as every young man does. We have no right, we, who expect to live for ever, to play about here as if we were mere flies, enjoying ourselves in the sunshine. We ought to have an earnest purpose outside of home, outside of our family relations. Then let the young girl fit herself for this. Let her be taught that she ought not to be married in her teens. Let her wait, as a young man does, if he is sensible, until she is twenty-five or thirty. She will then know how to choose properly, and probably she will not be deceived in her estimate of character; she will have had a certain life-discipline, which will enable her to control her household matters with wise judgment, so that, while she is looking after her family, she may still keep her great life purpose, for which she was educated, and to which she has given her best energies, steadily in view. She need not absorb herself in her home, and God never intended that she should; and then, if she has lived according to the laws of physiology, and according to the laws of common sense, she ought to be, at the age of fifty years, just where man is, just where our great men are, in the very prime of life! When her young children have gone out of her home, then let her enter in earnest upon the great work of life outside of home and its relations. It is a shame for our women to have no steady purpose or pursuit, and to make the mere fact of womanhood a valid plea for indolence; it is a greater shame that they should be instructed thus to throw all the responsibility of working for the general good upon the other sex. God has not intended it. But as long as you make women helpless, inefficient beings, who never expect to earn a farthing in their lives, who never expect to do any thing outside of the family, but to be cared for and protected by others throughout life, you cannot have true marriages; and if you try to break up the old ones, you will do it against the woman and in favor of the man. Last week, I went back to a town where I used to live, and was told that a woman, whose husband was notoriously the most miserable man in the town, had in despair taken her own life. I asked what had become of the husband, and the answer was, "Married again." And yet, every body there knows that he is the vilest and most contemptible man in the whole neighborhood. Any man, no matter how wretched he may be, will find plenty of women to accept him, while they are rendered so helpless and weak by their whole education that they must be supported or starve. The advantage, if this theory of marriage is adopted, will not be on the side of woman, but altogether on the side of man. The cure for the evils that now exist is not in dissolving marriage, but it is in giving to the married woman her own natural independence and self-sovereignty, by which she can maintain herself. Yes, our women and our men are both degenerate; they are weak and ignoble. "Dear me!" said a pretty, indolent young lady, "I had a great deal rather my husband would take care of me, than to be obliged to do it for myself." "Of course you would," said a blunt old lady who was present; "and your brother would a great deal rather marry an heiress, and lie upon a sofa eating lollypops, bought by her money, than to do any thing manly or noble. The only difference is, that as heiresses are not very plenty, he may probably have to marry a poor girl, and then society will insist that he shall exert himself to earn a living for the family; but you, poor thing, will only have to open your mouth, all your life long, like a clam, and eat."

So long as society is constituted in such a way that woman is expected to do nothing if she have a father, brother, or husband, able to support her, there is no salvation for her, in or out of marriage. When you tie up your arm, it will become weak and feeble: and when you tie up woman, she will become weak and helpless. Give her, then, some earnest purpose in life, hold up to her the true ideal of marriage, and it is enough—I am content!

VIEWPOINT 7

"Let every class have its rights the very moment the world is ready to recognize them."

Feminists Should Not Object to the Fifteenth Amendment

Wendell Phillips (1811–1884)

After the Civil War, the U.S. Congress began to consider legislation and constitutional amendments that would guarantee black men the right to vote. The Fourteenth Amendment, proposed in 1866 and adopted in 1868, specifically protected the voting rights of "male citizens" alone. Objecting to this wording, a number of feminists organized petition drives in an attempt to include women in the amendment—an attempt that was ultimately unsuccessful. The Fifteenth Amendment, proposed in February 1869, ensured that suffrage would not be denied "on account of race, color, or previous condition of servitude." Again, many women's rights advocates argued that the Fifteenth Amendment should not be passed unless it also granted the vote to women.

Other reformers, however, worried that this opposition to the Fifteenth Amendment only served to impede the movement to guarantee civil rights for black men. Among these reformers was Wendell Phillips, a prominent abolitionist and publisher of the *Anti-Slavery Standard*. Phillips was also an active supporter of the women's rights movement, but he disagreed with the faction that opposed passage of the civil rights amendments. The following viewpoint is excerpted from Phillips's July 1869 article in the feminist journal the *Woman's Advocate*. The country can only deal with one reform at a time, Phillips argues: To add the question of women's suffrage at this point would only confuse the issue and

From "The Fifteenth Amendment" by Wendell Phillips, *Woman's Advocate*, vol. 2, no. 1, July 1869.

jeopardize black men's voting rights. Phillips contends that feminists should support the passage of the Fifteenth Amendment rather than selfishly placing their demands above the needs of the former slaves. If women work now to secure the franchise for black men, Phillips concludes, surely black men will cast their votes in favor of women's suffrage.

There is a wide opposition to the Fifteenth Amendment among the advocates of Women's Rights; especially among those who have not been trained in the Anti-Slavery cause. The fact does not much surprise us. Education in reform is such a slow process, simple faith in absolute right is so very rare an element, that it is natural beginners should be confused by the crafty demagogues about them and shrink from what seems such a perilous step. A little experience and a more profound consideration will, we believe, lift them to the level of a full faith in principles.

What is the Fifteenth Amendment? It runs thus:

ARTICLE 15.—The right of the citizens of the United States to vote shall not be denied or abridged by the United States or by any State, on account of race, color, or previous condition of servitude.

SEC. 2. The Congress shall have power to enforce this article by appropriate legislation.

The form is unexceptionable. If the thing sought is good, the language used could not be better. There is no word "*male*" (odious to us all, in laws and constitutions) to be found here. Wherever and whenever women vote it will protect their rights as fully as those of men, and be as valuable to them as to men. The object sought is to oblige the States to allow black *persons* to vote on the same conditions that white *persons* do. As men only are now allowed to vote, of course the immediate effect will be to oblige the States to allow black *men* to vote just as white *men* do.

This is *all its effect*. The talk about its giving the vote to Chinamen, Irish, Germans and other "ignorant foreigners," is wholly out of place. It does not admit one such to the ballot-box; does not affect them in any way. Such men are excluded from the ballot-box, until they are naturalized, on account of their *birthplace*, not on account of their *race*. These are totally distinct elements. It is *foreigners* not *races* (excepting in the Negro's case) that we exclude from voting.

Race means *blood*. Nationality means *birthplace*. Englishmen are men of a dozen *races*, all *born* in England. *Americans* are made up of a score of *races*, all *born* here. All *races* here are equal, all Americans vote—except the black. The object of this Amendment is to abolish that inequality. A Jew born in New York does not change his race: he is still a Jew. This Amendment provides that he shall not, *on account of his race*, be denied his vote. A Jew born in Paris is still a Jew in race. He cannot vote, however, till naturalized, because he is a *foreigner*. This Amendment does not hasten his right to vote at all, does not in the least change his present rights as to voting. So of all other foreigners—Irish, Chinese, and the rest.

A Matter of Life and Death

Frederick Douglass, a former slave and a renowned abolitionist, was a dedicated supporter of women's rights. However, at the May 12, 1869, meeting of the American Equal Rights Association, Douglass maintained that the right to vote was more crucial for black men than for women.

I must say that I do not see how any one can pretend that there is the same urgency in giving the ballot to women as to the negro. With us, the matter is a question of life and death. It is a matter of existence, at least, in fifteen states of the Union. When women, because they are women, are hunted down through the cities of New York and New Orleans; when they are dragged from their houses and hung upon lamp-posts; when their children are torn from their arms, and their brains dashed out upon the pavement; when they are objects of insult and outrage at every turn; when they are in danger of having their homes burnt down over their heads; when their children are not allowed to enter schools; then they will have an urgency to obtain the ballot equal to our own.

Let us omit therefore all this idle talk, which only confuses the question at issue. The whole object of this Amendment is to prevent a person's being shut out from voting because he is a Jew, or a Celt, or a Negro. Its immediate effect will be to prevent negro men from being forbidden to vote.

Justice Cannot Be Delayed

What then is the objection to it? We are told that if these negro men vote they will tyrannize over their wives just as white men do; and that so large an ignorant class voting, will make it still more difficult to get woman's right to the ballot recognized. Suppose all this were true—what then? Does it authorize us to resist the recognition, by Government, of the negro man's right to vote?

A man has the same "inherent, unalienable" right to vote that a woman has. We humbly presume that the marvellous progress of these last few months has not upset that principle, or produced any woman so terribly in earnest as to deny it.

If that be so, is there any intelligent reformer prepared to maintain that we have a right to deny to any human being his, or her, *natural rights* because we fear he, or she, will misuse them? I should like to see the Abolitionist, of thirty years standing, who will look his own record in the face and maintain such a proposition. All history laughs at it. The Pope said, "I cannot allow men to read the Bible, each in his own language and pick out his own faith—the 'right will certainly be misused.'" Tories say, "we cannot let poor and unlearned men vote, 'they will misuse the right.'" What said the Declaration of Independence to that? . . .

Slaveholders said, "the black has a right to liberty, but we cannot recognize it, 'he will misuse the right.'" Ask the last thirty years and the war how God answered that. . . .

If the negro man should therefore, in his ignorance, misuse *his right* and delay woman's recognition many a year, we are not authorized *on that account*, to forbid Government to recognize his natural and inalienable right to vote; that is, to oppose the Fifteenth Amendment.

It was one of the great promises of MAGNA CHARTA, extorted from the King by his Barons, that he would "neither *delay* nor refuse Justice." God lays the same duty on all of us.

We were not sent into the world responsible that negroes, or any other race, should behave themselves. But God will hold us responsible if we presume to deny to our fellow man any of his natural rights.

Fashion—woman's realm—was one of the strongest bulwarks of slavery; sometimes equal to Church and State combined. It is to-day the special bulwark of negro hate. *Woman* could extinguish that scourge in half-a-dozen years. Suppose twenty years ago when fashion laughed at us, it had been proposed to give women the vote and that Abolitionists had cried out "no—we've enough to convert now, selfish merchants and bigoted church-members; do not throw contemptuous and silly women into the scale. It is an 'infamous' proposition." Should we have been justified?

But leaving this argument with those who recognize and fully trust all God-given rights, let us come down to those who settle this question by reasons of expediency.

One Reform at a Time

Those friends say it is not wise to recognize these rights piecemeal. The Amendment is faulty because it does not cover the whole ground, man and woman's vote too, all that relates to voting. Well then, here is Mr. A——, he believes the vote is a snare and a strengthening of the Aristocracy unless every voter is secured a homestead, his natural right. Here is Mr. B——, he believes voting only plays into the hands of Capital, unless our whole system of finance is changed and Government allowed to issue paper money at discretion, without interest. Here is Mr. C——, who believes no drunkard should be allowed to vote and no convicted criminal, as is sometimes the law abroad. Here is Mr. D——, who believes the whole method of choosing the Senate is a violation of natural right.

Why Stand in Their Way?

In her August 1869 editorial in the Woman's Advocate, *social reformer Frances D. Gage expressed her support for the Fifteenth Amendment—a view that was shared by many feminists.*

Could I with breath defeat the Fifteenth Amendment, I would not do it. That Amendment will let the colored men enter the wide portals of human rights. Keeping them out, suffering as now, would not let me in all the sooner, then in God's name why stand in their way? It is my earnest wish that the Fifteenth Amendment may be ratified. Let us apply the Golden Rule now and forever.

Shall we wait till the whole country gets educated up to all these ideas and make no change till we can settle the subject in its whole breadth? Absurd. Man gets forward step by step—the recognition of half a truth helping him to see the other half. First we had individual liberty, then separate property, then right of inheritance, then freedom of opinion, then freedom of speech, then voting: thus, one by one, ray by ray, men got able to bear the full light of day. In what order these steps shall be taken—which first, which second—is God's ordaining, not of our plan. Every change large and distinct enough to serve as a point upon which to rally the nation, should have a separate discussion and be decided by itself. This is the most economical and speediest method of reform. . . .

In the present instance this great rule holds. We have drawn the weight so far up; fasten it there; and thus get a purchase to lift it still higher. There have been several different tests excluding men from voting in this country. Church membership, property, book-learning, race, sex. The first we have got rid of everywhere. The second is almost gone, except in obsolete corners like Rhode Island. Book learning is fast vanishing as a test. The abolition of each one has helped to get rid of his comrade. Race and sex alone are left. Abolish the first and you will clear the ground and simplify the question. It will leave the naked, bare, intolerable, and illogical test of sex so monstrous as it stands isolated, that it will almost topple over of its own weight.

No doubt the ignorant prejudice of the working class is one of the great obstacles to the recognition of Woman's Rights. Some over-sanguine advocates seem to forget this, and imagine that when a Legislature is carried the work is mainly done. Not so by any means. When the first line of the enemy's works—the Legislature—is carried, there remain two behind—the Church and the laboring class. Whether the Church line will contest the fight remains to be seen. It looks sometimes and in some places as if it would not. But there's no trustworthy evidence on that point. The working men will, without doubt. And with that whole class the same thorough and weary work is to be done as fell to the lot of the Abolitionists between 1830 and 1850, with the mass of the Nation; patient lecturing, line upon line, precept upon precept, "without haste, without rest." But the enfranchisement of the negro need not give us the alarm which Democrats, masquerading in Woman's Rights uniform, try to create.

This reform—woman's voting—will never probably be carried by national action. It will be granted State by State. Slavery would have been abolished so but for the war. It was the "war power" which brought and enabled the Nation to kill slavery. Abolitionists looked forward to the peaceful action of successive States. This will probably be the course relative to woman's voting.

The addition therefore of seventy thousand black votes in South Carolina will not retard the action of Iowa or Massachusetts on this question. It will rather hasten their action. Desirous to guard as fully as possible against any conceivable ill consequence from such sudden increase of voters, the Northern States will be spurred to call, all the sooner into the field, whatever there is of good and conservative and well intentioned in woman. Just as the lager beer infatuation of the German Republicans out West moves the Republican Temperance men there to accept woman's rights in order to correct that bias in the party, so the negro vote will operate in this case. Once carry this reform in half-a-dozen Northern States, and the negro looks so much to us for his example that his vote will be sure to follow ours. If the North once accepts our principles, the time will come when Woman will find her best friend in the negro, as the Union did. You may be sure he will keep step to the music of any improvement his trusted North initiates.

Let ignorance then believe that the only way to improve the world is to do everything at once—"I shall never get to the top of the hill by single steps; the only way is to wait till I can leap the whole way at one bound." Let selfishness cry—"He shall not have his rights till I get mine." The true reformer will say, "Let every class have its rights the very moment the world is ready to recognize them. Thus and thus only will every other class get one step nearer to the recognition of its own. 'First the blade, then the ear, after that the full corn in the ear.'"

"In fitness for the franchise, the white women, especially of the North, are eminently superior to the average of Southern men, of any color."

The Fifteenth Amendment Should Include Women

Parker Pillsbury (1809–1898)

The Fourteenth and Fifteenth Amendments to the U.S. Constitution were designed to protect the citizenship and voting rights of black men, especially the recently freed slaves of the South. Many politicians believed that these measures were important not only to secure civil rights for the freedmen but also to ensure that the Republican Party would continue to hold a majority in Congress. Before and during the Civil War, most Democrats had advocated the continuation of slavery and southern secession, while Republicans largely had sought to preserve the nation and abolish slavery. Supporters of the amendments maintained that the freed slaves, grateful to the political party that had freed them and fearing subjugation by the southern Democrats, would consistently vote Republican. In turn, they argued, the Republicans would continue to pass legislation that would uphold the civil rights of blacks.

The women's rights movement had been closely associated with the abolitionists and the Republican Party; many reformers had been equally active in working for the rights of both blacks and women. However, dissension over the exclusion of women from the civil rights amendments eventually split this coalition as reformers chose sides. Parker Pillsbury, for example, was a minis-

From "Fifteenth Amendment—Its Ludicrous Side" by Parker Pillsbury, *Revolution*, July 22, 1869. Reprinted in *History of Woman Suffrage*, vol. 2, edited by Elizabeth Cady Stanton, Susan B. Anthony, and Matilda Joslyn Gage (Rochester, NY: Charles Mann, 1881).

ter who served as editor for Wendell Phillips's newspaper, the *Anti-Slavery Standard*, and lectured on women's rights. Unlike Phillips, Pillsbury believed that the Fifteenth Amendment should not be passed unless it was rewritten to include women's suffrage. In 1868, Pillsbury resigned his position at the *Anti-Slavery Standard* over this issue and became the coeditor of the *Revolution*, a feminist newspaper published by Elizabeth Cady Stanton and Susan B. Anthony.

The following viewpoint is excerpted from Pillsbury's July 22, 1869, editorial in the *Revolution*. The vote should be extended to all Americans, regardless of sex or color, Pillsbury contends. He accuses Wendell Phillips and other abolitionists of demanding that women sacrifice their civil rights for the sake of party politics. Reformers should refuse to endorse the Fifteenth Amendment as long as it withholds suffrage from women, Pillsbury concludes.

Almost every question has its ludicrous side. The champions of the Fifteenth Amendment to the Constitution present an illustration. Conceding woman's equal right to the ballot with man, they still resist her claims on the ground that this is not her hour, but man's hour. "The black man's hour." As though justice and right were determined by clocks and almanacs. And as though some sort of terrible crisis could not be urged always. Admitting even that in fitness for the franchise, the white women, especially of the North, are eminently superior to the average of Southern men, of any color, they still demand that woman's claim be postponed to their favorite Fifteenth Amendment, which presumes every man in the nation of whatever color, grade, or race, the superior of woman, however exalted by culture, by wealth, by refinement, by patriotism, or whatever virtues, gifts, or graces. An Amendment, it is called, while preparing the way to lift into lordship absolute, every man, however mean and vile, over every woman, however divine her character!

And then these "Amenders" presume to charge with "selfishness," "ignorance," "conservatism," and nobody knows what else, those who are laboring night and day, in season, out of season, and at all seasons, under a banner on which was inscribed at the formation of their [Equal Rights] Association, "Equal Rights to all citizens; ESPECIALLY THE RIGHT OF SUFFRAGE, IRRESPECTIVE OF RACE, COLOR OR SEX." Without pretending that the Association, or any of its members, has violated, in letter or in spirit, a word of this constitutional pledge, leading Abolitionists are charging "injustice," "insincerity," and "treachery to the cause of liberty," on actors in the Equal Rights Association, besides ignorance, selfishness, and conservatism, because they will not turn aside from their holy purpose to promote a measure that basely, grossly insults one-half, and that the best half of the human race. Were the subject not too serious for mirth, such accusations, coming from such a source, would be simply ludicrous. As it is, many will laugh at such absurdity. The Fifteenth Amendment, at best, is but a trick, a device (as was the Fourteenth with its word *male* three times burned into a single period), of as corrupt and unprincipled a school of politicians as ever disgraced the name of legislation, to save themselves and their party in place and power. It is told us in all seriousness, that the word *male* is not in the Fifteenth Amendment, as though that atoned for its infamy, and rendered it worthy of woman's support. Why should the word *male* be in it? Three times solemnly muttered in the Fourteenth, it needed no repetition in the Fifteenth.

Another ludicrous view of this subject, is the zeal with which so many women are laboring to hoist all mandom into power over them. Power as omnipotent as ignorance, prejudice, and love of domination can possibly create. A little reflection, one would think, might show and satisfy the blindest that the opposition they encounter already is quite sufficient, without augmenting it a thousand fold, and anchoring it fast in the constitution of the country. True, they are assured by radical Republicans that as soon as the negro man is secured, the colored woman and the white woman also shall be equally distinguished. Had this age an Aesop, he would tell again his story of the goat and the fox at the bottom of the well. How to get out, of course, was the question. After long and anxious thought, a happy expedient struck the fox. "Do you, friend goat, rear yourself up against the wall, as near the top as possible, and from the tip of your horns I can spring out, and then it will be quite easy to pull you up by the horns also." No quicker spoken than done. Out leaped the fox, and was safe. Then the goat demanded his release, as promised. "You old fool!" answered Reynard! "Had you half as much brain as beard, you would know that I would never risk my life to save yours," and away he ran. The whole history of American politics is assurance, but pre-eminently so is the history of present parties, that a party victory would scarcely be risked to save all womankind from consuming fire. . . .

Abolitionists Then and Now

But most ludicrous of all is it to hear old anti-slavery leaders and teachers referring to the past for defense of their present hostility, and challenging us to re-read that history and be ashamed of our present course. But when in the past did Wendell Phillips ever teach that a half loaf is better than no bread, if poisoned, or if it were snatched or stolen from a family of starving orphans? It was not in 1839, nor '49, nor '59, that he held or inculcated such a philosophy. The motto of [Wendell Phillips's abolitionist periodical] the Anti-Slavery *Standard* was and is "Without Concealment—Without Compromise." Now under that sublime evangel women are instructed to bridge over the gulf to colored male enfranchisement with their own imperiled, nay, sacrificed equal rights. Better now the "half loaf," festering, putrid with the poison of compromise, than no bread! Better that the black man have his half loaf, though he steal it from his mother and sisters, more hungry, starving, and dying, than himself!

Rights for All

Black abolitionist Robert Purvis objected to the exclusion of women from the Fifteenth Amendment in his January 6, 1870, letter to the Revolution.

As a colored man, and a victim to the terribly tyranny inflicted by the injustice and prejudice of the Nation, I ask no right that I will not give to every other human being, without regard to sex or color. I cannot ask white women to give their efforts and influence in behalf of my race, and then meanly and selfishly withhold countenance of a movement tending to their enfranchisement.

Oh, no! it was never so in the past. Terrible to conservatism as to slavery itself, was the mighty war-cry of the Abolitionists for twenty years. "No union with slaveholders!" No compromise with injustice for an election, or for an hour, not even for a good ultimate purpose! Colonization proposed a double purpose, the final extinction of slavery, and a meanwhile redemption of Africa from the midnight gloom and horror of heathenism. "Get thee behind me, Satan," was the thundering response and just rebuke of it by the Abolitionists! "Let us compromise with the South, and buy up their slaves," said [abolitionist] Elihu Burritt. . . . "Our curse on your slave trade, foreign and domestic," was the answering response of the Garrisonian Invincibles. Many of the oldest leaders and officers of the society refused even to help an escaped slave-mother buy her children of her old master. "Let us form a Republican party," said foxy politicians, and fight the extension of slavery into Kansas, or any other new territory with ballot, bullet, and battle-axe, if need be, but leaving the damnable system in the States with its 4,000,000 of victims and their posterity still chained under constitutional guarantee and the army and navy of the nation. "No union with slaveholders," rung out the lips and lungs of the Abolitionists, in tones that shook the land from Maine to Mexico! . . .

Now what do we behold? Wendell Phillips has shivered the English language all to pieces in attempts to describe the baseness and utter worthlessness of the Republican party. The president [Ulysses S. Grant] has sold "the poisonous porridge called his soul," to Virginia rebels and New York and Pennsylvania aristocrats and bondholders, and yet Mr. Phillips persists in demanding that woman lay her own right of suffrage at the presidential and Republican party feet, while they so mould and manipulate the black male element, as by it, if possible, to save themselves from utter rout and destruction. Thanks be to God, some of us learned the old anti-slavery lesson from Wendell Phillips better. And we dare take our appeal from the Wendell Phillips of to-day, to him of twenty years ago. And we do "dare to look our past history in the face." And moreover, we look with triumph, and with hearts swelling with fervent gratitude that our anti-slavery teachers schooled us so well. What is it but ludicrous (if mirth be possible on such a question) for those who are thus seeking the enfranchisement of but half of even the fragmentary colored race, to charge with selfishness, compromise, and treachery, the association, or any of its members, that are earnestly laboring to extend the ballot to every American citizen, irrespective of all distinctions of race, complexion or sex? Can such accusers look each other in the face and not laugh? [The Roman statesman] Cato wondered that two augurs could meet with gravity. What would he do here? And still more preposterous, if not ludicrous, is it, when woman voluntarily stops and becomes the agent of her own degradation, and with her own hands builds barriers against her own advancement; piling up opposition, . . . when the majority against her, even in New York and New England, is already appalling? And then for us to be referred to the teachings and experiences of the past for lessons in compromise, cold, calculating compromise, such as Abolitionists ever blasted with the breath of their nostrils, and scourged from their presence with fiery indignation! The Equal Rights Association is not to be turned aside by any seductive devices from its high and holy purpose of enfranchisement for all American citizens, KNOWING NO RACE, NO COLOR, NO SEX.

CHAPTER 3

The Era of the "New Woman"

Chapter Preface

The role of women in American society broadened substantially throughout the late nineteenth and early twentieth centuries. This expansion of women's boundaries resulted in part from the efforts of the early feminists as well as from other cultural and societal factors. Most women in the generations of Lucretia Mott and Elizabeth Cady Stanton had never attended college, voted, worked outside the home, or taken part in any public reform movements. During the 1870s, however, increasing numbers of women became actively involved in social reform causes such as women's rights and temperance. Several women's colleges were founded and other universities instituted coeducational classes, providing young women with a much greater opportunity for higher education. By 1890, the number of women in the workforce was rapidly rising, and women were marrying at an older age and bearing fewer children than previous generations. Whereas women in the beginning of the nineteenth century were expected to be mild, delicate, and retiring, the women of the 1890s more often were, as historian Nancy Woloch writes, "forthright, frank, and energetic."

The term "New Woman" was first coined in the 1890s to describe the confident and self-sufficient young women whose lifestyles differed so radically from preceding generations. The New Woman of the late nineteenth and early twentieth centuries was portrayed in periodical articles of the time as being sophisticated and city-dwelling, usually college educated, and interested in social issues. Instead of tight corsets and hoop skirts, she wore loose-fitting shirtwaists with straight, short skirts that allowed her more freedom of movement. This modified attire enabled the New Woman to be physically active and competitive in sports. As a single woman, she worked to support herself; as a married woman, she wanted a small family and a calling beyond housework—either a career or a social cause. Although she might not be an active feminist, the New Woman tended to advocate suffrage and other advances (such as birth control or improvements in housekeeping devices) that could improve women's lives. Of course, not all women of this era fit the image of the New Woman, but the prevalence of the stereotype reveals that many American women were living, or were aspiring to live, with more freedom than previous generations had experienced.

At the same time that some women were carving out lives of economic and social independence, however, others were banding together against what they perceived as a threat to women's traditional roles as wives and mothers. In 1871, a number of prominent upper-class women founded the Anti-Suffrage Party in response to the establishment of such groups as the National Woman Suffrage Association (NWSA) and the American Woman Suffrage Association (AWSA). Organized opposition to suffrage gained momentum from the 1880s on with the formation of the National Association Opposed to Woman Suffrage, the National Anti-Suffrage Association, and similar groups.

Ida Tarbell, Josephine Dodge, Emily P. Bissell, and other leading antisuffragists employed several arguments against giving women the vote. Their most frequently repeated assertion was that suffrage would divert women's attention toward politics and the public sphere and draw women away from home and family. As historian Jane Jerome Camhi describes, "Antisuffrage campaign material often included posters depicting the evil effects of woman suffrage on the domestic scene. In the antisuffrage litany, motherhood and participation in public life were always presented as mutually exclusive." The antisuffrage movement also received considerable support from the liquor industry, which feared that if women were granted suffrage, they would vote in large numbers for the prohibition of alcohol. Antisuffragists fought against the enfranchisement of women both on a state-by-state basis and nationally. During the late nineteenth and early twentieth centuries, feminists concentrated on the passage of state suffrage amendments, and the majority of suffrage battles were therefore waged on the state level. In 1890, the NWSA, which had originally advocated a national suffrage amendment, merged with the AWSA to form the National American Woman Suffrage Association (NAWSA). This merger mended a twenty-year split between two factions of the women's rights movement and served to focus the movement's united energies on gaining suffrage state by state. Between 1869 and 1917, sixteen states and territories granted women full suffrage.

In 1913, suffragist Alice Paul renewed attempts to pass a federal suffrage amendment by establishing the National Woman's Party. Paul and the majority of the members of the National Woman's Party were young feminists who espoused the ideals of the New Woman. They employed attention-grabbing strategies such as picketing the White House and organizing marches of thousands of suffragists. In combination with the less radical tactics of older feminists, the activities of the National Woman's Party helped to revive the demand for a national suffrage amendment. After Congress approved the Nineteenth Amendment in 1919, moderate and radical suffragists joined forces to campaign in the states for ratification of the amendment. On August 26, 1920, the Nineteenth Amendment was signed into law; the following autumn, millions of American women voted for the first time.

Viewpoint 1

"Girls lose health . . . by [an educational] regimen that ignores the periodical tides and reproductive apparatus."

Higher Education Harms Women

Edward H. Clarke (1820–1877)

From the 1860s to 1900, the number of colleges that accepted both male and female students rose dramatically. Many of the universities founded during these years were coeducational from the start, and older colleges increasingly came under pressure to admit women. Among the latter was Harvard College in Boston, Massachusetts, which received a substantial amount of criticism during the early 1870s for its male-only admission policy.

Edward H. Clarke was a retired professor from Harvard Medical School, an active member of the Harvard Board of Overseers, and a practicing physician. The following viewpoint is excerpted from Clarke's 1873 book *Sex in Education; or, A Fair Chance for Girls*, in which he defended Harvard's policy. Following a course of higher education designed for boys can be physically harmful to pubescent girls, Clarke asserts. Too much mental exertion can redirect a young woman's energy away from the development of her reproductive system, he contends, and can lead to ill health and infertility. While Clarke does not entirely disapprove of higher education for women, he advocates a separate program that would allow for complete mental and physical rest during menstruation and require less overall studying time.

In the late 1880s, Harvard established Radcliffe College, a coordinate college for women. Harvard and Radcliffe discontinued the policy of holding separate classes for male and female students in 1947.

From *Sex in Education; or, A Fair Chance for Girls* by Edward H. Clarke (Boston: James R. Osgood & Co., 1873).

Obedient to the American educational maxim, that boys' schools and girls' schools are one, and that the one is the boys' school, the female schools have copied the methods which have grown out of the requirements of the male organization. Schools for girls have been modelled after schools for boys. Were it not for differences of dress and figure, it would be impossible, even for an expert, after visiting a high school for boys and one for girls, to tell which was arranged for the male and which for the female organization. Our girls' schools, whether public or private, have imposed upon their pupils a boy's regimen; and it is now proposed, in some quarters, to carry this principle still farther, by burdening girls, after they leave school, with a quadrennium of masculine college regimen. And so girls are to learn the alphabet in college, as they have learned it in the grammar-school, just as boys do. This is grounded upon the supposition that sustained regularity of action and attendance may be as safely required of a girl as of a boy; that there is no physical necessity for periodically relieving her from walking, standing, reciting, or studying; that the chapel-bell may call her, as well as him, to a daily morning walk, with a standing prayer at the end of it, regardless of the danger that such exercises, by deranging the tides of her organization, may add to her piety at the expense of her blood; that she may work her brain over mathematics, botany, chemistry, German, and the like, with equal and sustained force on every day of the month, and so safely divert blood from the reproductive apparatus to the head; in short, that she, like her brother, develops health and strength, blood and nerve, intellect and life, by a regular, uninterrupted, and sustained course of work. All this is not justified, either by experience or physiology. Girls lose health, strength, blood, and nerve, by a regimen that ignores the periodical tides and reproductive apparatus of their organization. . . .

The Dangers of Identical Co-Education

Co-education, then, signifies in common acceptation identical co-education. This identity of training is what many of the present day seem to be praying for and working for. Appropriate education of the two sexes, carried as far as possible, is a consummation most devoutly to be desired; identical education of the two sexes is a crime before God and humanity, that physiology protests against, and that experience weeps over. Because the education of boys has met with tolerable success, hitherto,—but only tolerable it must be confessed,—in developing them into men, there are those who would make girls grow into women by

Train Women for Motherhood

G. Stanley Hall was a psychologist and the president of Clark University in Massachusetts. In his 1905 book Adolescence, *Hall maintains that women should be educated to be wives and mothers.*

From the available data it seems . . . that the more scholastic the education of women, the fewer children and the harder, more dangerous, and more dreaded is parturition, and the less the ability to nurse children. Not intelligence but education by present man-made ways is inversely as fecundity. The sooner and the more clearly this is recognized as a universal rule, not, of course, without many notable and much vaunted exceptions, the better for our civilization. For one, I plead with no whit less earnestness and conviction that any of the feminists, and indeed with more fervor because on nearly all their grounds and also on others, for the higher education of women, and would welcome them to every opportunity available to men if they can not do better; but I would open to their election another education, which every competent judge would pronounce more favorable to motherhood, under the influence of female principals who do not publicly say that it is "not desirable" that women students should study motherhood, because they do not know whether they will marry; who encourage them to elect "no special subjects because they are women," and who think infant psychology "foolish.". . .

Now that woman has by general consent attained the right to the best that man has, she must seek a training that fits her own nature as well or better. So long as she strives to be manlike she will be inferior and a pinchbeck imitation, but she must develop a new sphere that shall be like the rich field of the cloth of gold for the best instincts of her nature.

the same process. Because a gardener has nursed an acorn till it grew into an oak, they would have him cradle a grape in the same soil and way, and make it a vine. Identical education, or identical co-education, of the sexes defrauds one sex or the other, or perhaps both. It defies the Roman maxim, which physiology has fully justified, *mens sana in corpore sano* [a healthy mind in a healthy body]. The sustained regimen, regular recitation, erect posture, daily walk, persistent exercise, and unintermitted labor that toughens a boy, and makes a man of him, can only be partially applied to a girl. The regimen of intermittance, periodicity of exercise and rest, work three-fourths of each month, and remission, if not abstinence, the other fourth, physiological interchange of the erect and reclining posture, care of the reproductive system that is the cradle of the race, all this, that toughens a girl and makes a woman of her, will emasculate a lad. A combination of the two methods of education, a compromise between them, would probably yield an average result, excluding the best of both. It would give a fair chance neither to a boy nor a girl. Of all compromises, such a physiological one is the worst. It cultivates mediocrity, and cheats the future of its rightful legacy of lofty manhood and womanhood. It emasculates boys, stunts girls; makes semi-eunuchs of one sex, and agenes [underdeveloped adults] of the others.

The error which has led to the identical education of the two sexes, and which prophecies their identical co-education in colleges and universities, is not confined to technical education. It permeates society. It is found in the home, the workshop, the factory, and in all the ramifications of social life. The identity of boys and girls, of men and women, is practically asserted out of the school as much as in it, and it is theoretically proclaimed from the pulpit and the rostrum. Women seem to be looking up to man and his development, as the goal and ideal of womanhood. The new gospel of female development glorifies what she possesses in common with him, and tramples under her feet, as a source of weakness and badge of inferiority, the mechanism and functions peculiar to herself. . . .

Brain Activity and Reproductive Functions

Put a boy and girl together upon the same course of study, with the same lofty ideal before them, and hold up to their eyes the daily incitements of comparative progress, and there will be awakened within them a stimulus unknown before, and that separate study does not excite. The unconscious fires that have their seat deep down in the recesses of the sexual organization will flame up through every tissue, permeate every vessel, burn every nerve, flash from the eye, tingle in the brain, and work the whole machine at highest pressure. There need not be, and generally will not be, any low or sensual desire in all this elemental action. It is only making youth work over the tasks of sober study with the wasting force of intense passion. Of course such strenuous labor will yield brilliant, though temporary, results. The fire is kept alive by the waste of the system, and soon burns up its source. The first sex to suffer in this exhilarating and costly competition must be, as experience shows it is, the one that has the largest amount of force in readiness for immediate call; and this is the female sex. At the age of development, Nature mobilizes the forces of a girl's organization for the purpose of establishing a function that shall endure for a generation, and for constructing an apparatus that shall cradle and nurse a race. These mobilized forces, which, at the technical educational period, the girl possesses and controls largely in excess of the boy, under the passionate stimulus of identical co-education, are turned from their divinely-appointed field of operations, to the region of brain activity. The result is a most brilliant show of cerebral pyrotechnics, and degenerations. . . .

That undue and disproportionate brain activity exerts a sterilizing influence upon both sexes is alike a doctrine of physiology, and an induction from experience. And both physiology and experience also teach that this influence is more potent upon the female than upon the male. The explanation of the latter fact—of the greater aptitude of the female organization to become thus modified by excessive brain activity—is probably to be found in the large size, more complicated relations, and more important functions, of the female reproductive apparatus. This delicate and complex mechanism is liable to be aborted or deranged by the withdrawal of force that is needed for its construction and maintenance. . . .

Experience teaches that a healthy and growing boy may spend six hours of force daily upon his studies, and leave sufficient margin for physical growth. A girl cannot spend more than four, or, in occasional instances, five hours of force daily upon her studies, and leave sufficient margin for the general physical growth that she must make in common with a boy, and also for constructing a reproductive apparatus. If she puts as much force into her brain education as a boy, the brain or the special apparatus will suffer. Appropriate education and appropriate co-education must adjust their methods and regimen to this law.

Another detail is, that, during every fourth week, there should be a remission, and sometimes an intermission, of both study and exercise. Some individuals require, at that time, a complete intermission from mental and physical effort for a single day; others for two or three days; others require only a remission, and can do half work safely for two or three days, and their usual work after that. The diminished labor, which shall give Nature an opportunity to accomplish her special periodical task and growth, is a physiological necessity for all, however robust they seem to be. The apportionment of study and exercise to individual needs cannot be decided by general rules, nor can the decision of it be safely left to the pupil's caprice or ambition. Each case must be decided upon its own merits. The organization of studies and instruction must be flexible enough to admit of the periodical and temporary absence of each pupil, without loss of rank, or necessity of making up work, from recitation, and exercise of all sorts. The periodical type of woman's way of work must be harmonized with the persistent type of man's way of work in any successful plan of co-education.

VIEWPOINT 2

"Does it not look a little more as if women were sick because they stopped studying?"

Higher Education Does Not Harm Women

Elizabeth Stuart Phelps (1844–1911)

Raised in Boston, Massachusetts, Elizabeth Stuart Phelps became a public lecturer in the 1870s. She spoke widely on social reform topics—primarily women's rights and temperance—and wrote numerous articles on these issues for the magazine the *Independent*. Health problems eventually led Phelps to retire from the lecture circuit, but she continued to write prolifically, authoring fifty-seven books in her lifetime.

The following viewpoint is taken from an essay Phelps wrote in response to Edward H. Clarke's 1873 book *Sex in Education; or, A Fair Chance for Girls*. In this highly controversial book, Clarke, a Boston physician and former Harvard medical professor, argued that the mental exertion required in college often caused young women to experience menstrual problems and ill health. Outraged by this contention, Phelps and several other feminists wrote rebuttals that were published in the 1874 compilation *Sex and Education: A Reply to Dr. E. H. Clarke's "Sex in Education."*

Phelps points out that thousands of women attend school or work outside the home without experiencing any of the physical ailments of which Clarke warns. Although she admits that some young women become invalids after finishing their education, Phelps contends that there is no solid scientific proof that schooling caused these women to become ill. In fact, Phelps asserts, the more likely possibility is that these female graduates become invalids because they no longer have an outlet for their intellect and ambitions.

From Elizabeth Stuart Phelps's untitled essay in *Sex and Education: A Reply to Dr. E.H. Clarke's "Sex in Education,"* edited by Julia Ward Howe (Boston: Roberts Bros., 1874).

It is to be hoped that, among the physicians whose professional rank may entitle them to a hearing as broad as Dr. [Edward H.] Clarke's, some one who joins issue with him upon his principal physiological theory, may find the leisure to remind us what a blessed fact it is that doctors always disagree. Without the least desire to undervalue either the culture or the skill of the man from whom we differ, a little inquiry into the effect produced upon brother and sister physicians by his essay will reveal the fact that its author is not without sufficiently important opponents. "Sex in Education" having once been written, another essay, equally to the point, if a little more regardful of the old-fashioned prejudices of non-medical society, should be written to mate it.

Meanwhile it remains possible for any of us to say, in deprecation of the notion of womanhood advanced by Dr. Clarke, two things.

1. The physician is not the person whose judgment upon a matter involving the welfare of women can possibly be final. His testimony, worth what it may be worth, should seek and fall into its proper place in the physical aspects of such a question; but it shall *stay* in its place. It is but a link in a chain. It is only a tint in a kaleidoscope. A question so intricate and shifting as that which involves the exact position of woman in the economy of a cursed world is not to be settled by the most intimate acquaintance with the proximate principles of the human frame, with the proportions of the gray and white matter in the brain, or with the transitional character of the tissues and the exquisite machinery of the viscera. The psychologist has yet his word to say. The theologian has a reason to be heard. The political economist might also add to experience knowledge. The woman who is physically and intellectually a living denial of every premise and of every conclusion which Dr. Clarke has advanced, has yet a right to an audience. Nor is he even the man whose judgment as to the *health* of women can be symmetrical. No *clinical* opinion, it will be remembered, bearing against the physical vigor of any class of people, is or can be a complete one. The physician knows sick women almost only. Well women keep away from him, and thank Heaven. If there be any well women he is always in doubt. Thousands of women will read that they are prevented by Nature's eternal and irresistible laws from all sustained activity of brain or body, but principally of brain, with much the same emotion with which we might read a fiat gone forth from the Royal College of Surgeons in London, that Americans could not eat roast beef, since their researches into morbid American anatomy had developed the fact that Americans had died of eating roast beef, as well as a peculiar

structure of the American stomach, to which roast beef was poisonously adapted. Thousands of women will not believe what the author of "Sex in Education" tells them, *simply because they know better*. Their own unlearned experience stands to them in refutation of his learned statements. They will give him theory for theory. They can pile up for him illustration on illustration. Statistics they have none; but no statistics has he. They and the Doctor are met on fair fight.

The Benefits of Education

In her 1908 speech "Present Tendencies in Women's College and University Education," M. Carey Thomas maintains that warnings of the ill effects of women's education are unfounded. Thomas was an English professor and president of Bryn Mawr College in Pennsylvania.

I had never chanced . . . upon a book that seemed to me so to degrade me in my womanhood as the seventh and seventeenth chapters on women and women's education, of [Clark University] President Stanley Hall's *Adolescence*. . . . Sickening sentimentality and horrible over-sexuality seemed to me to breathe . . . from every pseudoscientific page. But how vast the difference between then and now in my feelings, and in the feelings of every woman who has had to do with the education of girls! Then I was terror-struck lest I, and every other woman with me, were doomed to live as pathological invalids in a universe merciless to women as a sex. Now we know that it is not we, but the man who believes such things about us, who is himself pathological, blinded by neurotic mists of sex, unable to see that women form one-half of the kindly race of normal, healthy human creatures in the world; that women, like men, are quickened and inspired by the same study of the great traditions of their race, by the same love of learning, the same love of science, the same love of abstract truth; that women, like men, are immeasurably benefited, physically, mentally and morally, and are made vastly better mothers, as men are made vastly better fathers, by subordinating the distracting instincts of sex to the simple human fellowship of similar education and similar intellectual and social ideals.

Many a woman who stands at the factory loom eleven hours and a half a day, from year's end to year's end, from the age of eight to the age of forty-eight, knows better than he tells her. Every lady lecturer in the land, who unites the most exhausting kind of brain and body labor in her own experience, day and night after day and night, for the half of every year, and unites it in defiance of Dr. Clarke's prognostications, knows better. Every healthy woman physician knows better; and it is only the woman physician, after all, whose judgment can ever approach the ultimate uses of the physicist's testimony to these questions.

It should be said: 2. Almost every fact brought forward by Dr. Clarke goes to illustrate the exact opposite of his almost every conclusion in respect to the effect of *mental* labor upon the female physique. With the serene, not to say dogmatic, conviction of the physician whose own patients represent the world to him, he has copied for us from his note-books a series of cases exemplifying the remarkable unanimity with which girls, *after* leaving school, break down in health. . . .

He calls our consideration to his list of cases, arguing detachedly, by the way, and ingeniously constructing for our benefit very much such a syllogism as this. . . .

As long as girls are in school they are (with exceptions so rare that I have had great difficulty in finding them) in excellent health.

When girls leave school, they fall sick.

Therefore it is sustained study which injures girls.

Here, now, is the point of fair dispute. Why do girls so often become invalids within a few years after leaving school ? The fact is a familiar one. We needed no Dr. Clarke come from their graves to tell us this. We are well accustomed to the sight of a fresh young girl, a close student, a fine achiever, "sustained" in mental application, and as healthy in body as she is vigorous and aspiring in brain, sinking, after a period of out-of-school life, into an aching, ailing, moping creature, aimless in the spirit and useless in the flesh for any of life's higher purposes, with which her young soul was filled and fired a little while ago.

"You may be well enough now. Wait till you are twenty four or five. That is the age when girls break down." This is the doleful prophecy of friends and physicians cast cold on the warm hopes of our hard-working, ambitious girls. "It is because you keep late hours, dance too much, eat indigestible food, or exercise too little," says the hygienist. "It is because you wear corsets, long skirts, and chignons," says the dress reformer. "It is because you are a woman. Here is a mystery!" says the dunce. "It is because you study too much," says Dr. Clarke.

Another Reason for Female Invalidism

Who of us has yet suggested and enforced the suggestion of another reason more simple and comprehensive than any of these,—more probable, perhaps, than any which could be found outside of the effects of female dress?

Women sick because they study ? Does it not look a little more as if women were sick because they *stopped* studying?

Worn out by intellectual activity?

Let us suppose that they might be exhausted by the change

from intellectual activity to intellectual inanition. Made invalids because they go to school from fourteen to eighteen? Let us conceive that they might be made invalids because they *left* school at eighteen! Let us draw upon our imagination to the extent of inquiring whether the nineteenth-century girl—intense, sensitive, and developing, like her age, nervously and fast—might not be made an invalid by the plunge from the "healing influences" of systematic brain exertion to the broken, jagged life which awaits a girl whose "education is completed." Made an invalid by exchanging the wholesome pursuit of sufficient and worthy aims for the unrelieved routine of a dependent domestic life, from which all aim has departed, or for the whirl of false excitements and falser contents which she calls society. . . . Made an invalid by the sad and subtle process by which a girl is first inspired to the ideal of a life in which her personal culture has as honest and honorable a part of her regard as (and as a part of) her personal usefulness; and then is left to find out that personal culture substantially stopped for her when she tied the ribbon of her seminary diploma. Made an invalid by the prejudice that deprives her of the stimulus which every human being needs and finds in the pursuit of some one especial avocation, and confines that avocation for her to a marriage which she may never effect, and which may never help the matter if she does. Made an invalid by the change from doing something to doing nothing. Made an invalid by the difference between being happy and being miserable. Made an invalid, in short, for *just the reasons* (in whatever manner, the manner being a secondary point) *why a man would be made an invalid* if subjected to the woman's life when the woman's education is over. That wretched, mistaken life, that nervous, emotive, aimless, and exhausting life which women assume at the end of their school career would have killed Dr. Clarke, had it been his lot, quite too soon for his years and experience to have matured into the writing of "Sex in Education."

Girls know what I mean. Women who work for women have some chance to read the mind of women on such points. We could produce our own note-book over against the physician's, and the contents of it would be pitiful to see.

The sense of perplexed disappointment, of baffled intelligence, of unoccupied powers, of blunted aspirations, which run through the confidences of girls "left school," is enough to create any illness which nervous wear and misery can create. And the physician should be the first man to recognize this fact,—not the man to ignore or discredit it; not the man to use his professional culture to the neglect of any obvious appeal to his professional candor; not the man to veil within a few slippery flatteries a wilful ignorance or an unmanly sneer.

VIEWPOINT 3

"Experience has shattered . . . all the old predictions that [women's suffrage] would destroy the home [and] subvert the foundations of society."

American Women Should Have the Right to Vote

Julia Ward Howe (1819–1910)

A poet and author, Julia Ward Howe is perhaps best known for writing the lyrics to "The Battle Hymn of the Republic," which was first published in February 1862. During the Civil War, Howe worked in relief operations and joined the American Peace Society. Although she was initially opposed to women's suffrage, after the war Howe became a founding member of the American Woman Suffrage Association and several other women's rights organizations. In 1870, she established the feminist periodical the *Woman's Journal*, which she edited for two decades.

On April 3, 1909, Howe's essay "The Case for Woman Suffrage" appeared in *Outlook* magazine. At the time this article was published, four states—Wyoming, Colorado, Utah, and Idaho—had granted women equal suffrage in their state constitutions. In 1893, New Zealand had become the first nation to give women full voting rights, and in 1902 Australian women had won the right to vote in national elections. Describing the positive results of equal suffrage in these states and countries, Howe argues that all American women should have the right to vote. Women are more likely than men to vote for laws that aid society and the family, she contends, and they are less inclined to vote for corrupt or incompetent candidates. In addition, Howe maintains, when women are enfranchised, their opinions on public affairs become far more important to politicians and are no longer easily ignored.

From "The Case for Woman Suffrage" by Julia Ward Howe, *Outlook*, April 3, 1909.

The question of suffrage for women has passed out of the academic stage, and has become a matter of practical observation and experience in an ever-growing number of States and countries. Experience has shattered, like a house of cards, all the old predictions that it would destroy the home, subvert the foundations of society, and have a ruinous influence both on womanly delicacy and on public affairs. During many years the opponents of woman suffrage have been diligently gathering all the adverse testimony that they could find. So far as appears by their published literature, they have not found, in all our enfranchised States put together, a dozen respectable men, residents of those States, who assert over their own names and addresses that it has had any ill effects. A few say that it has done no good, and call it a failure on that ground. But the mass of testimony on the other side is overwhelming.

The fundamental argument for woman suffrage, of course, is its justice, and this would be enough were there no other. But a powerful argument can also be made for it from the standpoint of expediency. It has now been proved to demonstration, not only that woman suffrage has no bad results, but that it has certain definite good results.

1. It gives women a position of increased dignity and influence. On this point I will quote from . . . people whose word has weight in our own land and abroad.

Miss Margaret Long, daughter of the ex-Secretary of the Navy, who has resided for years in Denver, has written: "It seems impossible to me that any one can live in Colorado long enough to get into touch with the life here, and not realize that women count for more in all the affairs of this State than they do where they have not the power that the suffrage gives. More attention is paid to their wishes, and much greater weight given to their opinions and judgment."

Mrs. K.A. Sheppard, President of the New Zealand Council of Women, says: "Since women have become electors, their views have become important and command respect. Men listen to and are influenced by the opinions of women to a far greater degree than was the case formerly. There is no longer heard the contemptuous 'What do women know of such matters?' And so out of the greater civil liberty enjoyed by women has come a perceptible rise in the moral and humanitarian tone of the community. A young New Zealander in his teens no longer regards his mother as belonging to a sex that must be kept within a prescribed sphere. That the lads and young men of a democracy should have their whole conception of the rights of humanity broadened and measured by truer standards is in itself an incalculable benefit."

Mrs. A. Watson Lister, Secretary of the Woman's National Council of Australia, says: "One striking result of equal suffrage is that members of Parliament now consult us as to their bills, when these bear upon the interests of women. The author of the new divorce bill asked all the women's organizations to come together and hear him read it, and make criticisms and suggestions. I do not remember any such thing happening before, in all my years in Australia. When a naturalization bill was pending, one clause of which deprived Australian women of citizenship if they married aliens, a few women went privately to the Prime Minister and protested, and that clause was altered immediately. After we had worked for years with members of Parliament for various reforms, without avail, because we had no votes, you cannot imagine the difference it makes."

Ex-Premier Alfred Deakin, of the Commonwealth of Australia, says: "There is now a closer attention paid in Parliament to matters especially affecting the [feminine] sex or interesting them."

Improving the Laws

2. It leads to improvements in the laws. No one can speak more fitly of this than Judge Lindsey, of the Denver Juvenile Court. He writes: "We have in Colorado the most advanced laws of any State in the Union for the care and protection of the home and the children, the very foundation of the Republic. We owe this more to woman suffrage than to any one cause. It does not take any mother from her home duties to spend ten minutes in going to the polls, casting her vote, and returning to the bosom of her home; but during those ten minutes she wields a power which is doing more to protect that home, and all other homes, than any other power or influence in Colorado."

Mrs. Helen L. Grenfell, of Denver, served three terms as State Superintendent of Public Instruction for Colorado, and is highly esteemed by educators throughout the State. She introduced in Colorado the system of leasing instead of selling the lands set apart by the Government for the support of the public schools, thereby almost doubling the annual revenue available for education. Mrs. Grenfell was appointed by the Governor to represent Colorado at the Congress of the International Woman Suffrage Alliance at Amsterdam last summer. In her report to that Congress she enumerated a long list of improved laws obtained in Colorado since women were granted the ballot, and added: "Delegates of the Interparliamentary Union who visited different parts of the United States for the purpose of studying American institutions declared concerning our group of laws relating to child life in its various aspects of education, home, and labor, that 'they are the sanest, most humane, most progressive, most scientific laws relating to the child to be found on any statute-books in the world.'"

Wyoming, many years ago, passed a law that women teachers in the public schools should receive the same pay as men when the work done is the same. The news that Utah had granted full suffrage to women was quickly followed by the announcement of the passage of a bill providing that women teachers should have equal pay with men when they held certificates of the same grade. The State Superintendent of Public Instruction for Colorado says: "There is no difference made in teachers' salaries on account of sex."

In the early twentieth century, suffragists held a number of marches, such as this New York City parade on May 6, 1912.

Woman suffrage has also operated to take the schools out of politics. Mrs. Grenfell writes: "I have seen or heard of more party politics in school matters in one block in Albany, Buffalo, or Philadelphia than in the 103,928 square miles of Colorado soil."

Since women attained the ballot, all the four equal suffrage States have raised the age of protection for girls to eighteen. In Idaho and Wyoming the repeal of the laws that formerly licensed gambling is universally ascribed to the women. The Colorado statutes against cruelty to animals and against obscene literature are said to be models of their kind.

Within four years after equal suffrage was granted, the number of no-[saloon]-license towns in Colorado had more than quadrupled and it has increased much more largely since. The organ of the brewers of Denver says that Colorado made a great mistake in giving the ballot to women. So far as I am aware it is the only paper in Colorado which takes that ground.

Under the title "Fruits of Equal Suffrage," the National American Woman Suffrage Association has published a partial list of the improved laws passed in the four enfranchised States with the aid of women's votes, giving chapter and verse for each. It fills nearly eight pages.

Women's Influence

3. Women can bring their influence to bear on legislation more quickly and with less labor by the direct method than by the indirect. In Massachusetts the suffragists worked for fifty-five years before they succeeded in getting a law making mothers equal guardians of their minor children with the fathers. After half a century of effort by indirect influence, only twelve out of our forty-six States have taken similar action. In Colorado, when the women were enfranchised, the very next Legislature passed such a bill.

4. Equal suffrage often leads to the defeat of bad candidates. This is conceded even by Mr. A. Lawrence Lewis, whose article in *The Outlook* against woman suffrage in Colorado has been reprinted by the anti-suffragists as a tract. He says:

"Since the extension of the franchise to women, political parties have learned the inadvisability of nominating for public offices drunkards, notorious libertines, gamblers, retail liquor dealers, and men who engage in similar discredited occupations, because the women almost always vote them down." During the fifteen years since equal suffrage was granted no saloon-keeper has been elected to the Board of Aldermen in Denver. Before that it was very common. I quote . . . from Governor Shafroth, of Colorado: "Women's presence in politics has introduced an independent element which compels better nominations."

Ex-Chief Justice Fisher, of Wyoming, says: "If the Republicans nominate a bad man and the Democrats a good one, the Republican women do not hesitate a moment to 'scratch' the bad and substitute the good. It is just so with the Democrats."

Ex-Governor Hunt, of Idaho: "The woman vote has compelled not only State conventions, but more particularly county conventions, of both parties to select the cleanest and best material for public office."

And quoting once more from Judge Lindsey, of Denver: "One of the greatest advantages from woman suffrage is the fear on the part of the machine politicians to nominate men of immoral character. While many bad men have been elected in spite of woman suffrage, they have not been elected because of woman suffrage. If the women alone had a vote, it would result in a class of men in public office whose character for morality, honesty, and courage would be of a much higher order."

The recent re-election of Judge Lindsey by the mothers of Denver, against the opposition of both the political machines, is only a striking instance of what has happened in a multitude of less conspicuous cases in the various enfranchised States.

Women Should Govern Themselves

Carrie Chapman Catt served as the president of the National American Woman Suffrage Association from 1900 to 1902 and from 1915 to 1920. In her February 1902 speech, Catt defends women's right to the vote and self-government.

The opposition to the enfranchisement of women is the last defense of the old theory that obedience is necessary for women, because man alone is the creator of the race.

The whole effort of the woman movement has been to destroy obedience of woman in the home. That end has been very generally attained, and the average civilized woman enjoys the right of individual liberty in the home of her father, her husband, and her son. The individual woman no longer obeys the individual man. She enjoys self-government in the home and in society. The question now is, shall all women as a body obey all men as a body? Shall the woman who enjoys the right of self-government in every other department of life be permitted the right of self-government in the State? It is no more right for all men to govern all women than it was for one man to govern one woman. It is no more right for men to govern women than it was for one man to govern other men.

5. Equal suffrage broadens women's minds, and leads them to take a more intelligent interest in public affairs. President Slocum, of Colorado College, Enos A. Mills, the forestry expert, Mrs. Decker, and many others, bear witness to this. The Hon. W.E. Mullen, Attorney-General of Wyoming, who went there opposed to woman suffrage and has been converted, writes: "It stimulates interest and study, on the part of women, in public affairs. Questions of public interest are discussed in the home. As the mother, sister, or teacher of young boys, the influence of woman is very great. The more she knows about the obligations of citizenship, the more she is able to teach the boys." A leading bookseller of Denver says he sold more books on political economy in the first eight months after women were given the ballot than he had sold in fifteen years before.

6. It makes elections and political meetings more orderly. The Hon. John W. Kingman, of the Wyoming Supreme Court, says: "In caucus discussions the presence of a few ladies is worth a whole squad of police."

7. It makes it easier to secure liberal appropriations for educational and humanitarian purposes. In Colorado the schools are not scrimped for money, as they are in the older and richer States. So say Mrs. Grenfell, General Irving Hale, and others.

8. It opens to women important positions now closed to them because they are not electors. Throughout England, Scotland, Ireland, and a considerable part of Europe, a host of women are rendering admirable service to the community in offices from which women in America are still debarred.

9. It increases the number of women chosen to such offices as are already open to them. Thus, in Colorado women were eligible as county superintendents of schools before their enfranchisement; but when they obtained the ballot the number of women elected to those positions showed an immediate and large increase.

10. It raises the average of political honesty among the voters. Judge Lindsey says: "Ninety-nine per cent of our election frauds are committed by men."

11. It tends to modify a too exclusively commercial view of public affairs. G.W. Russell, Chairman of the Board of Governors of Canterbury College, New Zealand, writes: "Prior to women's franchise the distinctive feature of our politics was finance. Legislative proposals were regarded almost entirely from the point of view of (1) What would they cost? and (2) What would be their effect from a commercial standpoint? The woman's view is not pounds nor pence, but her home, her family. In order to win her vote, the politicians had to look at public matters from her point of view. Her ideal was not merely money, but happy homes and a fair chance in life for her husband, her intended husband, and her present or prospective family."

Suffrage and the Family

12. Last, but not least, it binds the family more closely together. I say this with emphasis, though it is in direct opposition to an argument much brought forward by the opponents of woman suffrage. Let us give ear to words that are written, like the last, from a region where equal suffrage has been tried and proved.

The Hon. Hugh Lusk, ex-member of the New Zealand Parliament, says: "We find that equal suffrage is the greatest family bond and tie, the greatest strengthener of family life. It seemed odd at first to find half the benches at a political meeting occupied by ladies; but when men have got accustomed to it they do not like the other thing. When they found that they could take their wives and daughters to these meetings, and afterwards go home with them and talk it over, it was often the beginning of a new life for the family—a life of ideas and interests in common, and of a unison of thought."

It is related that the Japanese Government many years ago sent a commission to the United States to study the practical working of Christianity, with a view to introducing it into Japan as the State religion if the report of the commission proved favorable. The commission saw many evils rampant in America, and went home reporting that Christianity was a failure. The opponents of woman suffrage argue in the same way. They find evils in the enfranchised States, and straightway draw the conclusion that woman suffrage is a failure. But it may be said with truth of woman suffrage, as of Christianity, that these evils exist not because of it but in spite of it; and that it has effected a number of distinct improvements, and is on the way to effect yet more.

I have sat in the little chapel at Bethlehem in which tradition places the birth of the Saviour. It seemed fitting that it should be adorned with offerings of beautiful things. But while I mused there a voice seemed to say to me: "Look abroad! This divine child is a child no more. He has grown to be a man and a deliverer. Go out into the world! Find his footsteps and follow them. Work, as he did, for the redemption of mankind. Suffer as he did, if need be, derision and obloquy. Make your protest against tyranny, meanness, and injustice!"

The weapon of Christian warfare is the ballot, which represents the peaceable assertion of conviction and will. Society everywhere is becoming converted to its use. Adopt it, O you women, with clean hands and a pure heart! Verify the best word written by the apostle—"In Christ Jesus there is neither bond nor free, neither male nor female, but a new creature," the harbinger of a new creation!

VIEWPOINT 4

"The suffrage is 'a reform against nature' and such reforms are worse than valueless."

American Women Should Not Have the Right to Vote

Emily P. Bissell (1861–1948)

Social reformer and lecturer Emily P. Bissell was primarily involved in public welfare activities. As the first president of the Consumers' League of Delaware, Bissell helped to secure passage of state laws that regulated child labor and established maximum hours for women workers. Bissell was also an active opponent of equal suffrage; she wrote articles, lectured in various states, and testified before Congress on antisuffrage issues.

The following viewpoint is taken from Bissell's 1909 antisuffrage pamphlet, which was published and widely distributed by the New York State Association Opposed to Woman Suffrage. Bissell argues that most women do not want to vote or are too busy to familiarize themselves with political affairs. At best, she contends, the majority of women would be indifferent and uninformed voters. Those women who are interested in public affairs and social reform do not need voting rights in order to successfully promote beneficial legislation, she asserts. The negative effects of equal suffrage in states such as Colorado and Utah prove that the nation would not benefit from granting women voting rights, Bissell concludes.

From "A Talk to Women on the Suffrage Question" by Emily P. Bissell, in *Selected Articles on Woman Suffrage*, 3rd rev. ed. (New York: H.W. Wilson, 1916).

There are three points of view from which woman today ought to consider herself—as an individual, as a member of a family, as a member of the state. Every woman stands in those three relations to American life. Every woman's duties and rights cluster along those three lines; and any change in woman's status that involves all of them needs to be very carefully considered by every thoughtful woman.

The proposal that women should vote affects each one of these three relations deeply. It is then a proposal that the American woman has been considering for sixty years, without accepting it. Other questions, which have been only individual, as the higher education for such individual women as desire it, or the opening of various trades and professions to such individual women as desire to enter them have not required any such thought or hesitation. They are individual, and individuals have decided on them and accepted them. But this great suffrage question, involving not only the individual, but the family and the state, has hung fire. There are grave objections to woman suffrage on all these three counts. Sixty years of argument and of effort on the part of the suffragists have not in the least changed these arguments, because they rest on the great fundamental facts of human nature and of human government. The suffrage is "a reform against nature" and such reforms are worse than valueless.

Let us take these three points of view singly. Why, in the first place, is the vote a mistake for women as individuals? I will begin discussing that by another question. "How many of you have leisure to spare now, without the vote?" The claims upon a woman's time, in this twentieth century, are greater than ever before. Woman, in her progress, has taken up many important things to deal with, and has already overloaded herself beyond her strength. If she is a working-woman, her day is full—fuller than that of a workingman, since she has to attend, in many cases, to home duties or to sewing and mending for herself when her day's toil is over. If she is a wife and mother, she has her hands full with the house and the children. If she is a woman of affairs and charities, she has to keep a secretary or call in a stenographer to get through her letters and accounts. Most of the self-supporting women of my acquaintance do not want the ballot. They have no time to think about it. Most of the wives and mothers I know do not want to vote. They are too busy with other burdens. Most of the women of affairs I know do not want to vote. They are doing public work without it better than they could with it, and consider it a burden, not a benefit. The ballot is a duty, a responsibility; and most intelligent, active women today believe that it is man's duty and responsibility, and that they are not called to take it up in addition to their own share. The suffragists want the ballot individually. They have a perfect right to want it. They ask no leisure. And if it were only an individual question, then I should say heartily "Let them have it, as individuals, and let us refuse to take it, as individuals, and then the whole matter can be individually settled." But that is impossible, for there are two other aspects. The suffragists cannot get the vote without forcing it on all the rest of womankind in America; for America means unrestricted manhood suffrage, and an equal suffrage law would mean unrestricted womanhood suffrage, from the college girl to the immigrant woman who cannot read and the negro woman in the cotton-field, and from the leader of society down to the drunken woman in the police court. The individual aspect is only one of the three, and after all, the least important.

For no good woman lives to herself. She has always been part of a family as wife or sister or daughter from the time of Eve. . . . The American home is the foundation of American strength and progress. And in the American home woman has her own place

In this 1909 cartoon, women's suffrage leads to a complete reversal of gender roles.

142

and her own duty to the family.

It is an axiom in physics that two things cannot be in the same place at the same time. Woman, as an individual, apart from all home ties, can easily enough get into a man's place. There are thousands of women in New York to-day—business women, professional women, working girls, who are almost like men in their daily activity. But nearly all these women marry and leave the man's place for the woman's, after a few years of business life. It is this fact which makes their wages lower than men's, and keeps them from being a highly skilled class. They go back into the home, and take up a woman's duties in the family. If they are wise women, they give up their work; they do not try to be in a man's place and a woman's too. But when they do make this foolish resolve to keep on working the home suffers. There are no children; or the children go untrained; housekeeping is given up for boarding; there is no family atmosphere. The woman's place is vacant—and in a family, that is the most important place of all. The woman, who might be a woman, is half a man instead.

The family demands from a woman her very best. Her highest interests, and her unceasing care, must be in home life, if her home is to be what it ought to be. Here is where the vote for woman comes in as a disturbing factor. The vote is part of man's work. Ballot-box, cartridge box, jury box, sentry box, all go together in his part of life. Woman cannot step in and take the responsibilities and duties of voting without assuming his place very largely. The vote is a symbol of government, and leads at once into the atmosphere of politics; to make herself an intelligent voter (and no other kind is wanted) a woman must study up the subjects on which she is to vote and cast her ballot with a personal knowledge of current politics in every detail. She must take it all from her husband, which means that he is thus given two votes instead of one, not equal suffrage, but a double suffrage for the man.

A Man's Place

Home is meant to be a restful place, not agitated by the turmoil of outside struggles. It is man's place to support and defend the family, and so to administer the state that the family shall flourish in peace. He is the outside worker. Woman is the one whose place it is to bear and rear the children who shall later be the citizens of the state. As I have shown, she can, if she wishes, go into man's place in the world for a while. But man can never go into hers. (That proves she is superior, by the way.) He cannot create the home. He is too distracted by outside interests, too tired with his own duties, to create an atmosphere of home. The woman who makes the mistake of trying to do his work and hers too, cannot create a home atmosphere, either. She cannot be in two places at once. I have known even one outside charity become so absorbing in its demands on a woman's time and thought that her children felt the difference, and knew and dreaded the day of the monthly meeting, and the incessant call of the telephone. There are certain times in a wife and mother's life, such as children's illnesses, the need of care for an over-worked husband, the crisis of some temptation or wrong tendency in a child's life, and so on, when all outside interests must abdicate before the family ones, and be shut out for a while. The vote, which means public life, does not fit into the ideal of family life. The woman who is busy training a family is doing her public service right in the home. She cannot be expected to be in two places at the same time, doing the work of the state as the man does.

Individualism and Family Life

The individualism of woman, in these modern days, is a threat to the family. There is one divorce in America nowadays to every dozen marriages. There are thousands of young women who crowd into factory or mill or office in preference to home duties. There is an impatience of ties and responsibilities, a restlessness, a fever for "living one's own life," that is unpleasantly noticeable. The desire for the vote is part of this restlessness, this grasping for power that shall have no responsibility except to drop a paper into a ballot box, this ignorant desire to do "the work of the world" instead of one's own appointed work. If women had conquered their own part of life perfectly, one might wish to see them thus leave it and go forth to set the world to rights. But on the contrary, never were domestic conditions so badly attended to. Until woman settles the servant question, how can she ask to run the government?

This brings us to the third point, which is, the effect on the state of a vote for women. Let us keep in mind, always, that in America we cannot argue about municipal suffrage, or taxpaying suffrage, or limited suffrage of any kind—"to one end they must all come," that of unrestricted woman suffrage, white and colored, illiterate and collegebred alike having the ballot. America recognizes no other way. Do not get the mistaken idea—which the suffragists cleverly present all the while—that the English system of municipal or restricted suffrage, or the Danish system, or any other system, is like ours. It is *not*. Other countries have restricted forms of suffrage by which individual women can be sorted out, so to speak. But America has equal manhood suffrage ingrained in her very state, in her very law. Once begin to give the suffrage to women, and there is but one end in this country. The question is always with us, "What effect will unrestricted female suffrage have on the state?" We must answer that question or beg the subject.

Duties of Enfranchised Citizens

Alice Duffield Goodwin was the author of the 1903 book Anti-Suffrage: Ten Good Reasons. *In the following excerpt, Goodwin argues that women will not be able to perform the responsibilities that come with suffrage.*

The ballot carries with it the duty of bearing arms in time of war, and of jury duty in times of peace. If women are granted the ballot the governmental system will have to be reconstructed to free us from these duties, or we shall have to attend to them while doing our own peculiar and non-transferable tasks. . . . Absence from home and children during prolonged jury service will not materially help the state. Women are everywhere today suffering from exhaustion of vital force, due to the incessant demands of a life crowded with claims outside the home, either in social obligations, philanthropic or civic interests, or the taxing strain of industrial life. Between these two comes the large percentage of American women, far larger than any other class, who need all their strength for necessary household tasks. The watchful and intelligent observer fails to see the surplus of strength to be expended in a man's way for the good of the state, and he does see the good of the state seriously menaced at its source by the inroads upon feminine vitality which will be made when political duties are added to those bound upon our shoulders first by nature, second by a highly developed civilization.

One thing sure—the women's vote would be an indifferent one. The majority of women do not want to vote—even the suffragists acknowledge that. Therefore, if given the vote, they would not be eager voters. There would be a number of highly enthusiastic suffrage voters—for a while. But when the coveted privilege became a commonplace, or even an irksome duty, the stay-at-home vote would grow larger and larger. The greatest trouble in politics today is the indifferent vote among men. Equal suffrage would add a larger indifferent vote among women.

A Corrupt Vote

Then there is the corrupt vote to-day. Among men it is bad enough. But among women it would be much worse. What, for example, would the Tenderloin [red-light district] woman's vote be in New York? for good measures and better city politics? . . . Unrestricted suffrage must reckon with all kinds of women, you see—and the unscrupulous woman will use her vote for what it is worth and for corrupt ends.

Today, without the vote, the women who are intelligent and interested in public affairs use their ability and influence for good measures. And the indifferent woman does not matter. The unscrupulous woman has no vote. We get the best, and bar out the rest. The state gets all the benefit of its best women, and none of the danger from its worst women. The situation is too beneficial to need any change in the name of progress. We have now two against one, a fine majority, the good men and the good women against the unscrupulous men. Equal suffrage would make it two to two—the good men and the good women against the unscrupulous men and the unscrupulous women—a tie vote between good and evil instead of a safe majority for good.

Then, beside the indifferent vote and the corrupt vote, there would be, in equal suffrage, a well-meaning, unorganized vote. But government is not run in America by unorganized votes—it is run by organized parties. To get results, one vote is absurd. An effectual vote means organization; and organization means primaries and conventions, and caucuses and office-holding, and work, and work, and more work. A ballot dropped in a box is not government, or power. This is what men are fighting out in politics, and we women ought to understand their problem. One reason that I, personally, do not want the ballot is that I have been brought up, in the middle of politics in a state that is full of them, and I know the labor they entail on public-spirited men. Politics, to me, does not mean unearned power, or the registering of one's opinion on public affairs—it means hard work, incessant organization and combination, continual perseverance against disappointment and betrayal, steadfast effort for small and hard-fought advance. I have seen too many friends and relatives in that battle to want to push any woman into it. And unless one goes into the battle the ballot is of no force. The suffragists do not expect to. They expect and urge that all that will be necessary will be for each woman to "register her opinion" and cast her ballot and go home.

Where would the state be then—with an indifferent vote, a corrupt vote, and a helpless, unorganized vote, loaded on to its present political difficulties? Where would the state be with a doubled negro vote in the Black Belt? Where would New York and Chicago be with a doubled immigrant vote? I have two friends, sisters, one of them living in Utah, the other in Colorado—both suffrage states. The one in Colorado belongs to the indifferent vote. She is too busy to vote, and doesn't believe in it anyhow. The one in Utah goes to the polls regularly, not because she wants to vote, but because as she says "The Mormons vote all their women solidly, and we Gentiles have to vote as a duty—and how we wish we were back again under manhood suffrage." Is the state benefited by an unwilling electorate such as that?

146

VIEWPOINT 5

"If the average family . . . contained but two children the Nation as a whole would . . . in two or three generations . . . be on the point of extinction."

Family Size Should Not Be Limited

Theodore Roosevelt (1858–1919)

The United States experienced a sustained decline in its birthrate during the end of the nineteenth century and the beginning of the twentieth. Many people believed that this decrease in fertility was linked in part to the women's rights movement. For example, they noted that the 1890 U.S. census revealed not only that families were having fewer children but that increasing numbers of women were entering the labor force. These working women were either remaining single, the argument ran, or they were limiting the number of children they had.

The following viewpoint is excerpted from a speech delivered by Theodore Roosevelt to the National Congress of Mothers on March 13, 1905. In his speech, Roosevelt maintains that, if the decrease in the birthrate continues, the nation will suffer. Parents who limit the size of their families are not fulfilling their duty to raise up more citizens, Roosevelt avers. Women in particular, he contends, should willingly devote themselves to raising a family rather than deliberately choosing not to have children.

At the time of this speech, Roosevelt had recently been elected to his second term as president of the United States. During his tenure as governor of New York at the turn of the century, Roosevelt had actively supported attempts to obtain equal suffrage in the state. However, during his presidency he angered feminist leaders by refusing to publicly advocate national suffrage for women.

From Theodore Roosevelt's "Address Before the National Congress of Mothers, Washington, D.C., March 13, 1905," in *Presidential Addresses and State Papers*, vol. 3 (New York, n.p., 1910).

In our modern industrial civilization there are many and grave dangers to counterbalance the splendors and the triumphs. It is not a good thing to see cities grow at disproportionate speed relatively to the country; for the small landowners, the men who own their little homes, and therefore to a very large extent the men who till farms, the men of the soil, have hitherto made the foundation of lasting national life in every State; and, if the foundation becomes either too weak or too narrow, the superstructure, no matter how attractive, is in imminent danger of falling.

But far more important than the question of the occupation of our citizens is the question of how their family life is conducted. No matter what that occupation may be, as long as there is a real home and as long as those who make up that home do their duty to one another, to their neighbors, and to the state, it is of minor consequence whether the man's trade is plied in the country or the city, whether it calls for the work of the hands or for the work of the head.

But the Nation is in a bad way if there is no real home, if the family is not of the right kind; if the man is not a good husband and father, if he is brutal or cowardly or selfish; if the woman has lost her sense of duty, if she is sunk in vapid self-indulgence or has let her nature be twisted so that she prefers a sterile pseudo-intellectuality to that great and beautiful development of character which comes only to those whose lives know the fulness of duty done, of effort made and self-sacrifice undergone.

The State and the Family

In the last analysis the welfare of the state depends absolutely upon whether or not the average family, the average man and woman and their children, represent the kind of citizenship fit for the foundation of a great nation; and if we fail to appreciate this we fail to appreciate the root morality upon which all healthy civilization is based.

No piled-up wealth, no splendor of material growth, no brilliance of artistic development, will permanently avail any people unless its home life is healthy, unless the average man possesses honesty, courage, common-sense, and decency, unless he works hard and is willing at need to fight hard; and unless the average woman is a good wife, a good mother, able and willing to perform the first and greatest duty of womanhood, able and willing to bear, and to bring up as they should be brought up, healthy children, sound in body, mind, and character, and numerous enough so that the race shall increase and not decrease.

There are certain old truths which will be true as long as this world endures, and which no amount of progress can alter. One of these is the truth that the primary duty of the husband is to be the homemaker, the breadwinner for his wife and children, and that the primary duty of the woman is to be the helpmeet, the housewife, and mother. The woman should have ample educational advantages; but save in exceptional cases the man must be, and she need not be, and generally ought not to be, trained for a lifelong career as the family breadwinner; and, therefore, after a certain point the training of the two must normally be different because the duties of the two are normally different. This does not mean inequality of function, but it does mean that normally there must be dissimilarity of function. On the whole, I think the duty of the woman the more important, the more difficult, and the more honorable of the two; on the whole I respect the woman who does her duty even more than I respect the man who does his. . . .

Protecting the Sacredness of Life

In his 1917 book Woman, *antisuffragist Vance Thompson contends that women should not use contraception or regulate the size of their families.*

It is certainly possible "artificially to sterilize matrimony" in certain people—the paupers science keeps, like rabbits, for experiment; it is quite possible; but only blind ignorance could fancy it would stop the ebb and flow of the cosmic tide of life. All this ignorant clamor about sex-control belongs to the maudlin and sentimental science, which reached its climax in the last century and is, fortunately, dying down with decent rapidity. It has done its worst. You and I, whether man or Woman Emergent, may safely assume it will soon be buried in the grave of filthy and abandoned heresies against life. It is a bad thing to blaspheme against life; and that pseudo-scientific theory of birth-prevention was the foulest blasphemy of all—begotten by the dark and sterile powers of life-denial. . . .

I hail Woman's entrance, as a peer, into the rule and government of earth-life, because I know that she will indeed guard—with drawn sword—the sacredness and honor of [newborn] life.

She will have none of man's silly and criminal way of muddling the babies out of life; she will, instead, make a fair, large room for them in it. Already she has taught man a little of the spiritual significance of marriage; she must teach him also the sacred significance of the birth of a little child.

Just as the happiest and most honorable and most useful task that can be set any man is to earn enough for the support of his wife and family, for the bringing up and starting in life of his children, so the most important, the most honorable and desirable task which can be set any woman is to be a good and wise mother in a home marked by self-respect and mutual forbearance, by willingness to perform duty, and by refusal to sink into self-indulgence or avoid that which entails effort and self-sacrifice. Of course, there are exceptional men and exceptional women who can do and ought to do much more than this, who can lead and ought to lead great careers of outside usefulness in addition to—not as substitute for—their home work; but I am not speaking of exceptions; I am speaking of the primary duties, I am speaking of the average citizens, the average men and women who make up the Nation. . . .

There are many good people who are denied the supreme blessing of children, and for these we have the respect and sympathy always due to those who, from no fault of their own, are denied any of the other great blessings of life. But the man or woman who deliberately foregoes these blessings, whether from viciousness, coldness, shallow-heartedness, self-indulgence, or mere failure to appreciate aright the difference between the all-important and the unimportant—why, such a creature merits contempt as hearty as any visited upon the soldier who runs away in battle, or upon the man who refuses to work for the support of those dependent upon him, and who though able-bodied is yet content to eat in idleness the bread which others provide.

The existence of women of this type forms one of the most unpleasant and unwholesome features of modern life. . . . That [she] also exists in American life is made unpleasantly evident by the statistics as to the dwindling families in some localities. It is made evident in equally sinister fashion by the census statistics as to divorce, which are fairly appalling; for easy divorce is now, as it ever has been, a bane to any nation, a curse to society, a menace to the home, an incitement to married unhappiness and to immorality, an evil thing for men and a still more hideous evil for women. These unpleasant tendencies in our American life are made evident by articles such as those which I actually read not long ago in a certain paper, where a clergyman was quoted, seemingly with approval, as expressing the general American attitude when he said that the ambition of any save a very rich man should be to rear two children only, so as to give his children an opportunity "to taste a few of the good things of life.". . .

The way to give a child a fair chance in life is not to bring it up in luxury, but to see that it has the kind of training that will give it strength of character. Even apart from the vital question of national life, and regarding only the individual interest of the children themselves, happiness in the true sense is a hundredfold more apt to come to any given member of a healthy family of healthy-minded children, well brought up, well educated, but taught that they must shift for themselves, must win their own way, and by their own exertions make their own positions of usefulness, than it is apt to come to those whose parents themselves have acted on and have trained their children to act on, the selfish and sordid theory that the whole end of life is "to taste a few good things."

Race Suicide

The intelligence of the remark is on a par with its morality, for the most rudimentary mental process would have shown the speaker that if the average family in which there are children contained but two children the Nation as a whole would decrease in population so rapidly that in two or three generations it would very deservedly be on the point of extinction, so that the people who had acted on this base and selfish doctrine would be giving place to others with braver and more robust ideals. Nor would such a result be in any way regrettable; for a race that practiced such doctrine—that is, a race that practiced race suicide—would thereby conclusively show that it was unfit to exist, and that it had better give place to people who had not forgotten the primary laws of their being.

To sum up, then, the whole matter is simple enough. If either a race or an individual prefers the pleasures of mere effortless ease, of self-indulgence, to the infinitely deeper, the infinitely higher pleasures that come to those who know the toil and the weariness, but also the joy, of hard duty well done, why, that race or that individual must inevitably in the end pay the penalty of leading a life both vapid and ignoble. No man and no woman really worthy of the name can care for the life spent solely or chiefly in the avoidance of risk and trouble and labor. Save in exceptional cases the prizes worth having in life must be paid for, and the life worth living must be a life of work for a worthy end, and ordinarily of work more for others than for one's self.

The man is but a poor creature whose effort is not rather for the betterment of his wife and children than for himself; and as for the mother, her very name stands for loving unselfishness and self-abnegation, and, in any society fit to exist, is fraught with associations which render it holy.

The woman's task is not easy—no task worth doing is easy—but in doing it, and when she has done it, there shall come to her the highest and holiest joy known to mankind; and having done it, she shall have the reward prophesied in Scripture; for her husband and her children, yes, and all people who realize that her work lies at the foundation of all national happiness and greatness, shall rise up and call her blessed.

VIEWPOINT 6

"No woman can call herself free until she can choose consciously whether she will or will not be a mother."

Women Should Have Access to Birth Control

Margaret Sanger (1883–1966)

In the early 1910s, Margaret Sanger worked as a public health nurse in the tenements of New York City. Sanger's life was radically changed in 1912 when a young mother, who had previously begged her for information about contraceptives, died in her arms from a self-induced abortion. The next year, Sanger went to Europe to study contraceptive devices. On her return to New York, she opened the first birth-control clinic in the United States and published pamphlets containing detailed information on birth control. In 1917, Sanger founded the National Birth Control League, which later became Planned Parenthood.

The following viewpoint is taken from Sanger's 1920 book *Woman and the New Race*. Sanger contends that access to birth control will improve women's lives by allowing them to choose if and when they will have children. Women will never be able to fully achieve equal rights without the ability to control their own fertility, she argues. Although ideally both men and women should share responsibility for limiting the size of their families, Sanger maintains, women are most affected by childbearing and therefore should take measures to protect themselves. Neither individual men nor the government have the right to force women to bear unwanted children, Sanger concludes.

From *Woman and the New Race* by Margaret Sanger (New York: Brentano, 1920).

The problem of birth control has arisen directly from the effort of the feminine spirit to free itself from bondage. Woman herself has wrought that bondage through her reproductive powers and while enslaving herself has enslaved the world. The physical suffering to be relieved is chiefly woman's. Hers, too, is the love life that dies first under the blight of too prolific breeding. Within her is wrapped up the future of the race—it is hers to make or mar. All of these considerations point unmistakably to one fact—it is woman's duty as well as her privilege to lay hold of the means of freedom. Whatever men may do, she cannot escape the responsibility. For ages she has been deprived of the opportunity to meet this obligation. She is now emerging from her helplessness. Even as no one can share the suffering of the overburdened mother, so no one can do this work for her. Others may help, but she and she alone can free herself.

Birth Control and Freedom

The basic freedom of the world is woman's freedom. A free race cannot be born of slave mothers. A woman enchained cannot choose but give a measure of that bondage to her sons and daughters. No woman can call herself free who does not own and control her body. No woman can call herself free until she can choose consciously whether she will or will not be a mother.

It does not greatly alter the case that some women call themselves free because they earn their own livings, while others profess freedom because they defy the conventions of sex relationship. She who earns her own living gains a sort of freedom that is not to be undervalued, but in quality and in quantity it is of little account beside the untrammeled choice of mating or not mating, of being a mother or not being a mother. She gains food and clothing and shelter, at least, without submitting to the charity of her companion, but the earning of her own living does not give her the development of her inner sex urge, far deeper and more powerful in its outworkings than any of these externals. In order to have that development, she must still meet and solve the problem of motherhood.

With the so-called "free" woman, who chooses a mate in defiance of convention, freedom is largely a question of character and audacity. If she does attain to an unrestricted choice of a mate, she is still in a position to be enslaved through her reproductive powers. Indeed, the pressure of law and custom upon the woman not legally married is likely to make her more of a slave than the woman fortunate enough to marry the man of her choice.

Look at it from any standpoint you will, suggest any solution you will, conventional or unconventional, sanctioned by law or in defiance of law, woman is in the same position, fundamentally, until she is able to determine for herself whether she will be a mother and to fix the number of her offspring. This unavoidable situation is alone enough to make birth control, first of all, a woman's problem. On the very face of the matter, voluntary motherhood is chiefly the concern of the woman.

The Causes of Race-Suicide

Medical doctor and minister Anna Howard Shaw served as president of the National American Woman Suffrage Association from 1904 to 1915. On June 29, 1905, Shaw delivered a speech in which she defended women's right to choose to bear fewer children.

When the cry of race-suicide is heard, and men arraign women for race decadence, it would be well for them to examine conditions and causes, and base their attacks upon firmer foundations of fact. Instead of attacking women for their interest in public affairs and relegating them to their children, their kitchen, and their church, they will learn that the kitchen is in politics; that the children's physical, intellectual, and moral well-being is controlled and regulated by law; that the real cause of race decadence is not the fact that fewer children are born, but to the more fearful fact that, of those born, so few live, not primarily because of the neglect of the mother, but because men themselves neglect their duty as citizens and public officials. If men honestly desire to prevent the causes of race decadence, let them examine the accounts of food adulteration, and learn that from the effect of impure milk alone, in one city 5,600 babies died in a single year. . . .

It is infinitely more important that a child shall be well born and well reared than that more children shall be born. It is better that one well-born child shall live than that two shall be born and one die in infancy. That which is desirable is not that the greatest possible number of children should be born into the world; the need is for more intelligent motherhood and fatherhood, and for better born and better educated children.

It is persistently urged, however, that since sex expression is the act of two, the responsibility of controlling the results should not be placed upon woman alone. Is it fair, it is asked, to give her, instead of the man, the task of protecting herself when she is, perhaps, less rugged in physique than her mate, and has, at all events, the normal, periodic inconveniences of her sex?

We must examine this phase of her problem in two lights—that of the ideal, and of the conditions working toward the ideal. In an ideal society, no doubt, birth control would become the concern

154

of the man as well as the woman. The hard, inescapable fact which we encounter to-day is that man has not only refused any such responsibility, but has individually and collectively sought to prevent woman from obtaining knowledge by which she could assume this responsibility for herself. She is still in the position of a dependent to-day because her mate has refused to consider her as an individual apart from his needs. She is still bound because she has in the past left the solution of the problem to him. Having left it to him, she finds that instead of rights, she has only such privileges as she has gained by petitioning, coaxing and cozening. Having left it to him, she is exploited, driven and enslaved to his desires.

While it is true that he suffers many evils as the consequence of this situation, she suffers vastly more. While it is true that he should be awakened to the cause of these evils, we know that they come home to her with crushing force every day. It is she who has the long burden of carrying, bearing and rearing the unwanted children. . . . It is her heart that the sight of the deformed, the subnormal, the undernourished, the overworked child smites first and oftenest and hardest. It is *her* love life that dies first in the fear of undesired pregnancy. It is her opportunity for self expression that perishes first and most hopelessly because of it.

A Woman's Responsibility

Conditions, rather than theories, facts, rather than dreams, govern the problem. They place it squarely upon the shoulders of woman. She has learned that whatever the moral responsibility of the man in this direction may be, he does not discharge it. She has learned that, lovable and considerate as the individual husband may be, she has nothing to expect from men in the mass, when they make laws and decree customs. She knows that regardless of what ought to be, the brutal, unavoidable fact is that she will never receive her freedom until she takes it for herself.

Having learned this much, she has yet something more to learn. Women are too much inclined to follow in the footsteps of men, to try to think as men think, to try to solve the general problems of life as men solve them. If after attaining their freedom, women accept conditions in the spheres of government, industry, art, morals and religion as they find them, they will be but taking a leaf out of man's book. The woman is not needed to do man's work. She is not needed to think man's thoughts. She need not fear that the masculine mind, almost universally dominant, will fail to take care of its own. Her mission is not to enhance the masculine spirit, but to express the feminine; hers is not to preserve a man-made world, but to create a human world by the infusion of the feminine element into all of its activities.

155

Woman must not accept; she must challenge. She must not be awed by that which has been built up around her; she must reverence that within her which struggles for expression. Her eyes must be less upon what is and more clearly upon what should be. She must listen only with a frankly questioning attitude to the dogmatized opinions of man-made society. When she chooses her new, free course of action, it must be in the light of her own opinion—of her own intuition. Only so can she give play to the feminine spirit. Only thus can she free her mate from the bondage which he wrought for himself when he wrought hers. Only thus can she restore to him that of which he robbed himself in restricting her. Only thus can she remake the world. . . .

Woman must have her freedom—the fundamental freedom of choosing whether or not she shall be a mother and how many children she will have. Regardless of what man's attitude may be, that problem is hers—and before it can be his, it is hers alone.

She goes through the vale of death alone, each time a babe is born. As it is the right neither of man nor the state to coerce her into this ordeal, so it is her right to decide whether she will endure it. That right to decide imposes upon her the duty of clearing the way to knowledge by which she may make and carry out the decision.

Birth control is woman's problem. The quicker she accepts it as hers and hers alone, the quicker will society respect motherhood. The quicker, too, will the world be made a fit place for her children to live.

CHAPTER 4

The Women's Liberation Movement

Chapter Preface

During the last surge of effort to ratify the Nineteenth Amendment, suffragists had mobilized a large and strong coalition of women's organizations to work for the single cause of suffrage. When the amendment was ratified in 1920, however, this coalition rapidly disbanded. Many Americans assumed the battle for equal rights had been won when women were granted the vote, and accordingly most women's rights organizations suffered losses in active membership and interest. Some suffrage organizations completely dissolved; others shifted their focus to new concerns. The National American Woman Suffrage Association, for instance, renamed itself the League of Women Voters and lobbied for a variety of political causes, not all of which were related to women's rights. A few groups did continue to work specifically for women's rights but were unable to muster the same concentrated force of the former suffrage coalition. One such group was the National Woman's Party, which spent the 1920s advocating the passage of an equal rights amendment that would remove all legal distinctions between men and women. The feminist movement did not unite behind this new amendment as it had done for the suffrage amendment; instead, the League of Women Voters and other major women's rights organizations opposed the equal rights amendment on the grounds that it would ultimately work to women's detriment.

The Great Depression of the 1930s further affected the women's rights movement. The unprecedented national economic collapse and its devastating repercussions on most Americans' lives meant that few women had time, energy, or resources to dedicate to the feminist cause. Furthermore, working women were often viewed as taking jobs away from men. Some unions, businesses, and government agencies passed regulations that restricted married women from working if their husbands were also employed. Public opinion tended to support such measures; for instance, a 1939 Gallup poll revealed that 78 percent of Americans agreed that married women should not work outside the home. Nevertheless, the economic realities of the Depression era compelled numerous women—married or single—to enter the workforce.

World War II brought about a reversal both of public opinion toward working women and of policies that excluded married women from working outside the home. With the majority of the male labor force now in the military, it became vital for women to fill jobs in heavy industry, weapons manufacturing, transportation, and other professions that had traditionally been reserved for men. Recruitment literature and the media presented a new ideal woman: Rosie the Riveter, capable of succeeding at a "man's job" while simultaneously fulfilling her "female duties" of child rearing and housekeeping. This image was not intended to permanently alter women's attitudes towards work. According to professors Winston E. Langley and Vivian C. Fox, "Women were told that once the war was over men would reclaim their jobs. Propaganda posters portrayed women as temporarily sacrificing their duties at home for patriotic reasons." Indeed, at the start of World War II, 95 percent of women workers intended to quit their jobs once the war was over.

By the end of the war, however, surveys revealed that more than 80 percent of women workers preferred to keep their jobs. Although three million women left the workforce soon after the war, a substantial proportion did not quit of their own volition but were fired or forced out by the resumption of prewar labor restrictions. In what some historians characterize as a direct propaganda attempt to persuade women to quit their jobs, Rosie the Riveter was replaced by the new image of a full-time suburban housewife raising four or five children. Throughout the 1950s, the popular media, psychiatrists, sociologists, and child care experts promoted traditional theories of women's sphere. American women as a whole embraced this ideal, marrying at a younger age and having more children than preceding generations. Fewer women attended college, and the college graduation rates for women dropped substantially. During the postwar era, women's rights organizations such as the League of Women Voters experienced a marked decrease in membership and support. Overall, during the period from the end of World War II to the early 1960s, American women immersed themselves in domesticity.

While some women derived great satisfaction from housework and motherhood, others suffered from a growing sense of malaise and discontent, a condition that in 1963 Betty Friedan would term "the problem that has no name." Moreover, as increasing numbers of American families were unable to maintain the ideal of the full-time housewife, the initial postwar decline in the female labor force reversed. In the 1950s and 1960s, most women who took a job outside the home did so for financial reasons rather than because of feminist ideology. However, according to historian Barbara J. Harris, "many of these women reported receiving more gratification from their jobs than they did from their roles as wives and mothers." This growing dissatisfaction with the 1950s ideal of women led directly to the revitalization of feminism—the women's liberation movement of the 1960s and 1970s.

VIEWPOINT 1

"My office job was only a substitution for the real job I'd been 'hired' for: that of being purely a wife and mother."

Women Should Be Housewives and Mothers

Jennifer Colton (dates unknown)

During World War II, the proportion of American women in the labor force rose from 25 to 36 percent. An unprecedented number of these women worked in industries essential to the war effort, such as aircraft plants, shipyards, and munitions factories. When the war ended in 1945, however, many women quit or were laid off from their jobs and returned to being full-time housewives. As the male combatants returned home and reentered the workforce, an increasing number of psychologists, sociologists, and others began arguing that women could best find personal fulfillment by concentrating all their time and effort on raising their children and creating a pleasant home environment.

The following viewpoint is excerpted from Jennifer Colton's 1951 *Good Housekeeping* article entitled "Why I Quit Working." In this article, Colton, a young mother who resigned from her office job in 1950 in order to devote more time to her family, describes the effects that her decision has had. Colton admits that she misses some aspects of her outside job, but she maintains that being a full-time homemaker has added new richness to her life and given her a sounder relationship with her children. Furthermore,

From "Why I Quit Working" by Jennifer Colton, *Good Housekeeping*, September 1951.

Colton asserts, the free time she has gained has enabled her to take better care of her household chores, to develop her own interests, and to reduce the tension in her life. Although Colton believes that it is acceptable for housewives to earn money from home-based jobs (in her case, freelance writing), she concludes that a woman's primary career should be that of wife and mother.

Just over a year ago, I was suffering from that feeling of guilt and despondency familiar to most working mothers who have small children. During the hours I spent in the office, an accusing voice chanted continuously, "You should be home with the children." I couldn't have agreed more, which only created an additional tension: the frustrated anger of one who knows what is right but sees no way of doing it. Children need clothes as well as attention; they must be nourished with food as well as love.

Some mothers can eventually talk themselves out of this feeling; they conclude that the material advantages they can provide are worth more than their presence in the home. Some, unable to rationalize this way, gradually grow more despondent. . . .

One day in 1950, I finally worked out a compromise: a way to be at home with the children and still do some work for which I'd be paid. At that moment, I knew only two things: that I would never again rage against a delayed subway for costing me my painfully brief hour with the children, and that at last I would be able to serve a dinner that took more than half an hour to prepare and put on the table.

A year has passed, and I've had time to judge the advantages and disadvantages of leaving my office job. How they will total up ten years from now, I don't know. But here is my balance sheet of the results to date.

Lost

The great alibi: work. My job, and the demands it made on me, were my always accepted excuses for everything and anything: for spoiled children, neglected husband, mediocre food; for being late, tired, preoccupied, conversationally limited, bored, and boring.

The weekly check. And with that went many extravagances and self-indulgences. I no longer had the pleasure of giving showy gifts (the huge doll, the monogrammed pajamas) and the luxury of saying "My treat." And without the extra money, I couldn't rectify or camouflage such mistakes as an unbecoming hat, a too-big canasta debt, a too-small pair of shoes.

The special camaraderie and the common language. The warm but impersonal and unprying relationship among working people is one of the most rewarding things about having a job. People who work, even in unallied fields, speak rather the same language, which can't be translated for the uninitiated without going into the whole psychology of business. I missed the crutch of shoptalk when, later, I struggled to reach people through interests outside the business world.

The Masculinization of Women

Social historian Ferdinand Lundberg and psychiatrist Marynia F. Farnham delineated the harmful effects of women's working outside the home in their 1947 book Modern Woman: The Lost Sex.

Work that entices women out of their homes and provides them with prestige only at the price of feminine relinquishment, involves a response to masculine strivings. The more importance outside work assumes, the more are the masculine components of the woman's nature enhanced and encouraged. In her home and in her relationship to her children, it is imperative that these strivings be at a minimum and that her femininity be available both for her own satisfaction and for the satisfaction of her children and husband. She is, therefore, in the dangerous position of having to live one part of her life on the masculine level, another on the feminine. It is hardly astonishing that few can do so with success. One of these tendencies must of necessity achieve dominance over the other. The plain fact is that increasingly we are observing the masculinization of women and with it enormously dangerous consequences to the home, the children (if any) dependent on it, and to the ability of the woman, as well as her husband, to obtain sexual gratification.

One pretty fallacy. For some reason most working mothers seem to think they could retire with perfect ease; that they could readily adjust themselves to their new role. I don't think so. When you start to devote all your time to homemaking, you run into a whole new set of problems. The transition from part-time to full-time mother is difficult to make.

One baseless vanity. I realize now (and still blush over it) that during my working days I felt that my ability to earn was an additional flower in my wreath of accomplishments. Unconsciously—and sometimes consciously—I thought how nice it was for my husband to have a wife who could *also* bring in money. But one day I realized that my office job was only a substitution for the real job I'd been "hired" for: that of being purely a wife and mother.

The sense of personal achievement. A working woman is someone in her own right, doing work that disinterested parties consider valuable enough to pay for. The satisfactions of housekeeping are many, but they are not quite the same.

The discipline of an office. The demands made on you by business are much easier to fulfill than the demands you make on yourself. Self-discipline is hard to achieve.

Praise for a good piece of work. No one can expect her husband to tell her how beautifully clean she keeps the house or how well she makes the beds. And other people take her housewifely arts for granted. But a business coup attracts attention.

Found

A role. At first I found it hard to believe that being a woman is something in itself. I had always felt that a woman had to do something more than manage a household to prove her worth. Later, when I understood the role better, it took on unexpected glamour. Though I still wince a little at the phrase "wife and mother," I feel quite sure that these words soon will sound as satisfying to me as "actress" or "buyer" or "secretary" or "president."

New friends and a wider conversational range. It was sad to drift apart from my office colleagues, but their hours and, alas, their interests were now different from mine. So I began to make friends with people whose problems, hours, and responsibilities were the same as mine. I gratefully record that my friendship with them is even deeper than it was with business associates. Although we share the same pattern of life, we are not bound by it. As for conversation, I had been brought up on the satirical tales of the housewife who bored her husband with tiresome narratives about the grocer and the broken stove. Maybe it was true in those days. But not any more. I've had to exercise my mind to keep up with these new friends of mine. They have presented me with that handsome gift of expanded interests.

Normalcy. The psychiatrists say there is no such thing, but that's what it feels like. My relationship with my children is sounder, for instance. I have fewer illusions about them. I have found I can get bored with them. Exhausted by them. Irritated to the point of sharp words. At first I was shocked, and then I realized that when I worked and we had so little time together, we had all played our "Sunday best." The result: strained behavior and no real knowledge of one another. Now I'm not so interesting to them as I was. I'm not so attentive and full of fun because I'm myself. I scold, I snap, I listen when I have time. I laugh, I praise, I read to them when I have time. In fact, I'm giving a pretty good representation of a human being and as the children are going to spend most of their lives trying to get along with human beings, they

163

might as well learn right now that people's behavior is variable.

The luxury of free time. This is one of the crown jewels of retirement. The morning or afternoon that occasionally stretches before me, happily blank, to be filled with a visit to a museum or a movie, a chat with a friend, an unscheduled visit to the zoo with the children, the production of the elaborate dish I'd always meant to try, or simply doing nothing, is a great boon.

Leisure. The pleasure of dawdling over a second cup of coffee in the morning can be understood only by those who have, sometime in their lives, gulped the first cup, seized gloves and bag, and rushed out of the house to go to work.

Handwork. This may seem trivial, but making things at home is one of the pleasures the businesswoman is usually deprived of. Homemade cookies, presents, dresses, parties, and relationships can be worth their weight in gold.

Intimacy. The discovery of unusual and unexpected facets in the imaginations of children, which rarely reveal themselves in brief, tense sessions, is very rewarding.

Improved Appearance. Shinier hair, nicer hands, better manicures, are the products of those chance twenty-minute free periods that turn up in the busiest days of women who don't go to business. Of course, such periods crop up in an office, too; but you're not allowed to make use of them for personal affairs.

Proof Positive. If I hadn't retired, I would have remained forever in that thicket of self-delusion, called thwarted potentials. It was almost too easy: the shrug, the brave little smile, and the words "Of course, I've always *wanted* to write (or paint or run for Congress) but since I'm *working*, I never have time." And it's time that gives you proof positive of what you can and cannot do.

Relaxation. Slowly, I'm learning to forget the meaning of the word tension. While I was working, I was tense from the moment I woke up in the morning until I fell into bed at night.

There is no way of measuring or comparing unrelated work. I don't know whether I work harder or less hard now. I walk farther, but there are often free periods during the day to enjoy as I like. I do a greater variety of things, but at my own speed, and without the pressure common to all offices. I get sleepy instead of tired.

Sometimes I ask myself, "What would persuade me to go back?" And my answer is, "Barring big medical expenses or a real need for something for the children or my husband, nothing." And I mean it.

"The only way for a woman, as for a man, to find herself, to know herself as a person, is by creative work of her own."

Women Should Work Outside the Home

Betty Friedan (b. 1921)

From the late 1940s to the early 1960s, the prevailing opinion of American society was that women should devote themselves to being wives and mothers. Most psychologists and sociologists argued that women could only find complete fulfillment by rejecting the "masculine world" of work and embracing their true feminine role of homemaker and nurturer. By the early 1960s, however, it was becoming increasingly clear that many middle-class housewives were dissatisfied with their lives. A spate of magazine articles and television programs reported women's general unhappiness, often blaming it on the overeducation of housewives or sexual dysfunction.

In her 1963 book *The Feminine Mystique*, from which the following viewpoint is excerpted, Betty Friedan refers to this dissatisfaction as "the problem that has no name." According to Friedan, women's discontent arises from their inability to live up to the ideal of the "feminine mystique," which she defines as the belief that women should derive their sole personal satisfaction in being wives and mothers. Friedan argues that, to be truly fulfilled, women must be dedicated to a career as well as a family. The intellectual stimulation and sense of achievement that work brings is as essential to women's well-being as to men's, Friedan contends.

At the time she wrote *The Feminine Mystique*, Friedan was a freelance writer and suburban housewife. In 1966 she helped to found the National Organization for Women and served as its first president. Friedan became one of the foremost leaders of the women's liberation movement, both as an author and a political activist.

It is easier to live through someone else than to become complete yourself. The freedom to lead and plan your own life is frightening if you have never faced it before. It is frightening when a woman finally realizes that there is no answer to the question "who am I" except the voice inside herself. She may spend years on the analyst's couch, working out her "adjustment to the feminine role," her blocks to "fulfillment as a wife and mother." And still the voice inside her may say, "That's not it." Even the best psychoanalyst can only give her the courage to listen to her own voice. When society asks so little of women, every woman has to listen to her own inner voice to find her identity in this changing world. She must create, out of her own needs and abilities, a new life plan, fitting in the love and children and home that have defined femininity in the past with the work toward a greater purpose that shapes the future.

To face the problem is not to solve it. But once a woman faces it, as women are doing today all over America without much help from the experts, once she asks herself "What do I want to do?" she begins to find her own answers. Once she begins to see through the delusions of the feminine mystique—and realizes that neither her husband nor her children, nor the things in her house, nor sex, nor being like all the other women, can give her a self— she often finds the solution much easier than she anticipated. . . .

The Solution Is Meaningful Work

The only way for a woman, as for a man, to find herself, to know herself as a person, is by creative work of her own. There is no other way. But a job, any job, is not the answer—in fact, it can be part of the trap. Women who do not look for jobs equal to their actual capacity, who do not let themselves develop the lifetime interests and goals which require serious education and training, who take a job at twenty or forty to "help out at home" or just to kill extra time, are walking, almost as surely as the ones who stay inside the housewife trap, to a nonexistent future. . . .

The only kind of work which permits an able woman to realize

166

her abilities fully, to achieve identity in society in a life plan that can encompass marriage and motherhood, is the kind that was forbidden by the feminine mystique; the lifelong commitment to an art or science, to politics or profession. Such a commitment is not tied to a specific job or locality. It permits year-to-year variation—a full-time paid job in one community, part-time in another, exercise of the professional skill in serious volunteer work or a period of study during pregnancy or early motherhood when a full-time job is not feasible. It is a continuous thread, kept alive by work and study and contacts in the field, in any part of the country.

The women I found who had made and kept alive such long-term commitments did not suffer the problem that has no name. Nor did they live in the housewife image. But music or art or politics offered no magic solution for the women who did not, or could not, commit themselves seriously. The "arts" seem, at first glance, to be the ideal answer for a woman. They can, after all, be practiced in the home. They do not necessarily imply that dreaded professionalism, they are suitably feminine, and seem to offer endless room for personal growth and identity, with no need to compete in society for pay. But I have noticed that when women do not take up painting or ceramics seriously enough to become professionals—to be paid for their work, or for teaching it to others, and to be recognized as a peer by other professionals—sooner or later, they cease dabbling; the Sunday painting, the idle ceramics do not bring that needed sense of self when they are of no value to anyone else. The amateur or dilettante whose own work is not good enough for anyone to want to pay to hear or see or read does not gain real status by it in society, or real personal identity. These are reserved for those who have made the effort, acquired the knowledge and expertise to become professionals. . . .

The picture of the happy housewife doing creative work at home—painting, sculpting, writing—is one of the semi-delusions of the feminine mystique. There are men and women who can do it; but when a man works at home, his wife keeps the children strictly out of the way, or else. It is not so easy for a woman; if she is serious about her work she often must find some place away from home to do it, or risk becoming an ogre to her children in her impatient demands for privacy. Her attention is divided and her concentration interrupted, on the job and as a mother. A no-nonsense nine-to-five job, with a clear division between professional work and housework, requires much less discipline and is usually less lonely. Some of the stimulation and the new friendships that come from being part of the professional world can be lost by the woman who tries to fit her career into the physical confines of her housewife life. . . .

The most powerful weapon of the feminine mystique is the argument that [a woman] rejects her husband and her children by working outside the home. If, for any reason, her child becomes ill or her husband has troubles of his own, the feminine mystique, insidious voices in the community, and even the woman's own inner voice will blame her "rejection" of the housewife role. It is then that many a woman's commitment to herself and society dies aborning or takes a serious detour. . . .

Homemakers protested their status as unpaid workers during a 1975 national women's strike.

UPI/Bettmann

In other instances, however, women told me that the violent objections of their husbands disappeared when they finally made up their own minds and went to work. Had they magnified their husband's objections to evade decision themselves? Husbands I have interviewed in this same context were sometimes surprised to find it "a relief" to be no longer the only sun and moon in their wives' world; they were the object of less nagging and fewer insatiable demands and they no longer had to feel guilt over their wives' discontent. As one man put it: "Not only is the financial burden lighter—and frankly, that is a relief—but the whole burden of living seems easier since Margaret went to work.". . .

For the women I interviewed who had suffered and solved the problem that has no name, to fulfill an ambition of their own, long buried or brand new, to work at top capacity, to have a sense of achievement, was like finding a missing piece in the puzzle of their lives. The money they earned often made life easier for the whole family, but none of them pretended this was the only reason they worked, or the main thing they got out of it. That sense of being complete and fully a part of the world—"no longer an island, part of the mainland"—had come back. They knew that it did not come from the work alone, but from the whole—their marriage, homes, children, work, their changing, growing links with the community. They were once again human beings, not "just housewives.". . .

Complete Fulfillment

When enough women make life plans geared to their real abilities, and speak out for maternity leaves or even maternity sabbaticals, professionally run nurseries, and the other changes in the rules that may be necessary, they will not have to sacrifice the right to honorable competition and contribution anymore than they will have to sacrifice marriage and motherhood. It is wrong to keep spelling out unnecessary choices that make women unconsciously resist either commitment or motherhood—and that hold back recognition of the needed social changes. It is not a question of women having their cake and eating it, too. A woman is handicapped by her sex, and handicaps society, either by slavishly copying the pattern of man's advance in the professions, or by refusing to compete with man at all. But with the vision to make a new life plan of her own, she can fulfill a commitment to profession and politics, and to marriage and motherhood with equal seriousness. . . .

Who knows what women can be when they are finally free to become themselves? Who knows what women's intelligence will contribute when it can be nourished without denying love? Who knows of the possibilities of love when men and women share not only children, home, and garden, not only the fulfillment of their biological roles, but the responsibilities and passions of the work that creates the human future and the full human knowledge of who they are? It has barely begun, the search of women for themselves. But the time is at hand when the voices of the feminine mystique can no longer drown out the inner voice that is driving women on to become complete.

VIEWPOINT 3

"It is . . . the responsibility and right of the woman to decide; and a private affair between woman and doctor."

Abortion Should Be Legalized

Marya Mannes (1904–1990)

In the 1960s, most states prohibited abortion except under special medical circumstances, such as saving the life of the mother. The movement to liberalize abortion laws originated among medical and legal professionals who wanted to allow doctors more freedom in deciding when an abortion was necessary. In particular, these professionals were concerned about the high rate of illegal abortions (estimated at between 200,000 and 1,200,000 a year), which were often performed under unsanitary conditions by incompetent abortionists. By the late 1960s, abortion had become a key issue among feminists, who demanded that abortion laws be completely repealed rather than reformed.

Marya Mannes was a journalist, novelist, and lecturer who wrote prolifically for a number of periodicals, including the *New York Times Magazine*, *Vogue*, and the *Reporter*. In her 1967 article "A Woman Views Abortion," Mannes argues that legalizing abortion will improve women's lives. Women should not be forced to run the risk of dying from a hazardous illegal abortion, she insists, nor should they be compelled to bear unwanted children. Instead, Mannes contends, women should have the legal right to decide whether to have an abortion.

On January 22, 1973, the U.S. Supreme Court handed down its decision in the case of *Roe v. Wade*, ruling that the states could not bar first-trimester abortions and could regulate second-trimester abortions only to protect women's health. This decision effectively overturned most state laws that had made abortion illegal.

From "A Woman Views Abortion" by Marya Mannes, in *The Case for Legalized Abortion Now*, edited by Alan F. Guttmacher, M.D. (Berkeley, CA: Diablo Press, 1967). Reprinted with permission of the publisher.

Some years ago I helped a young woman get an illegal abortion in New York City. Divorced, earning her living, she found herself pregnant as the result of a passing affair and—she could only assume—defective precautions.

Her doctor said there was nothing he could do, so all *we* could do was to ask trusted friends until we finally found the names and addresses of two abortionists. The first was in such a filthy west-side brownstone apartment that she whispered "Oh, no!" to me, in despair, so we went far downtown to the second, who proved efficient and quick and was kind enough to let her rest for twenty minutes before leaving. I took her home with me for the weekend and she was back at her job Monday morning.

She was one of the lucky ones. No physical complications, no psychic scars after the first anguish of shock. But because I knew her as well as I know myself, I can say that a large part of that shock and pain was the furtive, ugly fact of illegality. For a woman, the decision to stop life is pain enough, and penalty enough. To add to it not only the risk of butchery but the humiliation of subterfuge and the squalor of crime is, I believe, indefensible: the result of archaic laws, social hypocrisy, religious pressure, and the refusal to accept present realities.

As I said, this was a lucky case, compared with many of the 10,000 or more illegal abortions performed in New York City alone each year. For the lucky people now are white, upper-class and able to reach and afford the psychiatrists or physicians who can refer them to private hospitals for what are called "therapeutic" abortions.

But ask the doctors in Harlem hospitals about the hundreds of bleeding and butchered women who come to them yearly, sick or dying from cheap or self inflicted abortions because they cannot endure one more unwanted child without father or future.

Even worse—yes, much worse—visit a Harlem tenement, as I have, where a pregnant woman lives with nine children on relief, most of whom should never have been born into the kind of world they inhabit there. And *would* not have been, had society not left such women in a swamp of ignorance about their bodies, their lives, their road to survival.

The sanctity of life. Whose life? The child's? The child of poverty and squalor and disease and crime? The child without a father, the child of a mother so overburdened that she has nothing left to give him? The child of a rapist, a degenerate, an incestuous father, a mental retardate? . . .

Men Made the Laws

What sanctity? And where, in all this talk of centuries—is the sanctity of women?

Ah, there's the crux. Who decided that life began—and was therefore sacred—when sperm and ovum met? Men of the cloth, who never bore or suckled a child. Who drew up the laws that determined, in effect, that woman had no control over the uses of her own body? The inseminators, not the bearers. Who governed the states and nations, who saw that these laws were sustained and enforced? Man, of course. And for what reason? In their terms, for the good of society. For the sake of the soul. For the preservation of the family, the state, the agriculture, the economy, the wars of conquest.

Abortion Rights Benefit Black Women

Shirley Chisholm became the first black woman member of the U.S. House of Representatives in 1969. In the following excerpt from her 1970 book Unbought and Unbossed, *Chisholm maintains that abortion rights will not result in black genocide.*

There is a deep and angry suspicion among many blacks that even birth control clinics are a plot by the white power structure to keep down the numbers of blacks, and this opinion is even more strongly held by some in regard to legalizing abortions. But I do not know any black or Puerto Rican *women* who feel that way. To label family planning and legal abortion programs "genocide" is male rhetoric, for male ears. It falls flat to female listeners, and to thoughtful male ones. Women know, and so do many men, that two or three children who are wanted, prepared for, reared amid love and stability, and educated to the limit of their ability will mean more for the future of the black and brown races from which they come than any number of neglected, hungry, ill-housed and ill-clothed youngsters. Pride in one's race, as well as simply humanity, supports this view. . . .

Which is more like genocide, I have asked some of my black brothers—this, the way things are, or the conditions I am fighting for in which the full range of family planning services is freely available to women of all classes and colors, starting with effective contraception and extending to safe, legal termination of undesired pregnancies, at a price they can afford?

But whose society? Whose land? Whose state? Whose markets? Whose wars? Not women's. Through all these thousands of years, with a handful of exceptions, the laws that governed the lives of women were never written by women; and the matter of life never held subject to the decision of the bearers of life. That a man should be master of his own body was never questioned. That a woman should be mistress of hers was *out* of the question. She was a vessel to be filled, a field to be planted. Such was the natural law, such was the will of God—such was the convenience (couched in the loftiest, most spiritual terms) of men.

Until now, in the more civilized countries of the world. And maybe, at long last, here.

But why now? And why here? Because, finally, the realities are catching up with us. Because the bearing of unwanted life is taking its terrible toll on life itself. You hardly need to be told that overpopulation is as great a threat to the world as the Bomb itself. That poverty, overcrowding, famine, and overwhelming needs of millions not only for food and shelter and space and education but for human dignity itself, are the most explosive mixture we face everywhere, anywhere.

All right, you say, but the answer to that is birth control—the pill, the coil, the funds to provide and educate. And you cite the great advances made by Planned Parenthood in the last decade, the increasing enlightenment of the public majority.

All this is true, although pockets of resistance still exist, not only in religious doctrines and in political and medical timidity, but in the minds of self-appointed moralists whose eyes are resolutely shut to living realities. Many of the men and women—oh, yes, women—who have consistently opposed any liberalization of the laws concerning birth control are animated less by religious conviction than by a self-righteousness that points accusing fingers at women supposedly less virtuous than they.

And abortion? The word itself sets off shudders of distaste. The definition of the word is simply "the expulsion of the fetus from the womb before it is viable" and only subsequently as " 'criminal abortion' when unlawful." Who says it's criminal? Why, those who call it unlawful. Suddenly, the expulsion of a tiny piece of a woman's body is called criminal because long ago, after learned discussions, men determined that this tiny piece was Life, and its expulsion murder.

But other men—among them the Jews—have long believed that life did not occur until the quickening, in the third and fourth month of pregnancy, and others that life began only when the child emerged from the womb.

And the woman? I think most women would agree that the child lives when it moves in the body, and that after that, only grave illness or danger to the life of either would warrant its removal.

But before that? What right has anyone but the woman herself to decide? Whose life does this still non-life so deeply affect but hers? For it is grossly inadequate, as in the present law, to make abortion legal only when the birth of the child threatens the life of mother or child. Life is far more than existence. A woman may be physically perfectly capable of having a fifth or sixth or seventh child, but what will bearing them do to her *and* to themselves if she hasn't the money or space or time to take proper care of them or, even worse, doesn't *want* them? What, I ask you, *is* worse than an unwanted child? Can you really, in all compassion, answer: abortion is worse?

I Am Not Ashamed

William Henrie, a physician who had been imprisoned for performing illegal abortions, asserted in a speech at the 1966 San Francisco Conference on Abortion and Human Rights that his actions had benefited many women.

It is always an honor for an ex-convict to be asked to speak to any group on any subject. It is especially so in this case.

I have been told not to say that I am an ex-convict but I ask, why should I be ashamed of being an ex-convict if I am not ashamed of the things I did that caused me to become a convict? I am ashamed of a law that must be broken to save the honor and respect of many women. I am ashamed of a law that must be violated to help other women live better lives, and I am certainly ashamed of a law that must be disobeyed in order to make a better world in which to live and to help people live better in that world.

I am not ashamed that I took the time to listen to those pleading women for now I can stand proud and erect, as I do, to give thanks that I had the heart to understand their problems; and I am glad that I had the courage to abandon the ethics of my training to practice the convictions of my conscience and perform the services those patients demanded.

And quite aside from the woman already unable to cope with more children, what about the teen-agers, the unmarried girls who are expected to pay for one accident, or one fleeting love, with the anguish of giving the child for adoption—or in the case of Negroes—the anguish of having almost no chance for adoption? Or the equal penance of a marriage which neither man nor woman wants?

Is your answer that she should have known better? Can you really maintain in the face of the present sexual freedom, whether you approve of it or not, that sex without marriage is illegal, and that therefore the accidental results of such casual unions are subject to legislation?

Can you really believe that legalized abortion will increase promiscuity, when even with the harsh existent laws, one out of every five births in this country is aborted—and that out of these, every four abortions are illegal?

Do you honestly think you can legislate morality by forcing this kind of illegality? For don't you know that a woman will do almost anything to rid herself of an unwanted child, and do you really think she should endanger or ruin her life to do so?

If you do think this, then keep the present laws and watch the illegal abortions mount and mount. If you don't—if you have any regard for, or knowledge of, the nature of man—then there is one clear course open. The World Health Organization has already taken this course. It has defined the word "health"—("the life *or* health") to include "social health" along with health of body or mind—i.e., "Health is not merely the absence of disease, but a state of complete physical, mental and *social* well-being."

For social health means the *kind* of life we live—as women, as mothers, as individuals—in the world. A life which, in turn, deeply affects, for good or bad, the kind of life our children will lead.

A Woman's Decision

In a good marriage, it naturally affects the man as well, and ideally such great decisions of life—or non-life—should be mutual ones. But in the last analysis, it is still the responsibility and right of the woman to decide; and a private affair between woman and doctor. No priest, no minister, certainly no committee, can assume this right.

Women have been told by others, through long centuries, what they should be and do, what rights they should have, or be denied. Bit by bit, and with the great help of courageous and enlightened men,—(for without your kind we could never move ahead)—we have gained civic and legal rights long withheld.

But this most important one of all has so far been denied us: the right to control what takes place within our own body. This is our citadel, our responsibility, our mental, emotional, and physical being. If biological accident—and those who find this indefensible and needless have little knowledge and less compassion for the human condition—threatens to alter this being and effect the new life begun without the will of either—then steps taken for the good of both should be our profound—and prime—concern.

Impregnation through mutual love and will can be called a sanctified act demanding fruition. When neither love nor will are present, why should the bitter seeds of this negation be required to flower?

As Lawrence Lader wrote in his eloquent book, *Abortion*, "The right to abortion is the foundation of society's long struggle to guarantee that every child comes into this world wanted, loved, and cared for. The right to abortion, along with all birth control measures, must establish the Century of the Wanted Child."

This is the *true* sanctity of life—this the imperative human need.

175

VIEWPOINT 4

"[A] fetus has an inherent and inviolable right to be born . . . even if its birth results in the impairment of the physical health of its mother."

Abortion Should Not Be Legalized

Robert F. Drinan (b. 1920)

In the mid-1960s to early 1970s, advocates of abortion law reform pressured both the individual states and the federal government to liberalize the conditions under which a woman could obtain a legal abortion. Up to this time, most states only allowed legal abortions to be performed when the life of the mother was directly endangered. Between 1967 and 1970, however, twelve states enacted reform statutes that allowed legal abortions under other special circumstances, including rape, incest, and impairment of the mother's mental health. In 1970, three states—New York, Hawaii, and Alaska—completely abolished their criminal laws against early stage abortions. The U.S. Supreme Court's 1973 decision in the case of *Roe v. Wade* invalidated any state laws that prohibited first-trimester abortions or that banned second-trimester abortions for any reason other than protecting a woman's health.

The following viewpoint is excerpted from Robert F. Drinan's article "The Inviolability of the Right to Be Born," which was written shortly before the *Roe v. Wade* ruling was handed down. Drinan expresses his concern over the underlying ethics of the arguments in favor of liberalizing abortion laws. The fetus is a living human being, Drinan contends, and therefore has a inalienable right to live. Abortion law reforms that would place the physical health or mental well-being of the mother over the unborn child's right to exist are immoral, Drinan asserts.

From "The Inviolability of the Right to Be Born" by Robert F. Drinan, in *Abortion, Society, and the Law*, edited by David F. Walbert and J. Douglas Butler. (Cleveland: Press of Case Western Reserve University, 1973). Reprinted by permission of Dr. Butler.

A Jesuit priest, lawyer, and law professor, Drinan served as a congressman in the U.S. House of Representatives from 1971 to 1981. He writes and lectures frequently on legal issues, particularly church-state relations.

Every discussion of abortion must, in the final analysis, begin and end with a definition of what one thinks of a human embryo or fetus. If one has, by the application of several principles, come to the conviction that a fetus, viable or not, can be extinguished for the benefit of its mother or its own welfare, rational debate on changing or "liberalizing" existing laws forbidding abortion is not really possible or necessary. For if a person argues from the premise that a human fetus may have its existence terminated for any valid reason, then the only point about which to argue is the validity of the reasons asserted to be sufficient to justify the voluntary extinction of a human fetus. . . .

The Health of the Mother

All states permit a therapeutic abortion in order to save the life of the mother. Although there is no meaningful decisional law on this matter, it is clear that this policy allows a physician to make the indisputably moral judgment that the life of the mother is to be preferred over the life of her unborn child. It could be argued that, since the law permits physicians to act upon their own moral judgments when a mother's life is at stake, the law should logically permit physicians to make similar moral judgments when the mother's future health, rather than her survival, is in question. If this line of reasoning is correct, it may be that those who oppose the legalization of abortion must urge that the right of physicians to perform an abortion to save the life of a mother be either abrogated or logically extended to a granting of permission to perform an abortion in order to save the health of the mother. On the assumption which permeates the case of those seeking the legalization of abortion—that society should concentrate on the quality rather than the quantity, of life it preserves—there would seem to be no reason why a doctor should *not* be allowed to preserve the health of the mother by performing an abortion.

The medical hypothesis running through this line of argumentation is, of course, open to question. Assuming reasonably modern medical techniques, in how many instances is it likely that the birth of a child will permanently impair the *physical* health of a mother?

177

Some cases, of course, do exist where the continuation of a pregnancy may bring about a substantial risk, not to the mother's life, but to her future physical health. If there is an inherent right in basic justice for a mother in this situation to request an abortion—and this case is probably the most appealing and compelling reason for a justifiable abortion—how should the law regulate the exercise of this right? The various proposals for changes in America's law regulating abortions silently suggest that the mother's right not to have her health impaired is paramount in this instance and that the state has no duty to speak for, or to protect, the fetus. However appealing such a solution may appear, its implications and consequences need examination.

The Best for Mother and Child

*In their 1972 article "Is Abortion the Best We Have to Offer?"
Thomas W. Hilgers, Marjory Mecklenburg, and Gayle Riordan argue
against legalizing abortion.*

The paradox of modern man is his assumption that he can turn on and turn off, seemingly at will, the respect for human life. He assumes that he can offer a woman the very best while denying her child the very least. These assumptions are invalid because they are inconsistent. Human life is a continuum; and to be consistent in its respect, we must value the whole of this continuum. We cannot promote the quality of life while arbitrarily denying any aspect of our common humanity. We cannot kill a child and then say that this is the best we have to offer the mother.

Every married couple possesses a moral and a legal right to privacy from any undue interference from the state. This right, emphasized by the United States Supreme Court in *Griswold v. Connecticut*, involving the Connecticut birth control statute, should be as broad and as inclusive as is consistent with the good of society. The right to have, or not to have, children and to determine the number of such children are matters in which the state, by general agreement, should not interfere. The welfare of children born to any marriage, however, is, by equally general agreement, a matter of grave concern for the state. Recent controversies over the advisability of statutes designed to curb the physical abuse or the battering of children by mentally upset or emotionally disturbed parents indicate that society feels a deep responsibility to protect children even at the expense of restricting the right to privacy enjoyed by married couples.

For at least a century and a half, this same concern of society and the law for children too young to speak for themselves has been extended to the unborn child by Anglo-American law. The law has taken the position that a married couple may refrain from having children or may restrict the number of their children but that a child, once conceived, has rights which its parents may not extinguish, even if the parents seek only to prevent a permanent impairment of the physical health of the mother.

Once again, the advocates of the right of a mother to an abortion, when confronted with the interest of the state in the child, born or unborn, will take refuge in the medically questionable and logically indefensible position that the unborn child is so different from a child after birth that the state has no right to interfere with a mother's desire to extinguish the life of her unborn child. It appears, however, that if Anglo-American law is to retreat from its present position of extending some, though not total, protection to the fetus, it must logically say that the right to marital privacy precludes state interference with an abortion or that the nonviable fetus is not yet sufficiently a human being to merit the protection of the law.

The advocates of the abolition of anti-abortion laws will no doubt urge, as one of the principal arguments, the right to marital privacy as that right is explained in the *Griswold* decision. I submit, however, that even the broadest dicta in *Griswold*, and even the most sweeping language in other judicial decisions on the right to marital privacy, do not justify the exclusion of the interest of the state *after* a child has been conceived but not yet delivered. It may be, of course, that courts in the future will extend the right of marital privacy to exclude state interference with an abortion decided upon by a couple. But such a decision would be entirely different from existing decisional law and would, at least logically, have to reject the underlying assumption of present laws forbidding abortion, which is, of course, that a nonviable fetus has an inherent and inviolable right to be born even if it is physically or mentally defective and even if its birth results in the impairment of the physical health of its mother.

A Mother's Mental Health or Happiness

The various proposals designed to liberalize America's abortion laws, including that of the American Law Institute (ALI), do not attempt to restrict the right to have an abortion to women who might otherwise have an impairment of their *physical* health. Those who would ease existing abortion laws recognize the fact that physical and mental health are so interdependent that it would be unrealistic to state that an abortion is allowable only for threatened damage to *either* the physical *or* mental health of the mother.

When the meaning and scope of mental health are evaluated, however, many problems arise. The legislative history of the section on abortion of the Model Penal Code of the ALI suggests that the term "mental health" is not meant to be used in the proposed law in a narrow or technical sense but, rather, in a comprehensive way which would permit two physicians to authorize an abortion if in their judgment an operation of this nature would be best for the long-range happiness of the mother. Hence, the term "mental health" is not intended to be restricted to cases where there is a diagnosis that severe mental depression or some similar psychiatric phenomenon will follow childbirth.

Black Genocide

In the July 4, 1970, issue of the Black Panther, *Brenda Hyson contends that laws liberalizing abortion, such as the one passed three days earlier in New York, are designed to eliminate the black race.*

Black women love large families, and the only reason that they would want to eliminate them is to rid them of the pain and the agony of trying to survive. Why in a country where farmers . . . are given large sums of public funds to not grow food; where food is actually burned, must Black mothers kill their unborn children? So they won't go hungry? Absurd! Eliminating ourselves is not the solution to the hunger problem in America nor any other problem that could exist from a so-called unwanted pregnancy in the context of this capitalistic society. The solution lies in overthrowing this system and returning the means of production back to the people—REVOLUTION. . . .

The [1970 New York] abortion law hides behind the guise of helping women, when in reality it will attempt to destroy our people. How long do you think it will take for voluntary abortion to turn into involuntary abortion, into compulsory sterilization? Black people are aware that laws made supposedly to ensure our well-being are often put into practice in such a way that they ensure our deaths.

Therefore, in view of the broad authorization which would result if the mental health of the mother became a norm for judging the advisability of abortions, it may be that the married and unmarried mother should be treated differently.

There is not much scientifically compiled information available on the number and nature of unwed mothers in America. Even less is known about those unwed mothers who terminate their pregnancy by an abortion. As a result, any writer moves into a sea of ambiguities when he attempts to analyze the factors involved in reaching a prudential judgment on the question of whether more relaxed abortion laws would promote the mental health of unwed mothers. Among the many factors which should be weighed in coming to a decision regarding the basic legal-moral policy which America should adopt with respect to the availability of abortion for unwed mothers are the following.

(a) *Promiscuity among single persons.* To what extent would more relaxed abortion laws promote promiscuity among single persons?

(b) *Adoption of children of unwed mothers.* Should law and society give greater consideration to childless couples (one out of ten) who seek an adoptable child? If so, should the nation's public policy tend to encourage unwed mothers not to destroy their unborn child but to arrange that the child be born and placed for adoption?

(c) *Guilt feelings of the unwed mother.* Who is to assess the nature and the consequences of the guilt which, according to reliable and virtually universal reports, comes to an unwed mother who resolves her problem by abortion? If accurate psychiatric testimony showed that the vast majority of unwed mothers who abort their child experience guilt that may have adverse consequences in their lives and their future marriages, would society be morally obliged to counsel unwed mothers about the likelihood of guilt before an easy method of abortion were made available to them? If, in other words, the mental health of the mother is to be the norm by which the advisability of an abortion is to be judged, then the assessment of the unwed mother's prospective mental health following an abortion must include the most careful and comprehensive evaluation of the impact which a feeling of guilt may have on her life.

(d) *"Happiness" of the unwed mother.* Since the term "mental health" in the Model Penal Code actually translates into "happiness," how and by whom is this broad norm to be interpreted and applied, not merely to the present predicament of the unwed mother but, more importantly, to her entire future life?

Some may object to the relevance of some or all of these factors and urge that the desire of the unwed mother for an abortion should be controlling. As much as one must be sympathetic to this apparently simple solution to a most difficult problem, it should never be forgotten that in modern society the unwed mother is in a position of shame, humiliation, and anguish which is possibly worse than any other human predicament. One may feel that society's attitude of disdain towards the unwed mother is one of hypocrisy, but the fact remains that the pressures and problems confronted by an unwed mother are such that it is not likely that she will be in a position to make rational decisions substantially uninfluenced by fear or panic. Society, therefore, has a very special and unique duty to furnish the most careful counselling to unwed mothers before it allows them to employ a legally approved method of abortion. . . .

The Sanctity of Life

The integrity, the untouchableness, the inviolability of every human life by any other human being has been the cardinal principle and the centerpiece of the legal institutions of the English-speaking world and, to a large extent, of every system of law devised by man. However convenient, convincing, or compelling the arguments in favor of abortion may be, the fact remains that the taking of a life, even though it is unborn, cuts out the very heart of the principle that *no one's* life, however unwanted and useless it may be, may be terminated in order to promote the health or happiness of another human being. If the advocates of legalized abortion desire to have an intellectually honest debate about the fundamental change they seek in the moral and legal standards of American life, they should not fall back on the error of fact that a fetus is not a human being. They should, rather, face the fact that they are stating that the rights of one or more human beings to health or happiness may in some circumstances become so important that they take precedence over the very right to exist of another human being.

The inescapable moral issues in the emerging struggle over the wisdom and fairness of America's abortion laws deserve to be discussed and dissected and eventually resolved. It will be a tragedy beyond description for America if the question of legislation on abortion is resolved on sentiment, utilitarianism, or expediency rather than on the basic ethical issue involved—the immorality of the destruction of any innocent human being carried out by other human beings for their own benefit.

VIEWPOINT 5

"Woman's liberation [cannot] free women without facing the basic heterosexual structure that binds us in one-to-one relationship with our oppressors."

A Lesbian Perspective on Women's Liberation

Radicalesbians

One of the most divisive issues in the women's liberation movement was the relationship between feminism and lesbianism. During the early years of the movement, most feminists tried to distance themselves from accusations of lesbianism, and lesbians within women's rights organizations usually kept quiet about their sexual orientation. With the rise of the gay rights movement in the late 1960s, however, many lesbian feminists began to demand that women's rights groups publicly recognize and accept their lesbian members. Some went a step further, arguing that lesbians were the most dedicated feminists because they committed themselves wholly to women in all aspects of their lives.

The Radicalesbians was a New York City collective that consisted of members of both the women's liberation and gay rights movements. In 1970, the Radicalesbians issued the following position paper, entitled "The Woman-Identified Woman." According to the Radicalesbians, lesbians are inherently feminists because they reject traditional female roles and refuse to accept a subordinate relationship to men. The collective argues that heterosexual feminists should not let the stigma of the word "lesbian" prevent them from concentrating their energies solely on women. A woman-identified lifestyle, which may include choosing to love other women, will enable feminists to find alternatives to the oppressive male culture, the collective concludes.

From "The Woman-Identified Woman," by Radicalesbians, *Notes from the Third Year*, 1971; ©1970 by Radicalesbians.

What is a lesbian? A lesbian is the rage of all women condensed to the point of explosion. She is the woman who, often beginning at an extremely early age, acts in accordance with her inner compulsion to be a more complete and freer human being than her society—perhaps then, but certainly later—cares to allow her. These needs and actions, over a period of years, bring her into painful conflict with people, situations, the accepted ways of thinking, feeling and behaving, until she is in a state of continual war with everything around her, and usually with her self. She may not be fully conscious of the political implications of what for her began as personal necessity, but on some level she has not been able to accept the limitations and oppression laid on her by the most basic role of her society—the female role. The turmoil she experiences tends to induce guilt proportional to the degree to which she feels she is not meeting social expectations, and/or eventually drives her to question and analyze what the rest of her society more or less accepts. She is forced to evolve her own life pattern, often living much of her life alone, learning usually much earlier than her "straight" (heterosexual) sisters about the essential aloneness of life (which the myth of marriage obscures) and about the reality of illusions. To the extent that she cannot expel the heavy socialization that goes with being female, she can never truly find peace with herself. For she is caught somewhere between accepting society's view of her—in which case she cannot accept herself—and coming to understand what this sexist society has done to her and why it is functional and necessary for it to do so. Those of us who work that through find ourselves on the other side of a tortuous journey through a night that may have been decades long. The perspective gained from that journey, the liberation of self, the inner peace, the real love of self and of all women, is something to be shared with all women—because we are all women.

It should first be understood that lesbianism, like male homosexuality, is a category of behavior possible only in a sexist society characterized by rigid sex roles and dominated by male supremacy. Those sex roles dehumanize women by defining us as a supportive/serving caste *in relation to* the master caste of men, and emotionally cripple men by demanding that they be alienated from their own bodies and emotions in order to perform their economic/political/military functions effectively. Homosexuality is a by-product of a particular way of setting up roles (or approved patterns of behavior) on the basis of sex; as such it is an inauthentic (not consonant with "reality") category. In a society in which men do not oppress women, and sexual expression is allowed to follow feelings, the categories of homosexuality and heterosexuality would disappear.

Women Stepping Out of Bounds

But lesbianism is also different from male homosexuality, and serves a different function in the society. "Dyke" is a different kind of put-down from "faggot," although both imply you are not playing your socially assigned sex role . . . are not therefore a "real woman" or a "real man." The grudging admiration felt for the tomboy, and the queasiness felt around a sissy boy point to the same thing: the contempt in which women—or those who play a female role—are held. And the investment in keeping women in that contemptuous role is very great. Lesbian is the word, the label, the condition that holds women in line. When a woman hears this word tossed her way, she knows she is stepping out of line. She knows that she has crossed the terrible boundary of her sex role. She recoils, she protests, she reshapes her actions to gain approval. Lesbian is a label invented by the Man to throw at any woman who dares to be his equal, who dares to challenge his prerogatives (including that of all women as part of the exchange medium among men), who dares to assert the primacy of her own needs. To have the label applied to people active in women's liberation is just the most recent instance of a long history; older women will recall that not so long ago, any woman who was successful, independent, not orienting her whole life about a man, would hear this word. For in this sexist society, for a woman to be independent means she *can't be* a woman—she must be a dyke. That in itself should tell us where women are at. It says as clearly as can be said: women and person are contradictory terms. For a lesbian is not considered a "real woman." And yet, in popular thinking, there is really only one essential difference between a lesbian and other women: that of sexual orientation—which is to say, when you strip off all the packaging, you must finally realize that the essence of being a "woman" is to get fucked by men.

"Lesbian" is one of the sexual categories by which men have divided up humanity. While all women are dehumanized as sex objects, as the objects of men they are given certain compensations: identification with his power, his ego, his status, his protection (from other males), feeling like a "real woman," finding social acceptance by adhering to her role, etc. Should a woman confront herself by confronting another woman, there are fewer rationalizations, fewer buffers by which to avoid the stark horror of her dehumanized condition. Herein we find the overriding fear of many women toward being used as a sexual object by a woman, which not only will bring her no male-connected compensations,

185

but also will reveal the void which is woman's real situation. This dehumanization is expressed when a straight woman learns that a sister is a lesbian; she begins to relate to her lesbian sister as her potential sex object, laying a surrogate male role on the lesbian. This reveals her heterosexual conditioning to make herself into an object when sex is potentially involved in a relationship, and it denies the lesbian her full humanity. For women, especially those in the movement, to perceive their lesbian sisters through this male grid of role definitions is to accept this male cultural conditioning and to oppress their sisters much as they themselves have been oppressed by men. Are we going to continue the male classification system of defining all females in sexual relation to some other category of people? Affixing the label lesbian not only to a woman who aspires to be a person, but also to any situation of real love, real solidarity, real primacy among women, is a primary form of divisiveness among women: it is the condition which keeps women within the confines of the feminine role, and it is the debunking/scare term that keeps women from forming any primary attachments, groups, or associations among ourselves.

Lesbians and Feminism

Women in the movement have in most cases gone to great lengths to avoid discussion and confrontation with the issue of lesbianism. It puts people up-tight. They are hostile, evasive, or try to incorporate it into some "broader issue." They would rather not talk about it. If they have to, they try to dismiss it as a "lavender herring." But it is no side issue. It is absolutely essential to the success and fulfillment of the women's liberation movement that this issue be dealt with. As long as the label "dyke" can be used to frighten a woman into a less militant stand, keep her separate from her sisters, keep her from giving primacy to anything other than men and family—then to that extent she is controlled by the male culture. Until women see in each other the possibility of a primal commitment which includes sexual love, they will be denying themselves the love and value they readily accord to men, thus affirming their second-class status. As long as male acceptability is primary—both to individual women and to the movement as a whole—the term lesbian will be used effectively against women. Insofar as women want only more privileges within the system, they do not want to antagonize male power. They instead seek acceptability for women's liberation, and the most crucial aspect of the acceptability is to deny lesbianism—i.e., to deny any fundamental challenge to the basis of the female. It should also be said that some younger, more radical women have honestly begun to discuss lesbianism, but so far it has been primarily as a sexual "alternative" to men. This, however, is still giving primacy to men, both because the idea of relating more completely to women occurs as a negative reaction to men, and because the lesbian relationship is being characterized simply by sex, which is divisive and sexist. On one level, which is both personal and political, women may withdraw emotional and sexual energies from men, and work out various alternatives for those energies in their own lives. On a different political/psychological level, it must be understood that what is crucial is that women begin disengaging from male-defined response patterns. In the privacy of our own psyches, we must cut those cords to the core. For irrespective of where our love and sexual energies flow, if we are male-identified in our heads, we cannot realize our autonomy as human beings.

Until All Women Are Lesbians

Jill Johnston, author of Lesbian Nation: The Feminist Solution, *insists that true women's liberation cannot occur as long as women maintain heterosexual relationships.*

Feminism at heart is a massive complaint. Lesbianism is the solution. Which is another way of putting what Ti-Grace Atkinson once described as Feminism being a theory and lesbianism the practice. When theory and practice come together we'll have the revolution. Until all women are lesbians there will be no true political revolution. No feminist per se has advanced a solution outside of accommodation to the man. The complaints are substantial and articulate and historically sound and they contain by implication their own answers but the feminists refuse to acknowledge what's implicit in their own complaint or analysis. To wit: that the object of their attack is not going to make anything better than a *material* adjustment to the demands of their enslaved sex. There's no conceivable equality between two species in a relation in which one of the two has been considerably weakened in all aspects of her being over so long a period of historical time. The blacks in America were the first to understand that an oppressed group must withdraw into itself to establish its own identity and rebuild its strength through mutual support and recognition. The first unpublicized action of many feminists *was* in fact to withdraw from the man sexually. Feminists who still sleep with the man are delivering their most vital energies to the oppressor.

But why is it that women have related to and through men? By virtue of having been brought up in a male society, we have internalized the male culture's definition of ourselves. That definition consigns us to sexual and family functions, and excludes us from defining and shaping the terms of our lives. In exchange for our psychic servicing and for performing society's non-profitmaking functions, the man confers on us just one thing: the slave status which makes us legitimate in the eyes of the society in which we live. This is called "femininity" or "being a real woman" in our cultural lingo. We are authentic, legitimate, real to the extent that we are the property of some man whose name we bear. To be a woman who belongs to no man is to be invisible, pathetic, inauthentic, unreal. He confirms his image of us—of what we have to be in order to be acceptable by him—but not our real selves; he confirms our womanhood—as he defines it, in relation to him—but cannot confirm our personhood, our own selves as absolutes. As long as we are dependent on the male culture for this definition, for this approval, we cannot be free.

The consequence of internalizing this role is an enormous reservoir of self-hate. This is not to say the self-hate is recognized or accepted as such; indeed most women would deny it. It may be experienced as discomfort with her role, as feeling empty, as numbness, as restlessness, as a paralyzing anxiety at the center. Alternatively, it may be expressed in shrill defensiveness of the glory and destiny of her role. But it does exist, often beneath the edge of her consciousness, poisoning her existence, keeping her alienated from herself, her own needs, and rendering her a stranger to other women. They try to escape by identifying with the oppressor, living through him, gaining status and identity from his ego, his power, his accomplishments. And by not identifying with other "empty vessels" like themselves. Women resist relating on all levels to other women who will reflect their own oppression, their own secondary status, their own self-hate. For to confront another woman is finally to confront one's self—the self we have gone to such lengths to avoid. And in that mirror we know we cannot really respect and love that which we have been made to be.

As the source of self-hate and the lack of real self are rooted in our male-given identity, we must create a new sense of self. As long as we cling to the idea of "being a woman," we will sense some conflict with that incipient self, that sense of I, that sense of a whole person. It is very difficult to realize and accept that being "feminine" and being a whole person are irreconcilable. Only women can give to each other a new sense of self. That identity we have to develop with reference to ourselves, and not in relation to men. This consciousness is the revolutionary force from which all else will follow, for ours is an organic revolution. For this we must be available and supportive to one another, give our commitment and our love, give the emotional support necessary to sustain this movement. Our energies must flow toward our sisters, not backward toward our oppressors. As long as woman's liberation tries to free women without facing the basic heterosexual structure that binds us in one-to-one relationship with our oppressors, tremendous energies will continue to flow into trying to straighten up each particular relationship with a man, into finding how to get better sex, how to turn his head around—into trying to make the "new man" out of him, in the delusion that this will allow us to be the "new woman." This obviously splits our energies and commitments, leaving us unable to be committed to the construction of the new patterns which will liberate us.

Women Relating to Women

It is the primacy of women relating to women, of women creating a new consciousness of and with each other, which is at the heart of women's liberation, and the basis for the cultural revolution. Together we must find, reinforce, and validate our authentic selves. As we do this, we confirm in each other that struggling, incipient sense of pride and strength, the divisive barriers begin to melt, we feel this growing solidarity with our sisters. We see ourselves as prime, find our centers inside of ourselves. We find receding the sense of alienation, of being cut off, of being behind a locked window, of being unable to get out what we know is inside. We feel a real-ness, feel at last we are coinciding with ourselves. With that real self, with that consciousness, we begin a revolution to end the imposition of all coercive identifications, and to achieve maximum autonomy in human expression.

VIEWPOINT 6

"There is no magic that makes lesbianism proof positive of any high feminist motives."

Feminists Do Not Have to Adopt a Lesbian Lifestyle

Anne Koedt (dates unknown)

The relationship between feminism and lesbianism became one of the most volatile controversies inside the women's liberation movement. During 1969 and 1970, lesbians began to demand more visibility in the movement and serious consideration of lesbianism as a women's rights issue. Some lesbians also maintained that their lifestyle was inherently more feminist than one that allowed for sexual relationships with men. A number of feminists began to perceive lesbianism not as a sexual orientation but as a personal and political choice to commit fully to the women's movement. Women who continued in sexual relationships with men, some feminists argued, were guilty of "sleeping with the enemy."

Anne Koedt, a writer, editor, and artist, had personal experience with the practical effects of this philosophy. In 1968, Koedt was one of the founders of The Feminists, a militant women's liberation group that established a quota: No more than one-third of its membership could be married to or living with a man. The following viewpoint is excerpted from Koedt's 1971 article, "Lesbianism and Feminism," in which she critiqued the theories that led to the setting of such quotas. Arguing that lesbianism does not automatically make one a feminist, Koedt points out that women in lesbian relationships do not necessarily work against sexism in other facets of life. The dedication of bisexual and heterosexual women to the feminist cause should not be questioned simply because they have sexual relationships with men, Koedt maintains.

From "Lesbianism and Feminism" by Anne Koedt, *Notes from the Third Year*, 1971; ©1971 by Anne Koedt.

One position advanced by some lesbians is the idea that lesbians are the vanguard of the women's movement because 1) they broke with sex roles before there even was a feminist movement, and 2) they have no need for men at all. (Somehow they are the revolution.) The following [from a 1971 letter to *Everywoman*] is one example of this position:

> Feel the real glow that comes from "our" sisterhood. We can teach you something about being gentle and kind for we never felt competitive. Remember WE long before YOU have known discontent with male society and WE long before YOU knew and appreciated the full potential of everything female. . . . It is WE who say welcome to you, long blind and oppressed sisters, we have been fighting against male supremacy for a long time, join US! We are not intimidated by relational differences, for we have never felt mortgaged by society.

Several points seem to be ignored with this kind of argument. For one, there is a confusion of a personal with a political solution. Sex roles and male supremacy will not go away simply by women becoming lesbians. It will take a great deal of sophisticated political muscle and collective energy for women to eliminate sexism. So at best a lesbian relationship can give a woman more happiness and freedom in her private life (assuming both women are not playing roles). But a radical feminist is not just one who tries to live the good non-sexist life at home; she is one who is working politically in society to destroy the institutions of sexism.

Another assumption implicit in the argument of "lesbian-as-the-vanguard-feminist" is that having balked at one aspect of sexism—namely, exclusive heterosexuality—they are therefore radical feminists. Any woman who defies her role—be it refusing to be a mother, wanting to be a biochemist, or simply refusing to cater to a man's ego—is defying the sex role system. It is an act of rebellion. In the case of lesbianism, the act of rebellion often has earned the woman severe social ostracism. However, it becomes radical only if it is then placed in the context of wanting to destroy the system as a whole, that is, destroying the sex role system as opposed to just rejecting men. Indeed, there can be reformism within lesbianism too; when a lesbian says "I have nothing against men, I just don't want to be involved with them," she is really describing an accommodation within the sexist system even though she has performed the rebellious act of violating that system by being a lesbian. It is also in this context that a statement like "feminism is the theory; lesbianism is the practice" is erroneous. For not only is the sex of a woman's lover insufficient information to infer radical feminism, but there is also the false implication that to have no men in your personal life means you are therefore living the life of fighting for radical feminist change.

The notion that lesbians have no need for men at all also needs clarification. First of all, since we are all women living in a male society, we do in fact depend regularly upon men for many crucial things, even if we do not choose to have men in our personal relationships. It is for this reason that one woman alone will not be fully liberated until all women are liberated. However, taking the statement to mean having no need for men in *personal relationships* (which can be an important achievement for women, since one should obviously want the person, not the man), one must still ask the question: has the male role been discarded? Thus again the crucial point is not the sex of your bed partner but the sex role of your bed partner. . . .

Bisexuality

One position taken by some lesbians is that bisexuality is a cop-out. This is usually argued in terms like "until all heterosexuals go gay, we are going to remain homosexual," or "lesbianism is more than having sex with women; it is a whole life style and commitment to women. Bisexuality is a sign of not being able to leave men and be free. We are *women*- (not men-) identified women."

The first position mentioned is an apparently tactical argument (though it has also been used by some, I think, to dismiss the discussion of bisexuality altogether by safely pushing it off into the Millennium), and makes the case for politically identifying yourself with the most discriminated against elements—even though you might really believe in bisexuality.

Taking that argument at face value (and I don't completely), I think it is a dangerous thing to advocate politically. For by, in effect, promoting exclusive homosexuality, they lend political support to the notion that it *does* matter what the sex of your partner may be. While I recognize the absolute necessity for the gay movement to concentrate on the freedom of people to sleep with members of their own sex (since it is here that discrimination exists), it must at the same time always be referred back to its larger, radical perspective: that it is oppressive for that very question even to be asked. As a matter of fact, if "freedom of sexual preference" is the demand, the solution obviously must be a bisexuality where the question becomes irrelevant.

I think in fact that the reason why bisexuality has been considered such an unpopular word by most gays is not to be found primarily in the arguments just discussed, but rather in gay adherence to a kind of fierce homosexual counter-definition which has developed. That is, a counter identity—a "life style" and "world view"—has been created around the fact of their homosexuality. This identity is so strong sometimes that to even advocate or predict bisexuality is considered "genocide." The following is an example: In a response to a statement by Dotson Rader that "as bisexuality is increasingly accepted as the norm, the position of the homosexual *qua* homosexual will fade," one gay response was that "The homosexual, like the Jew, is offered the choice between integration or the gas chamber."

Destroying Heterosexual Domination

Longtime activist Charlotte Bunch was the editor of Quest: A Feminist Quarterly, *in which her 1975 article "Not for Lesbians Only" appeared. In the following excerpt, Bunch maintains that straight women can follow lesbian feminist ideology.*

The heart of lesbian feminist politics . . . is a recognition that heterosexuality as an institution and an ideology is a cornerstone of male supremacy. Therefore, women interested in destroying male supremacy, patriarchy, and capitalism must, equally with lesbians, fight heterosexual domination—or we will never end female oppression. This is what I call "the heterosexual question"—it is *not* the lesbian question.

Although lesbians have been the quickest to see the challenge to heterosexuality as a necessity for feminists' survival, straight feminists are not precluded from examining and fighting against heterosexuality. . . .

This analysis of the function of heterosexuality in women's oppression is available to any woman, lesbian or straight. Lesbian feminism is not a political analysis "for lesbians only." It is a political perspective and fight against one of the major institutions of our oppression—a fight that heterosexual women can engage in.

It is not with the actual gay counterculture that I want to quarrel; I think it is a very understandable reaction to an intolerable exclusion of homosexuals from society. To be denied the ordinary benefits and interaction of other people, to be stripped of your identity by a society that recognizes you as valid only if your role and your biology are "properly" matched—to be thus denied must of course result in a new resolution of identity. Since gays have been rejected on the basis of their homosexuality, it is not surprising that homosexuality has become the core of the new identity.

The disagreement with feminism comes rather in an attempt to make a revolutionary political position out of this adjustment. The often heard complaint from feminists that "we are being defined once again by whom we sleep with" is correct, I think. The lesson to be learned from a feminist analysis of sex roles is that there is no behavior implied from our biology beyond, as Wilma

Scott Heide has noted, the role of sperm donor and wet nurse. A woman has historically been defined, on the basis of biology, as incomplete without a man. Feminists have rejected this notion, and must equally reject any new definition which offers a woman her identity by virtue of the fact that she may love or sleep with other women.

It is for this reason, also, that I disagree with the Radicalesbian concept of the "woman-identified-woman." For we ought not to be "identified" on the basis of whom we have relationships with. And there is a confusion in such a term; it seems to mix up the biological woman with the political woman. I think the often used feminist definition of "woman-identified" as meaning having identified with the female *role* in society is more useful; it refers to a specific political phenomenon of internalization. So far as finding a term which describes women's solidarity or sisterhood on the basis of our common oppression, the term is feminism. Beyond that, what is left is the biological female—an autonomous being who gains her identity by virtue of her own achievements and characteristics, not by virtue of whom she has a love relationship with.

Once we begin to discuss persons as *persons* (a word which doesn't ask the sex of an individual), even the word "bisexuality" may eventually be dropped, since implicit in its use is still an eagerness to inform you that it is *both* sexes. Perhaps we will finally return to a simpler word like "sexuality," where the relevant information is simply "sex among persons."

The Personal and the Political

If you are a feminist who is not sleeping with a woman you may risk hearing any of the following accusations: "You're oppressing me if you don't sleep with women"; "You're not a radical feminist if you don't sleep with women"; or "You don't love women if you don't sleep with them." I have even seen a woman's argument about an entirely different aspect of feminism be dismissed by some lesbians because she was not having sexual relations with women. Leaving aside for a minute the motives for making such accusations, there is an outrageous thing going on here strictly in terms of pressuring women about their personal lives.

This perversion of "the personal is the political" argument, it must be noted, was not invented by those gay women who may be using it now; the women's movement has had sporadic waves of personal attacks on women—always in the guise of radicalism (and usually by a very small minority of women). I have seen women being told they could not be trusted as feminists because they wore miniskirts, because they were married (in one group quotas were set lest the group's quality be lowered by "unliberated women"), or because they wanted to have children. This rejection of women who are not living the "liberated life" has predictably now come to include rejection on the basis of the "unliberated" sex life.

The original genius of the phrase "the personal is political" was that it opened up the area of women's private lives to political analysis. Before that, the isolation of women from each other had been accomplished by labeling a woman's experience "personal." Women had thus been kept from seeing their common condition as women and their common oppression by men.

However, opening up women's experience to political analysis has also resulted in a misuse of the phrase. While it is true that there are political implications in everything a woman *qua* woman experiences, it is not therefore true that a woman's life is the political property of the women's movement. And it seems to me to show a disrespect for another woman to presume that it is any group's (or individual's) prerogative to pass revolutionary judgment on the progress of her life.

There is a further point: Even the most radical feminist is not the liberated woman. We are all crawling out of femininity into a new sense of personhood. Only a woman herself may decide what her next step is going to be. I do not think women have a political obligation to the movement to change; they should do so only if they see it in their own self-interest. If the women's movement believes that feminism *is* in women's self-interest, then the task at hand is to make it understood through shared insights, analysis, and experience. That is, feminism is an offering, not a directive, and one therefore enters a woman's private life at her invitation only. Thus a statement like "you don't love women if you don't sleep with them" must above all be dismissed on the grounds that it is confusing the right to discuss feminism with the right to, uninvited, discuss a woman's private life and make political judgments about it.

However, taking the issue presented in the above accusation (outside of its guilt-provoking personal context), there are several points to consider. One element of truth is that some women are unable to relate sexually to other women because of a strong self-hatred for themselves as women (and therefore all women). But there may also be many other reasons. A woman may not be interested in sleeping with anyone—a freedom women are granted even less often than the right to sleep with other women. She may not have met a woman she's attracted to. Or she may be involved with a man whom she likes as a person, without this necessarily being a rejection of women. It should also be noted that the women who suffer from strong self-hatred may not necessarily find it impossible to relate sexually to women. They may instead find that taking the male part in a lesbian relationship will symbolically remove them from their feminine role. Such a woman then may become one who "balls" women so as not to be one.

All in all, as has been noted earlier, there is no magic that makes lesbianism proof positive of any high feminist motives. Rather, what the woman brings to her relationship as far as relinquishing sex roles will, I think, determine her ultimate attitude about really loving other women. . . .

The larger political truth is still that we are women living in a male society where men have the power and we don't; that our "female role" is a creation that is nothing more than a male political expediency for maintaining that power; and that until the women's movement alters these ancient political facts we cannot speak of being free collectively or individually.

VIEWPOINT 7

"The equal rights amendment is necessary to establish unequivocally the American commitment to full and equal recognition of the rights of all its citizens."

The Equal Rights Amendment Should Be Passed

Margaret M. Heckler (b. 1931)

A Republican representative from Massachusetts, Margaret M. Heckler advocated women's rights and the adoption of the proposed Equal Rights Amendment (ERA) to the U.S. Constitution. A constitutional amendment banning discrimination on the basis of sex had first been proposed to Congress in 1923. It was not until 1970, however, that Congress held hearings on the matter. On May 5, 1970, Heckler delivered the following testimony to the U.S. Senate Subcommittee on Constitutional Amendments.

Heckler contends that the Equal Rights Amendment is necessary to protect American working women from sexual discrimination. Women earn substantially less than equally qualified men and are often employed at positions far below their capabilities, she asserts. By preventing women from fully contributing to society, Heckler argues, this discrimination negatively affects not only individual women but the nation as a whole. Because current laws have proven to be insufficient in safeguarding women's rights, Heckler concludes, the passage of a federal amendment is crucial.

In 1977, Heckler became the cofounder of the Congressional Caucus for Women's Issues. From 1983 to 1985 she served in President Ronald Reagan's cabinet as secretary of health and human services; in 1985 she was appointed U.S. ambassador to Ireland.

From Margaret M. Heckler, testimony before the U.S. Senate Subcommittee on Constitutional Amendments, Committee on the Judiciary, 91st Cong., 2nd sess. (May 5, 1970).

It is assumed today by many persons that women were granted equality with the passage of the 14th amendment, ratified in 1868. Only 50 years later, however, was woman suffrage guaranteed by the ratification of the 19th amendment. Half a century of waiting for the vote required a great deal of patience. In the temper of these turbulent times, I do not believe that total equality of opportunity for women can be further postponed.

Thus I speak out in support of the equal rights amendment—a measure that has been before each Congress since 1923. The fast pace of life in the world today fosters impatience. And when much is promised, failure to deliver becomes a matter of critical importance.

The Crusade for Equality

I am sure that every woman who has been in the position of "job seeker" identifies in some small measure with the fundamental complaints that have generated the crusade for equality in employment for women. The 42 percent of working women who are heads of household takes a serious economic interest in fair job opportunity, a basic goal in the cause for women's rights. And the women who have contributed their full share to social security, yet who receive the sum allotted widows, certainly have cause for contemplation.

The average woman in America has no seething desire to smoke cigars or to burn the bra—but she does seek equal recognition of her status as a citizen before the courts of law, and she does seek fair and just recognition of her qualifications in the employment market. The American working woman does not want to be limited in advancement by virtue of her sex. She does not want to be prohibited from the job she desires or from the overtime work she needs by "protective" legislation.

These types of discrimination must be stopped, and the forthright means of halting discrimination against women is passage of the equal rights amendment at the earliest possible time. In fact, I have heard it said quite often that the only discrimination that is still fashionable is discrimination against women.

Perhaps, as some say, it is derived from a protective inclination on the part of men. But women seek recognition as individual human beings with abilities useful to society—rather than shelter or protection from the real world.

John Gardner has said that our Nation's most underdeveloped resource is womanpower. The old saying "you can't keep a good man down" might well serve as a warning. It is safe to say, I think, that women are unlikely to stay down and out of the field of competition for much longer.

Legal remedies are clearly in order, and the equal rights amendment is especially timely. Although changes in social attitudes cannot be legislated, they are guided by the formulation of our Federal laws. This constitutional amendment must be passed so that discriminatory legislation will be overturned. That custom and attitude be subject to a faster pace of evolution is essential if we are to avoid revolution on the part of qualified women who seek equality in the employment world.

The Status of American Women

Time and again I have heard American men question the fact of discrimination against women in America. "American women," they say, "enjoy greater freedom than women of any other nation." This may be true with regard to freedom from kitchen labor—because the average American housewife enjoys a considerable degree of automation in her kitchen. But once she seeks to fill her leisure time gained from automated kitchen equipment by entering the male world of employment, the picture changes. Many countries we consider "underprivileged" far surpass America in quality and availability of child care available to working mothers, in enlightened attitudes about employment leave for pregnancy, and in guiding women into the professions.

Since World War II, nearly 14 million American women have joined the labor force—double the number of men. Forty percent of our Nation's labor force is now composed of women. Yet less than 3 percent of our Nation's attorneys are women, only about 7 percent of our doctors, and 9 percent of our scientists are women. Only a slightly higher percentage of our graduate students in these fields of study are women, despite the fact that women characteristically score better on entrance examinations. The average woman college graduate's annual earnings ($6,694) exceed by just a fraction the annual earnings of an average male educated only through the eighth grade ($6,580). An average male college graduate, however, may be expected to earn almost twice as much as the female—$11,795. Twenty percent of the women with 4 years of college training can find employment only in clerical, sales, or factory jobs. The equal pay provision [a 1963 amendment] of the Fair Labor Standards Act does not include administrative, executive, or professional positions—a loophole which permits the talents and training of highly qualified women to be obtained more cheaply than those of comparable qualified men.

Of the 7.5 million American college students enrolled in 1968, at least 40 percent were women. American parents are struggling to educate their daughters as well as their sons—and are sending them to the best colleges they can possibly afford. As many of these mothers attend commencement exercises this summer, their hearts will swell with pride as their daughters receive college degrees—and these mothers may realize their daughters will have aspirations for exceeding their own horizons.

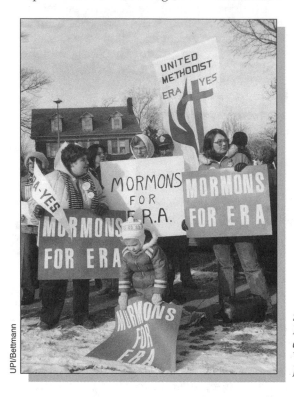

Supporters of the Equal Rights Amendment demonstrated in Washington, D.C., in January 1981.

Few of the fathers or mothers, enrolling their daughters in college several years ago, were at the time aware of the obstacles to opportunity their daughters would face. But today they are becoming aware that opportunity for their daughters is only half of that available to their sons. And they are justifiably indignant. Young women graduating with degrees in business administration take positions as clerks while their male counterparts become management trainees. Women graduating from law school are often forced to become legal secretaries, while male graduates from the same class survey a panorama of exciting possibilities.

The Nation's Needs

To frustrate the aspirations of the competent young women graduating from our institutions of higher learning would be a dangerous and foolish thing. The youth of today are inspired with a passion to improve the quality of life around us—an admirable and essential goal, indeed. The job is a mammoth one, however; and it would be ill-advised to assume that the role of women in the crusade of the future will not be a significant one. To the contrary, never before has our Nation and our world cried out for talent and creative energy with greater need. To deny full participation of the resources of women, who compose over half the population of our country, would be a serious form of neglect. The contributions of women have always been intrinsic in our national development. With the increasing complexity of our world, it becomes all the more essential to tap every conceivable resource at our command.

The time is thus ripe for passage of the equal rights amendment. The women of America are demanding full rights and full responsibilities in developing their individual potential as human beings in relationship to the world as well as to the home and in contributing in an active way to the improvement of society.

In this day of the urban crisis, when we seem to be running out of clean air and water, when the quantity of our rubbish defies our current disposal methods, when crime on the streets is rampant, when our world commitments seem at odds with our obligations here at home, when breaking the cycle of ongoing poverty requires new and innovative approaches, when increased lifespan generates a whole new series of gerontological problems—in these complicated and critical times, our Nation needs the fully developed resources of all our citizens—both men and women—in order to meet the demands of society today.

Women are not requesting special privilege—but rather a full measure of responsibility, a fair share of the load in the effort to improve life in America. The upcoming generation is no longer asking for full opportunity to contribute, however—they are demanding this opportunity.

The equal rights amendment is necessary to establish unequivocally the American commitment to full and equal recognition of the rights of all its citizens. Stopgap measures and delays will no longer be acceptable—firm guarantees are now required. The seventies mark an era of great promise if the untapped resource of womanpower is brought forth into the open and allowed to flourish so that women may take their rightful place in the mainstream of American life. Both men and women have a great deal to gain.

*"ERA [the Equal Rights Amendment] is an elitist
upper-middle class cause that has no relevance to the
big majority of working women."*

The Equal Rights
Amendment Should
Not Be Passed

Phyllis Schlafly (b. 1924)

In 1972, Congress passed the Equal Rights Amendment (ERA),
which guaranteed the equal rights of women and prohibited sexual discrimination. The amendment was then presented to the
states for ratification. Congress allowed seven years for the legislatures of three-fourths of the states to ratify the Equal Rights
Amendment. In the first year after Congress passed the amendment, thirty states out of the required thirty-eight voted to ratify it.

Conservative political activist Phyllis Schlafly was perhaps the
most well-known opponent of the Equal Rights Amendment. In
1972, Schlafly founded and became national chairman of Stop
ERA, an organization dedicated to preventing ratification of the
amendment. The following viewpoint is excerpted from her 1977
book, *The Power of the Positive Woman*, in which she delineated her
reasons for campaigning against the Equal Rights Amendment. If
the amendment is passed, Schlafly warns, it will eliminate protective labor laws that benefit women. Schlafly argues that women
are not as strong as men and therefore should not be expected to
do equal work in jobs that require physical labor. Because women
also put in long hours of housework and caring for children, she
contends, they need special legislation that regulates the amount
of overtime they may work. Although upper-class professional

women may feel hampered by protective labor laws, Schlafly asserts, the vast majority of working women oppose the elimination of these regulations.

In 1978, Congress extended the ratification deadline for the Equal Rights Amendment until 1982. By the 1982 deadline, only thirty-five of the necessary thirty-eight states had ratified the amendment. The Equal Rights Amendment has been reintroduced in Congress several times since 1983 but has never passed.

In business, professional, intellectual, and academic pursuits, women can compete equally with men because they are just as smart. In jobs that require physical labor, women cannot compete equally with men because their physical strength is not equal. . . . It is unfair to treat women the same as men in the millions of manual-labor jobs that keep our industrial economy functioning.

Protective Legislation for Working Women

In recognition of the physical differences between women and men—which are self-evident to everyone except women's liberationists our country has developed a fabric of protective labor legislation. This consists of the network of state laws designed to give women employees particular benefits and protections not granted to men.

This protective labor legislation varies from state to state, but generally includes provisions to protect women from being compelled to work too many hours a day, or days a week, or at night; weight-lifting restrictions; provisions that mandate rest areas, rest periods, protective equipment, or a chair for a woman who stands on her feet all day; laws that protect women from being forced to work in dangerous occupations; and laws that grant more generous workmen's compensation for injuries to more parts of a woman's body than to a man's.

Women and unions have worked hard over several generations to achieve such legislation to protect and benefit women who are required to join the labor force because of economic necessity, but who have no academic or professional qualifications.

If ERA [the Equal Rights Amendment] is ever ratified, all such protective labor laws will be wiped out in one stroke. ERA lawyers and witnesses do not dispute this fact. Instead, they resort to various diversionary arguments to sidestep the issue.

Congresswoman Martha Griffiths deals with the protective labor legislation issue by saying that all such legislation is already outlawed by Title VII of the Civil Rights Act of 1964. It is true that some labor legislation has been invalidated by the courts under the Civil Rights Act. But not all. Just because the courts have knocked out some good labor legislation is no reason to use the sledgehammer approach and knock it all out.

Phyllis Schlafly organized a successful movement to block ratification of the Equal Rights Amendment.

To any extent that protective labor legislation has been invalidated by the Civil Rights Act, it can be restored by amendment to the act. But anything knocked out by the United States Constitution cannot be restored except by the long and laborious process of another constitutional amendment.

ERA speakers confidently assure their uninformed audiences that "whenever the courts are confronted with a law that truly benefits women, the courts will extend the benefit to men instead of declaring it void." This does not happen in practice. In every case on record, particularly in the states of Washington, California, and Ohio, the courts have thrown out the protections of women and have not extended any benefits to men. Women have lost on every count. Most companies are delighted with the removal of the protections for women because they are generally expensive to management.

Syndicated columnist Georgie Anne Geyer reported from Seattle in December, 1976:

> Once the [Washington] state ERA was passed, the protective legislation for women and children dating from 1913, which restricted such things as enforced overtime work, provided for water and cots in restrooms, limited lifting of weights, etc., was voided.
>
> Fine, all the feminist organizations said, now we will go ahead and procure all of that protection for men, too.
>
> Only that is not what has happened.
>
> "The hearings that ensued were incredible," mused Mary Helen Roberts, executive director of the Washington State Women's Council. "On one side, we had workers talking about 'dying in the streets,' and on the other side, we had businessmen talking about being 'forced out of business.' It was unreal. . . ."
>
> As the protective legislation was voided, women complained of forced overtime because business found it cheaper to pay time and a half than to hire new workers. If work was considered "intermittent in nature," the women got no breaks—for lunch or toilet—at all.

Governor-elect Dixy Lee Ray of Washington was asked on "Meet the Press" on November 7, 1976, if the Washington state ERA had caused problems. She said, yes, it had removed the protective labor legislation from women that had formerly guaranteed them coffee breaks, lunch breaks, the right to leave company property at lunch time, and safeguards against heavy lifting.

Middle-Class Feminists and Factory Workers

The women who appear as ERA witnesses before state legislative committees usually argue that protective labor legislation doesn't really protect but instead keeps women from advancing. This is the cloistered attitude of a business or professional woman who sits at a desk all day in a clean and spacious office and never lifts anything heavier than a few books and papers. She is the type of woman who finds intellectual fulfillment in her job, and she may indeed want the opportunity to work longer hours for more pay and promotions. Protective labor legislation does not apply to her, anyway.

This is not the point of view of the factory woman, who works only to help supplement the family income, who stands on her feet all day in front of a machine, whose work may be sweaty or exhausting, and who is eager to go home to take care of her children. There are millions more factory women than there are business women. And it is grossly unfair to the factory woman to wipe out the legislation that now protects her from a company that may order her to work a second eight-hour shift, an extra four-hour shift, seven days a week, or assign her to heavy lifting, dangerous or unpleasant jobs as male employees are arbitrarily assigned according to the workload of the company.

Opposition from Union Women

Blanch Freedman was the executive secretary of the New York Women's Trade Union League during World War II. In the following statement, Freedman explains the league's opposition to an early version of the Equal Rights Amendment.

We oppose the so-called "Equal Rights" Amendment which is dangerous and vicious because:

The Proposed Amendment Deprives the State of Its Inherent Right to Protect Itself by Taking Cognizance of the Special Role of Women as Mothers or Potential Mothers.

On the statute books of most of the states of the Union, laws exist which prescribe conditions under which women shall work. They regulate the hours of employment and fix maximums; they sometimes establish minimum-wage rates; they often require the establishment of certain facilities for the maintenance of health. The purpose behind this legislation is readily understandable. Experience as well as scientific knowledge has demonstrated that unless the conditions under which women work are controlled there is grave danger that their health and well-being will be impaired to a degree that will affect their offspring injuriously.

It is no answer to say that all overtime should be voluntary. Of course, it should! But the fact is that it isn't. With a few minor exceptions, even the most powerful unions have not been able to make overtime for men a matter of choice. But protective labor laws protect women from involuntary overtime, and it is grossly unfair to deny them that protection. Most women in factory jobs have home duties, too. . . .

Only if ERA is permanently rejected will women in industry be able to work out a solution whereby overtime for women is a voluntary option. If ERA is ratified, there will be no way to achieve this.

It is no answer to say that the factory woman has the right to reject heavy and dangerous work. She may have this right in theory, but not in practice. Take, for example, a period of unemployment and layoffs. When a company lays off workers, it reassigns those remaining to other jobs as needed by the company. In states where the courts have ruled that there can be no sex discrimination in job assignment, women are now being placed on jobs for which they never applied, do not want, and consider too heavy or dangerous or hazardous to their health. If they refuse to take such jobs, they get a black mark on their records. If they resign, they cannot draw unemployment compensation.

If ERA is ever ratified, the women in the lower economic classes, the women who do the manual jobs, will get the short end of the stick. The best one-sentence description of ERA was given by Mrs. Jean Noble, executive secretary of the National Council of Negro Women, who said:

> I call the Equal Rights Amendment the liftin' and totin' bill. More than half of the black women with jobs work in service occupations; if the Amendment becomes law, we will be the ones liftin' and totin'.

At one state legislative hearing, a business woman appearing as a pro-ERA witness confidently argued that protective labor legislation is obsolete and unnecessary in this technological age, so women no longer need a law that requires a company to provide chairs. It comes with exceedingly poor grace for one who sits at a comfortable desk to brush off the legal right of a woman who stands on her feet all day to be provided with a chair.

Naomi McDaniel, . . . who founded Women of Industry, an organization of labor union women opposed to ERA, is an eloquent witness for the woman who has a double role in our society as wife/mother and factory worker. Mrs. McDaniel has eight children and works the night shift at a General Motors plant in Dayton, Ohio. In her testimony at many state legislative hearings she said:

> Women who work at desks or blackboards, where the heaviest loads they lift may be a pile of papers or a few books, are not representative of factory production workers who need protection of present laws, such as those limiting loads women must lift. The uninformed but noisy minority of ERA proponents— smooth-talking college women who have never even seen a factory production line—parrot the claim that some women can lift up to 75 pounds, and should have the "opportunity" to work alongside men.

> In their eagerness to, perhaps, get their boss' job as office manager, they are most generous in giving away those precious distinctions so badly needed by their harder-working sisters on the assembly line. While they point out that mothers easily lift 50-pound children, they do not realize or do not care that this is not like lifting 50 pounds every 60 seconds on an assembly line all day long. We Women in Industry know better than anyone else that we are simply not physically equal to men, but ERA permits no distinction.

When the women's liberationists ridicule the "restroom argument," they are simply proving that ERA is an elitist upper-middle class cause that has no relevance to the big majority of working women. The restroom argument is meaningful to the woman who works in industry. She knows that the women's restrooms are much pleasanter places than the men's and are often equipped with couches. They are places where she can escape for a few moments of rest each day from the drudgery of a manual labor job. She knows that protective labor legislation has mandated rest periods and rest areas for women, and that this is part of her right to be treated like a woman. In the states where the courts have voided all protective labor legislation, company after company has enthusiastically cut operating costs by removing the couches and reducing the size of women's restrooms.

The patronizing attitude of some business and professional women shows that they neither understand nor represent the needs or desires of women who work in industry or in manual-labor jobs. President Nixon's Council on the Status of Women, which endorsed ERA, was wholly dominated by business and professional women and had no representation from women in industry. . . .

Out of Touch with Reality

Some young and inexperienced proponents of ERA have argued that, if certain jobs are so hard, dangerous, and unpleasant, men should not be required to do them, either. Such an argument is out of touch with realities.

There are thousands of jobs in industry that are strenuous, hard, unpleasant, dirty, and dangerous that men can and will do and for which they receive good wages, but which women don't want to do and should not be compelled to do. To abolish these jobs would eliminate thousands of necessary and well-paying jobs that produce products Americans want and would significantly reduce our standard of living. Eliminating them would benefit neither women nor men. But legislation can and should protect women from being forced to take such jobs.

It is not only in factories but in retail stores and supermarkets that women are feeling the brunt of unwelcome equality. For example, in 1976 the government issued orders to many supermarkets and liquor stores that all clerks must be paid the same wage *and* perform the same duties, including unloading trucks filled with cases weighing thirty to fifty pounds each. You can guess how enthusiastic women clerks in their fifties and sixties are about this new equality. Yet, their appeals to be exempted from such enforced equality have fallen on deaf ears.

CHAPTER 5

Historical Evaluations of the Suffrage Movement

Chapter Preface

Suffrage was the primary goal of the women's rights movement for several decades. The lack of voting rights was one of the chief complaints voiced by early feminists, and the resolutions signed by attendees at the first women's rights convention in 1848 included a demand for women's enfranchisement. After the Civil War, when amendments protecting black men's right to vote were worded to specifically exclude women from voting, feminists concentrated with new urgency on fighting for women's suffrage. The National and American Woman Suffrage Associations may have disagreed over whether the vote would change women's lives more than other reforms, but in practice both organizations spent the majority of their energy and resources on suffrage campaigns. From the mid-1860s to the passage of the Nineteenth Amendment in 1920, the battle for suffrage was the defining characteristic of the women's rights movement.

Even during the midst of their drive for suffrage, however, feminists differed over the impact the vote would have on other aspects of women's rights. Most feminists agreed that women faced not merely a lack of voting rights but also a multitude of other problems and inequities. Once women had the right to vote, some women's rights advocates maintained, they would be able to use their votes to overcome other forms of sexual discrimination. This sentiment was expressed in the resolutions of the 1853 National Woman's Rights Convention: "Woman will soonest free herself from the legal disabilities she now suffers, by securing the right to the elective franchise—thus becoming herself a lawmaker." Other feminists argued that, while suffrage would be an important gain, it could not begin to improve every facet of women's lives. Charlotte Perkins Gilman, for example, asserted in her 1898 book *Women and Economics* that women would only achieve full equality if the entire social structure of marriage and family was reworked.

In retrospect, it seems clear that the Nineteenth Amendment did not immediately solve all the concerns of the women's rights movement. However, historians disagree over the extent to which the right to vote affected feminists' ability to attain subsequent reforms. Many historians contend that the suffragists hurt the women's rights cause by fixating single-mindedly on the passage of the Nineteenth Amendment instead of addressing deep-rooted attitudes about women's proper role in the family and in society.

Winning the vote did little to improve women's status or to broaden women's opportunities, they argue. On the other hand, some historians assert that the Nineteenth Amendment was a significant accomplishment that raised women's status by granting them the full rights of citizens. The right to vote was a crucial step in the women's rights movement, these historians argue, since it added considerably to women's power to influence legislation and politics. The following pair of viewpoints examines whether the suffrage campaign helped or hindered the larger objectives of the women's rights movement.

VIEWPOINT 1

"The vote [did not] change the lives of women as individuals nor greatly aid the causes in which organized women were most interested."

Suffrage Was Not a Radical Reform

William L. O'Neill (b. 1935)

William L. O'Neill is a professor of history at Rutgers University in New Brunswick, New Jersey. He is the author of several books, including *Everyone Was Brave: A History of Feminism in America,* and is the editor of *Women at Work* and *The Woman Movement: Feminism in the United States and England.*

In the following viewpoint, O'Neill contends that the women's rights movement did not go far enough when it concentrated on suffrage as its primary cause. Initially the leaders of the women's movement advocated reforms that would have revolutionized society, O'Neill argues, but scandal and Victorian mores prompted the majority of feminists to abandon their radical ideas. Suffragists concentrated instead on winning the right to vote, he asserts, even though enfranchisement would not greatly change the inequality of women's social status.

Because feminism was such a widespread, indistinct, poorly defined phenomenon, feminists never developed a precise vocabulary. Indeed, the vagueness of their language reflected larger confusions of thought and perception that kept them from building a successful ideology. No historian, to my knowledge, has found it necessary to remedy this defect, but, because I intend to show that there were several kinds of feminism, a word about terms is necessary.

The phrase most commonly used by women in the nineteenth and early twentieth centuries to describe their expanding activities was "the woman movement." This movement included not only those things pertaining to women's rights but almost any act or event that enlarged woman's sphere, increased her opportunities, or broadened her outlook. It covered everything from woman suffrage and social reform down to the individual accomplishments of gifted, ambitious women. "Feminism," a more limited word, related specifically to the advancement of women's legal and political rights. The feminist movement, in turn, was broadly divided into two wings, but, because feminists themselves did not recognize this until the very end of the period, i.e. in the 1920's, I have coined the phrases "social feminism" to describe that part of the movement that put social reform ahead of women's rights and "hard-core" or "extreme feminists" to describe those who put women's rights before all else. A "suffragist" was simply one who worked for equal suffrage, irrespective of her views on other questions.[1]

The Victorian Domestic System

During much of its history feminism was considered extremely radical; indeed, suffragists did not triumph until after they had persuaded the public that they constituted a "bourgeois, middle-class, . . . middle-of-the-road movement."[2] Although equal suffrage was an absurdly controversial issue, and there was little basis for the repeated charge that it was revolutionary, for a long time there was good reason to think that the feminist program—of which suffrage was only a part—had revolutionary implications. This was so because, by the Victorian era, women were locked into such a tight domestic system—their role so narrowly defined—that granting them real equality was impossible without overhauling the entire social structure. Full equality required drastic readjustments on two levels. If women were to have an equal chance with men to develop themselves, not only would they need equal educational and vocational opportunities but they would somehow have to be relieved of the domestic obligations that bound most of them to the home. And, because every system encourages the attitudes that are appropriate to it, the whole complex of ideas and assumptions that "justified" women's inferior status would have to be changed.

At the beginning of the nineteenth century the only acceptable roles for women were domestic; there was virtually nothing for them to do except stay at home or hire out as maids, governesses and, before long, teachers. A handful made other places for themselves, but until the middle of the century they were too few to affect the system. The cultural rationale that kept women in the home, however, was more complex and demands further attention. The Victorian woman was part of a network of ideas, prejudices, and religious emotionalism that simultaneously degraded and elevated her. "The cult of true womanhood" (as one historian calls it) emphasized women's piety, purity, submissiveness, and domesticity. Religious work was almost the only form of outside activity permitted women because it did not take them away from their "true sphere." "From her home woman performed her great task of bringing men back to God."[3] Woman, it was believed, was morally and spiritually superior to man because of her highly developed intuition, refined sensibilities, and especially because of those life-giving maternal powers that defied man's comprehension. But woman was physically weaker than man, inferior to him in cognitive ability, and wholly unsuited to the rough world outside the home. This was just as well, however, because women were largely responsible for "The Family," the chief adornment of Christian society and the foundation of civilized life.[4]

Although the concept of women as wan, ethereal, spiritualized creatures bore little relation to reality by mid-century, when women operated machines, worked in the fields, hand-washed clothing, and toiled over kitchen ranges, it was endorsed by science and by religion. A vast and constantly growing body of polemical literature was churned out by physicians, clergymen, and journalists in support of this thesis. Even fashion conspired to the same end; the bustles and hoops and the corsets and trailing skirts in which women were encased throughout much of the century seemed designed to hobble them and prevent all but the most desperate from leaving their homes for long. (The weight of metal, cloth, and bone that women were expected to bear should itself have disproved the notion that they were peculiarly delicate creatures, but of course it did not.) Feminine "delicacy" was considered the visible evidence of their superior sensibilities, the "finer clay" of which they were made. Women who were not delicate by nature became so by design. In the end, the fashion was self-defeating for it aroused fears that women would become so ornamental as to be incapable of discharging their essential functions. The Civil War helped wake middle-class women from "their dream of a lady-like uselessness," and in 1861, when Vassar College was founded, its trustees put physical education at the head of their list of objectives.[5]

The Victorian idealization of women was self-defeating in another and more important way. The Victorians attempted to compensate women for their domestic and pedagogic responsibilities by enveloping them in a mystique that asserted their higher status while at the same time guaranteeing their inferiority; hence the endless polemics on the moral purity and spiritual genius of woman that found its highest expression in the home and that had to be safeguarded at all costs from the hopelessly corrupting effects of the man-made society without. But, as William R. Taylor and Christopher Lasch have suggested,

> the cult of women and the home contained contradictions that tended to undermine the very things they were supposed to safeguard. Implicit in the myth was a repudiation not only of heterosexuality but of domesticity itself. It was her purity, contrasted with the coarseness of men, that made woman the head of the home (though not of the family) and the guardian of public morality. But the same purity made intercourse between men and women at last almost literally impossible and drove women to retreat almost exclusively into the society of their own sex, to abandon the very home which it was their appointed mission to preserve.[6]

Thus the "woman movement" had its origins in the sexual segregation that Victorians considered essential for an ideal domestic system. Beginning with church societies and a few women's clubs, associationism grew and grew, until by the end of the century millions of women were caught up in it, and their old isolation was broken.

As we noted earlier, the woman movement was not the same thing as feminism. Women who worked for their church or met in literary societies were, however, indirectly helping themselves by developing aspirations that promoted the larger growth to come. They began to press for more education and to manifest intellectual and literary interests. The acute Englishwoman, Harriet Martineau, noted that "in my progress through the country I met with a greater variety and extent of female pedantry than the experience of a lifetime in Europe would afford." This pedantry, she hastened to add, "was not to be despised in an oppressed class as it indicates the first struggle of intellect with its restraints; and it is therefore a hopeful symptom."[7]

Formulating a Movement

Even more hopeful, of course, was the next step that these developments made possible: the formulation of a distinct women's rights movement. In the 1830's women were stirred by the currents of reform that were sweeping the country, and those who were moved to action discovered that their status as women told against their ambitions as abolitionists, temperance workers, or whatever. Sarah M. Grimké was inspired to write the first American feminist tract of consequence[8] because some clergymen objected to her antislavery work. Elizabeth Cady Stanton was started on her career as a women's rights leader after she was denied a seat, by reason of her sex, at a World Anti-Slavery Convention in London. Susan B. Anthony became a feminist after she was discriminated against by her male colleagues in the temperance movement.

A Mainstream Movement

Aileen Kraditor is a professor emerita of history at Boston University. In the following excerpts from her book The Ideas of the Woman Suffrage Movement, *Kraditor asserts that the suffrage movement was a product of the mainstream middle class.*

The women took pride in the fact that their [suffrage] movement was in the mainstream of American history, seeking to realize and further the ideals of the Founding Fathers, but not to replace those ideals or overthrow the government of the glorious republic brought forth by their ancestors. . . . In placing their movement in the middle of the road, the suffragists were perfectly correct. They exhibited both the strengths and the weaknesses of other reform movements in American history, especially when in justifying their demand for the vote they voiced principles too extreme for their own consistent allegiance. The pioneers of the suffrage movement, living in a time when victory for their cause seemed eons away, did not have to concern themselves too much with tactics. They could afford to state their ideals in ringing declarations on democracy that would admit of no qualifications or exceptions. In fact, they had to do so, for only ideals that could inspire a martyr's dedication could sustain these women through the physical violence and almost unbearable ridicule to which they were subjected. Later, when victories could be won here and there at the cost of small concessions to political expediency, the hard facts of political life and the equivocal position in American society of these middle-class women exerted a pull away from the high ideals and ringing declarations. To win support from needed allies they compromised with those principles perhaps more than the requirements of the alliances dictated. More often than not they voiced the ideals and advocated the compromises at the same time.

In 1848 these separate streams of dissent came together at the first Woman's Rights Convention in Seneca Falls, New York. The "Declaration of Sentiments" that was adopted by the meeting indicated another element that infused the early feminist movement: the libertarianism of the age of reform. Modeled in part on the Declaration of Independence, this manifesto declared that "the history of mankind is a history of repeated injuries and usurpations on the part of man toward woman, having in direct object the establishment of an absolute tyranny over her."[9] It was, in fact, a decidedly radical document—not that it called for an end to private property, or anticipated a good society along socialist lines, but in storming against every iniquity from votelessness to the double standard of morals it made demands that could not be satisfied without profound changes in the social order. The most sophisticated feminists appreciated, in some measure at least, that they were not merely asking for their rights as citizens, that what they wanted called for new institutions as well as new ways of thinking. They seem to have been feeling their way toward a new domestic order. Mrs. Stanton, who denounced marriage as "opposed to all God's laws," wanted to begin its reformation by liberalizing divorce.[10] The magazine she and Susan B. Anthony ran after the Civil War, *Revolution*, was full of references to the "marriage question" at a time when no orthodox person was willing to admit that there was a marriage question.

Logic alone had forced extreme feminists to sail these dangerous waters because even then it was clear that if women were fully emancipated by law, their domestic obligations would nevertheless prevent them from competing with men on an equal basis. There were only two (by no means mutually exclusive) ways of dealing with this problem: Either women must be supported by the kind of welfare measures (guaranteed maternity leaves with pay, family allowances, and the like) that the advanced social democracies have devised, or marriage and the family must be more flexibly defined.

Because the first alternative did not exist in the mid–nineteenth century, far-sighted women had to consider how the essential domestic institutions could be revised to free women from the tyranny of home and family; they had some precedents to guide them. For their own reasons the Mormons practiced polygamy, while the Shaker communities went to the opposite extreme by abolishing not only marriage but sexual relations as well. A number of perfectionist groups explored the varieties of free love, such as John Humphrey Noyes, who (at Oneida, New York) combined the equality of the sexes, perfectionism, socialism, and "complex marriage" (the sharing of spouses) in a bizarre but strikingly successful way. In such an atmosphere it was natural for the boldest feminists to flirt with radical approaches to the domestic problem. It is impossible to tell where these speculations would have led Mrs. Stanton and her followers, but the Victoria Woodhull affair suggests a likely possibility.

Victoria Woodhull and her equally vivid sister, Tennessee Celeste Claflin, burst upon the New York scene in 1868. Although nominally lady stockbrokers, they were agitators and evangelists by persuasion, and enthusiasts for everything radical, or just plain wild—socialism, spiritualism or women's rights. Their magazine, *Woodhull and Claflin's Weekly*, promoted such causes, as well as the peculiar interests of their mentor, Stephen Pearl Andrews, a self-proclaimed universal philosopher and linguist. The surprising thing about the raffish sisters is that they rapidly became celebrated champions of the cause of women, admired by such shrewd and experienced figures as Elizabeth Cady Stanton and Susan B. Anthony. In 1871, for example, Victoria Woodhull persuaded a congressional subcommittee to hold hearings on woman suffrage, and she testified before it with great effect.

Their *Weekly* was interested in marriage from the beginning. Stephen Pearl Andrews believed in free love in the usual Victorian sense (that is, in extramarital sexual relationships contracted as a matter of principle), and the Claflin sisters had practiced free love long before they understood its theoretical possibilities. Having thrown out a good many hints, Mrs. Woodhull finally called a mass meeting and on the stage of Steinway Hall declared herself a free lover. She seems to have been genuinely astonished at the ferocious reaction to this public confession; newspapers hounded her, cautious feminists snubbed her, and the sisters fell on hard times, financially and emotionally. Victoria struck back by disclosing that Henry Ward Beecher, the most famous preacher of the day and a good friend of woman suffrage, had been having an affair with the wife of Theodore Tilton, Mrs. Woodhull's friend, her biographer, and perhaps her lover. The ensuing scandal destroyed the Claflins and the Tiltons; but Beecher survived it, thanks to his great reputation, considerable courage, and influential friends.[11]

The effect of this debacle on the suffrage movement's fortunes is hard to determine because the cause was already in bad shape when the Claflins took it in hand. Suffragists had been disappointed at the end of the Civil War when they were asked to sacrifice votes for women to secure votes for Negro men. Some of them refused to admit that the freedman's need was greater than theirs and, because of this and other frictions, the suffrage movement had divided into two organizations: the staid, Boston-based American Woman's Suffrage Association and the more aggressive National Woman's Suffrage Association, led by Miss Anthony and Mrs. Stanton. Both groups were tarnished by the Beecher-Tilton affair, but the AWSA suffered less because it had always been anti-Claflin. The NWSA came in for a larger measure of abuse because of its closer association with the sisters, but the unquestionable virtue and integrity of its leaders saved it from total eclipse. It used to be thought that the affair had set back equal suffrage for decades; today, however, the movement's temporary decline seems to have been only one feature of the conservative backlash of the Gilded Age. Suffragists had expected too big a reward for their services during the Civil War as nurses, propagandists and sanitary commission volunteers. The country was grateful to them, but not all that grateful—as the defeat of woman suffrage in the hotly contested Kansas referendum of 1866 demonstrated. In freeing and enfranchising the Negro, America, it seemed, had exhausted its supply of liberalism.

The Woodhull affair had one lasting effect, however: it reaffirmed the general conviction that suffrage politics and radical speculations, particularly those affecting marriage and the family, did not mix. In consequence the movement, although it never disowned the social goals that women's votes were presumably to implement, emphasized the most conservative aspects of the suffrage question. The vote was shown to be compatible with the existing domestic economy, and—at best—with those reforms that would elevate and refine domesticity to the level of perfection for which society yearned. Suffragists thereafter, vigorously resisting the temptation to think seriously about the domestic institutions that ruled their lives, made sexual orthodoxy their ruling principle.

A More Conservative Feminism

In the long run these shocks had two important consequences: feminism rapidly became more conservative and more altruistic. Its conservatism—not the doing of Victoria Woodhull—stemmed from the tightening up of morals and manners that occurred in the high Victorian era. Bills like the Comstock Act (1873) made it impossible for John Humphrey Noyes and other sexual radicals to use the mails, choking off the lively debate that had flourished earlier. The porous or open quality that had characterized American life in the age of reform gave way to the censorious prudery we associate with Victorianism. It is very likely that the extreme feminists would have had to abandon their tentative explorations, if only because of social purity. Earlier there had been sporadic attempts by organized women to eliminate the double standard of morals by holding men to a higher level of conduct. The radical feminists who toyed with free love approached the same goal from an opposite direction, by proposing a sort of convergence in which men and women would occupy a middle ground between the old extremes of absolute license and complete chastity. After the war, however, all doubts as to which line feminists would follow were relieved by the social purity movement, which enlisted the energies of public-spirited women all over the country in a crusade to abolish prostitution and infidelity.[12] Mrs. Stanton continued to advocate free divorce, to the great embarrassment of her younger followers, but she was very much the exception.

At the same time that feminists abandoned their more advanced positions they took on a great range of activities that often had little to do with women's rights. Extreme feminists, for example, displayed a keen sense of self-interest in the struggle over Negro suffrage after the Civil War. The Stantonites as a rule were more radical and more sensitive to the needs of others than the Boston faction, but when they were forced to choose between the Negroes' interests and their own they unflinchingly went down the line for feminist objectives.

The feminism of later years, however, was much more generous and diffuse. A hardy band of suffragists fought the good fight for the vote while most feminists devoted themselves to charities, philanthropies, and reforms. As social workers, settlement house residents, members of women's clubs, advocates of the reform of child labor and women's working conditions, of municipal government, public health, education and housing, and as temperance workers and conservationists they submerged their interests as women in a sea of worthy enterprises. These social justice activities became the principal justification for feminism, and are what historians most admire about the movement, but feminists paid a high price for their good deeds in two important ways. First, these activities drained off personnel from the women's rights movement and protracted the suffrage struggle. Second, they led to ideological confusions that played a large role in the collapse of feminism once the vote was won.

Social feminism also perpetuated the confusion between class and sex, that false sense of solidarity that characterized the entire woman movement. In a way this was natural, because all women suffered from disabilities that were imposed upon men only discriminatingly. It was not possible to have a "man movement" because most men enjoyed all the rights and opportunities that God and nature presumably intended them to have. Equal rights for women, however, did not mean the same thing to a factory girl that it meant to a college graduate, and feminists invariably refused to admit that differences in station among women were of any importance. In the beginning this hardly mattered, because the early feminists were mainly bourgeois intellectuals who were struggling to improve their own immediate circumstances. As the woman movement matured, however, its sociological evasions and self-deceptions attained critical proportions.

This analytic failure, which was characteristic of a movement that (with the notable exceptions of Elizabeth Cady Stanton and Charlotte Perkins Gilman) produced few intellects of the first

220

rank, was compounded by an insistence that women were united in a selfless sisterhood by their maternal capacities, real or potential. "Women," it was declared over and over again, "stand relatively for the same thing everywhere and their first care is naturally and inevitably for the child."[13] Maternity was not only a unifying force but the enabling principle that made the entrance of women into public life imperative. As another suffragist put it in 1878, "the new truth, electrifying, glorifying American womanhood today, is the discovery that the State is but the larger family, the nation the old homestead, and that in this national home there is a room and a corner and a duty for mother."[14] Not only was the nation a larger home in need of mothering, but, by impinging upon the domestic circle, it made motherhood a public role.

As Jane Addams saw it, "many women today are failing properly to discharge their duties to their own families and household simply because they fail to see that as society grows more complicated it is necessary that woman shall extend her sense of responsibility to many things outside of her own home, if only in order to preserve the home in entirety."[15] Thus the effort to escape domesticity was accompanied by an invocation of the domestic ideal: women's freedom road led in a circle, back to the home from which feminism was supposed to liberate them. Feminism was made respectable by accommodating it to the Victorian ethos that had forced it into being.

Given the plausibility and flexibility of this contention, women were (perhaps inevitably) lured into using it to secure their immediate aims; but in retrospect it does not seem to have been an unqualifiedly successful ploy. The Women's Christian Temperance Union is a case in point. Although one historian has hailed Frances Willard's "supreme cleverness" in using "this conservative organization to advocate woman suffrage and child labor laws and other progressive legislation always in the name of purity and the home,"[16] the history of the WCTU illustrates the weakness of an argument that begins by accepting the opposition's premise. In conceding that better homes were of equal importance to feminists and anti-feminists alike, these women reduced their case from one of principle to a mere quarrel over tactics. All the opposition had to do to redeem itself was prove that its tactics were superior. This apparently is what happened to the WCTU after the death of Frances Willard (which coincided with a significant change in its social composition), when new leaders came to believe that temperance was more crucial to the home than suffrage, child welfare, and other progressive causes. Perhaps this new orientation would have come about in any event, but surely such WCTU suffragists as Frances Willard made it much easier by their willingness to utilize the cult of domesticity in pursuit of quite separate and distinctively feminist objectives.

Hazards of the Emphasis on Motherhood

The truth was that while these feminists resented the demands made upon them in their roles as wives and mothers, they were insufficiently alert to the danger presented by even a partial accommodation to the maternal mystique. Gravely underestimating the tremendous force generated by the sentimental veneration of motherhood, they assumed they could manipulate the emotions responsible for the condition of women without challenging the principles on which these feelings rested. Moreover, while denying that under the present circumstances mothers could be held accountable for the failings of their children, they implied that, once emancipated, women could legitimately be indicted for their progenies' shortcomings. In 1901 Susan B. Anthony declared that "before mothers can rightfully be held responsible for the vices and crimes, for the general demoralization of society, they must possess all possible rights and powers to control the conditions and circumstances of their own and their children's lives."[17] Her remark would seem to mean that, once granted political equality, mothers would have to answer for all the ills of society. This was a great weight to lay on female posterity, and such statements contributed to the unhealthy and unrealizable expectations that feminism encouraged.

A further hazard of the feminist emphasis on motherhood was the support it lent the notion that women were not only different from men, but superior to men. Julia Ward Howe, a moderate and greatly admired feminist, persistently implied that emancipation was intended to make women better mothers as well as freer persons.

> Woman is the mother of the race, the guardian of its helpless infancy, its earliest teacher, its most zealous champion. Woman is also the home-maker, upon her devolve the details which bless and beautify family life. In all true civilization she wins man out of his natural savagery to share with her the love of offspring, the enjoyment of true and loyal companionship.[18]

Definitions like this left men with few virtues anyone was bound to admire, and inspired women to think of themselves as a kind of superrace that had been condemned by historical accident and otiose convention to serve its natural inferiors.

Such indeed was the case with women who, encouraged by the new social sciences (especially anthropology, which demonstrated that matriarchies had existed and may once have been common, if not universal), took themselves with a new seriousness that few men could share. Elizabeth Cady Stanton argued that prehistoric women had been superior to men, or at least equal to them, but that Christianity, and especially Protestantism, had driven the feminine element out of religion and had subordinated women to the rule of men. Society thereby had lost the beneficent moral and conservative forces of the female intellect and the mother instinct.[19]

With this line of argument [American clergyman] Walter Rauschenbush, no enemy of women's rights, was compelled to take issue. Alarmed by what he regarded as the feminists' moral pretensions, he wrote: "Many men feel that women are morally better than men. Perhaps it is right that men should instinctively feel so. But it is a different matter when women think so too. They are not better. They are only good in different ways than men."[20] Rauschenbush believed in the emancipation of women, but he reminded his readers that the feminine virtues could easily be exaggerated, and that in recent times both Christian Science and theosophy had demonstrated a particular appeal to women even though both stressed authority and unexamined belief.

As Rauschenbush's observation suggests, the attempt to demonstrate women's superior nature led nowhere. In essence it was just one more variation of the Victorian mystique, another way of exploiting the belief that woman's unique power was rooted in the mystery of her life-giving capacities. Taken one way, it led back to a preoccupation with motherhood. Read differently, it supported so complete a rejection of men that women could retain their integrity and spirituality only in spinsterhood. Or—by subscribing to the principles of Ellen Key, who elevated motherhood even above marriage and made the right to have illegitimate children the central aspect of feminism—women could have their cake and eat it too.[21] They could realize their generative and instinctual potential without an unseemly dependence on the contaminating male. Deliberately having an illegitimate child necessitated an act of masculine cooperation, and in a delicious reversal of ancient custom man became an instrument of woman's purpose and his ungoverned passion the means to her full emancipation. This was radicalism with a vengeance, but a radicalism that had curiously little to do with the normal objects of revolutionary ardor.

Special Interests and the Vote

Most organized women, however, were neither radical nor especially feministic. The woman movement as a whole, and most social feminists in particular, were satisfied with the comparatively modest programs of the WCTU and the General Federation of Women's Clubs. These programs, despite the fears of conservatives, were no threat to what Mrs. Gilman scornfully called the domestic mythology; in fact, they rested largely on the domestic and maternal mystique that was characteristic of the Victorian era. Not only did organized women continuously invoke "home and mother," for the most part their serious enterprises dealt with such related social matters as pure foods and drugs, child welfare, and working mothers. Whenever suffragists were able to tie in the ballot with a specific problem of special interest to women, they gained adherents. Through most of the nineteenth century suffragists maintained that women were entitled to vote as a matter of right and that they needed the vote to protect themselves and to advance the causes that were important to them. Neither argument was very persuasive in the age of Victoria, and always the suffragists' greatest obstacle was the indifference of their own sex.

As late as 1908 Theodore Roosevelt could comfortably, and quite rightly, say that "when women as a whole take any special interest in the matter they will have suffrage if they desire it."[22] But only a few years later the picture had changed entirely. In 1914 the General Federation of Women's Clubs endorsed woman suffrage in the name of its two million members; in 1917 membership in the NWSA soared to something like two million; and in that same year 500,000 women in New York City alone put their signatures to a suffrage petition. By 1917 it was obvious that women wanted the vote, and by 1920 they had it.

Few feminists seemed to realize that although winning the vote had been a feminist victory, it had not been won for feminist reasons. Suffragists had merely persuaded the organized middle-class women, who had become a potent force for reform in the Progressive era, that they needed the vote in order to secure the healthier and broader domestic life that was their main objective; feminists had not, however, convinced bourgeois women that they were greatly deprived and oppressed and that they had vast unrealized capabilities. From a strictly feminist point of view, the vote had been wrongly obtained. It neither reflected nor inspired a new vision of themselves on the part of most American women. Moreover, the suffrage could not but demoralize feminists who had worked so hard for so long, only to find that success had little effect upon the feminine condition.

The immediate consequence of feminine emancipation, then, was the fading away of the woman movement as it became apparent that the great organizations had less in common than they supposed. Moreover, the organizations themselves were changing in character. The WCTU was obsessed with prohibition (although it did not entirely lose interest in other social problems during the 1920's). The NWSA was transformed into the League of Women Voters; and although the league struggled valiantly to advance the old causes beloved of women reformers, it lacked the drive, funds, and numerical membership of its predecessor. The General Federation suffered least, because it had always been less committed to major reforms than its sister groups, and if its member clubs slackened their efforts, the national leadership continued to support the federation's traditional interests. The best evidence of the movement's decline was the fate of the Women's Joint Congressional Committee, which had been formed in 1920 to lobby for bills in which organized women took a special interest. Although it enjoyed some success (it helped keep Muscle Shoals out of private hands and it preserved a measure of federal support for mothers' pensions and other welfare programs), it lost more battles than it won, especially in the crucial struggle to ratify the Child Labor Amendment.

The Battle over Equal Rights

In the 1920's the split between social feminism and hard-core feminism emerged as a fundamental distinction. During the voteless years a common interest in women's suffrage and a general if vague commitment to women's and children's welfare had saved feminists from having to choose between equal rights and social reform. Then, in the twenties, a sharp cleavage opened between feminists in the League of Women Voters and the Joint Committee—which labored mainly for civic-virtue and welfare measures—and the militant Woman's Party, which singlemindedly pursued a narrow program that was signified by the title of its periodical *Equal Rights*. The most divisive feature of the Woman's Party program was its espousal of an equal rights amendment to the Constitution. Social feminists were alarmed by the Lucretia Mott Amendment (as the Woman's Party called it) because of the possibility that the courts would define equal rights as equal treatment. If this happened, the entire array of protective legislation that had been enacted for the benefit of working women during the Progressive era would be swept away. Inasmuch as the courts had . . . twice declared congressional child labor bills unconstitutional, and had struck down minimum wage laws for women, this was not an unreasonable fear. The Woman's Party insisted that equal rights and equal treatment would not be confused, or, if they were confused, so much the better: protective laws discriminated against working women by denying them the competitive advantages of men, who could work whatever jobs and hours they pleased. In reality the competition issue was relevant mainly to business and professional women who had to function in the job market as individuals. It hardly applied to wage-earning women, who could not bargain individually over wages, hours, or working conditions. Thus, feminists of every kind discovered that women did not constitute a real social class but were subject to the same distinctions that obtained among men.

Throughout the decade, and indeed long afterward, an unseemly struggle was waged over equal rights and protective legislation, but this quarrel was only symptomatic of the deeper confusions into which the entire movement had fallen as a result of the Nineteenth Amendment. It was not merely a question of whether complete equality was more risky than advantageous, nor even where, having won the vote, feminism ought to go, but what being a woman in America really meant. In short, feminists had traveled a long, circuitous, ascending path—to find themselves in 1920 about where they had been in 1830. They had not failed to better their condition along the way, but in avoiding fundamental questions for the sake of immediate advantages they had merely postponed the inevitable confrontation with themselves. Now the day of reckoning was at hand.

In the 1920's, then, it became clear that the anti-suffragists had been right all along in saying that the vote would neither change the lives of women as individuals nor greatly aid the causes in which organized women were most interested. Most women soon lost interest in overthrowing such remaining barriers to full emancipation as the WP urgently, and the LWV rather perfunctorily, called to their attention. The surviving hard-core feminists abandoned the fight for social justice (except for themselves), while the social feminists devoted themselves to such causes as peace, poverty, and prohibition, which had little to do with the status of women.

Under these circumstances it was no longer possible to speak with accuracy of a "woman movement," and the term fell into disuse, although such organizations as the International Woman's Suffrage Alliance and the International Council of Women perpetuated the cosmopolitan and cooperative spirit that had been such a striking and useful feature of the old movement. Hardcore feminism, on the other hand, contracted in size and spirit, so that it came to resemble its own mid-Victorian predecessor.

Notes

[1] "Suffragette" was the English equivalent of "suffragist." The former term was used in America mainly as a derisive term by critics of woman suffrage.

[2] "A Bourgeois Movement," *The Woman Citizen*, July 7, 1917, p. 99.

[3] Barbara Welter, "The Cult of True Womanhood: 1820–1860," *American Quarterly* 18 (Summer, 1966): 162.

[4] For a more complete description of this idea, see my *Divorce in the Progressive Era* (New Haven, 1967), pp. 58–61.

[5] Amy Louise Reed, "Female Delicacy in the Sixties," *Century* 68 (October, 1915): 258–70.

[6] "Two 'Kindred Spirits': Sorority and Family in New England, 1839–1846," *New England Quarterly* 36 (March, 1963): 35.

[7] In *Society in America*, 3 vols. (London, 1837), 3: 107.

[8] *The Equality of the Sexes and the Condition of Women* (Boston, 1838).

[9] *History of Woman Suffrage*, 1: 70. This immense documentary history of the suffrage movement from 1848 to 1920 ran to six fat volumes and was published between 1881 and 1922. The first three volumes (1881, 1882, 1887) were edited by Elizabeth Cady Stanton, Susan B. Anthony, and Matilda Joslyn Gage. Volume 4 (1902) was edited by Susan B. Anthony and Ida Husted Harper, and volumes 5 and 6 (1922, 1922) by Miss Harper.

[10] A letter to Lucy Stone, November 24, 1856, in *History of Woman Suffrage*, 1: 860.

[11] For a compact description of these events, see Robert E. Riegel, *American Feminists* (Lawrence, Kan., 1963), pp. 144–50. A biography of Victoria Woodhull is Johanna Johnston's *Mrs. Satan: The Incredible Saga of Victoria C. Woodhull* (New York, 1967). The best single source on these events is the *Weekly* itself, a fascinating publication that deserves more attention than most historians have given it.

[12] For this important but little-studied reform, see David Jay Pivar's "The New Abolitionism: The Quest for Social Purity, 1876–1900," (Ph.D. diss., University of Pennsylvania, 1965).

[13] Mrs. Ellis Meredith at the 1904 NWSA convention, in *History of Woman Suffrage*, 5: 101.

[14] Elizabeth Boynton Harbert, *ibid.*, 3: 78–79.

[15] "Woman's Conscience and Social Amelioration," in Charles Stelzle, ed., *Social Applications of Religion* (Cincinnati, 1908), p. 41.

[16] Andrew Sinclair, *The Better Half* (New York, 1965), p. 223.

[17] In *History of Woman Suffrage*, 5: 5–6.

[18] Florence Howe Hall, ed., *Julia Ward Howe and the Woman Suffrage Movement* (Boston, 1913), p. 158.

[19] See her paper, "The Matriarchate, or Mother-Age," in Rachel Foster Avery, ed., *Transactions of the National Council of Women of the United States* (Philadelphia, 1891), pp. 218–27.

[20] "Moral Aspects of the Woman Movement," *Biblical World* 42 (October, 1913): 197.

[21] See esp. Key's *Love and Marriage* (New York, 1911).

[22] In a letter to Lyman Abbott, dated November 10, 1908, published in "An Anti-Suffrage Meeting in New York," *Remonstrance* (January, 1909), p. 3.

VIEWPOINT 2

"The demand for the vote was the most radical program for women's emancipation possible in the nineteenth century."

Suffrage Was a Radical Reform

Ellen Carol DuBois (b. 1947)

Ellen Carol DuBois is a professor of history and women's studies at the University of California at Los Angeles. She has written extensively on the women's rights movement, including the book *Feminism and Suffrage: The Emergence of an Independent Women's Movement in America.* DuBois is also the editor of *The Elizabeth Cady Stanton–Susan B. Anthony Reader: Correspondence, Writings, Speeches.*

In the following viewpoint, DuBois refutes the argument made by William L. O'Neill and others that suffrage was not a significant reform. Women's suffrage was actually the most radical demand of the nineteenth-century women's rights movement, DuBois maintains, because it would allow women to break the social barriers that prevented them from entering the public sphere. Although DuBois admits that most suffragists did not concentrate directly on questioning the limitations of women's domestic roles, she argues the reformers believed women would gain the power to upgrade their condition once they had obtained the right to vote.

Ellen Carol DuBois, "The Radicalism of the Woman Suffrage Movement: Notes Toward the Reconstruction of Nineteenth-Century Feminism," *Feminist Studies*, vol. 3, 1975. Reprinted with permission.

The major theoretical contribution of contemporary feminism has been the identification of the family as a central institution of women's oppression. On the basis of this understanding we are seeing the beginnings of a revisionist history of American feminism which challenges the significance that has traditionally been attributed to the woman suffrage movement. Aileen Kraditor and William O'Neill have suggested that the woman suffrage movement did not lead to female emancipation because it accepted women's traditional position within the home. While attacking this "what-went-wrong" approach, Daniel Scott Smith has contended that suffragism should yield its claim to the central place in the history of nineteenth-century feminism to a phenomenon he calls "domestic feminism." Similarly, in her study of the female moral reform movement of the 1830s, Carroll Smith-Rosenberg argues that "it can hardly be assumed that the demand for votes for women was more radical than" the moral reform movement's attack on the sexual double standard.

These revisionist efforts are commendable in that they expand our sense of nineteenth-century feminism to include a much larger and more diverse group of women's activities than merely suffrage. On the other hand, I think they do an historical disservice to the woman suffrage movement. Nineteenth-century feminists and antifeminists alike perceived the demand for the vote as the most radical element in women's protest against their oppression and we are obligated to honor the perceptions of the historical actors in question. When considering nineteenth-century feminism, not as an intellectual tradition but as a social movement, as a politics that motivated people to action, twentieth century historians are in no position to redefine what was its most radical aspect. What we can do is analyze the position of nineteenth-century women and the nature of suffragism in order to understand why the demand for the vote was the most radical program for women's emancipation possible in the nineteenth century.

Public and Private Spheres

I would like to suggest an interpretation of nineteenth-century suffragism that reconciles the perceived radicalism of the woman suffrage movement with the historical centrality of the family to women's condition. My hypothesis is that the significance of the woman suffrage movement rested precisely on the fact that it bypassed women's oppression within the family, or private sphere, and demanded instead her admission to citizenship, and through it admission to the public arena. By focusing on the public sphere, and particularly on citizenship, suffragists demanded for women a kind of power and a connection with the social order not based on the institution of the family and their subordination within it.

Recent scholarship has suggested that the sharp distinction between public and private activities is a relatively modern historical phenomenon. In his work on the evolution of the idea of childhood in Western Europe, Phillipe Aries demonstrates that there was considerable overlap between family life and community life in the premodern period. He traces a gradual separation of public and private life from the sixteenth century to the nineteenth century when "family" and "society" came finally to be viewed as distinct, even hostile institutions. This development seems to be have been clear and compact in American history. In seventeenth-century New England, all community functions—production, socialization, civil government, religious life—presumed the family as the basic unit of social organization. The whole range of social roles drew on familial roles. The adult male's position as producer, as citizen, as member of the church, all flowed from his position as head of the family. Similarly, women's exclusion from church and civil government and their secondary but necessary role in production coincided with their subordinate position within the family. A few women enjoyed unusual economic or social privileges by virtue of their family connections, but, as Gerda Lerner has pointed out, this further demonstrated women's dependence on their domestic positions for the definition of their roles in community life.

By the nineteenth century, this relationship between family and society had undergone considerable change. Although the family continued to perform many important social functions, it was no longer the sole unit around which the community was organized. The concept of the "individual" had emerged to rival it. In the nineteenth century, we can distinguish two forms of social organization—one based on this new creature, the individual, the other based on the family. These overlapping but distinct structures became identified respectively as the public sphere and the private sphere. The emergence of a form of social organization not based on the family meant the emergence of social roles not defined by familial roles. This was equally true for women and men. But because women and men had different positions *within* the family, the existence of nonfamilial roles had different implications for the sexes. For women, the emergence of a public sphere held out the revolutionary possibility of a new way to relate to society not defined by their subordinate position within the family.

However, only men emerged from their familial roles to enjoy participation in the public sphere. Women on the whole did not. Women were of course among the first industrial workers, but it is important to remember that these were overwhelmingly unmarried women, for whom factory work was a brief episode before marriage. Adult women remained almost entirely within the private sphere, defined politically, economically, and socially by their familial roles. Thus, the public sphere became man's arena; the private, woman's. This gave the public/private distinction a clearly sexual character. This phenomenon, canonized as the nineteenth-century doctrine of sexual spheres, is somewhat difficult for us to grasp. We are fond of pointing out the historical durability of sexual roles into our own time and miss the enormous difference between the twentieth-century notion of sexual roles and the nineteenth-century idea of sexual spheres. The difference is a measure of the achievements of nineteenth-century feminism.

Different Paths, Same Goals

The following passage is taken from historian Jack S. Blocker's article "Separate Paths: Suffragists and the Women's Temperance Crusade," which appeared in the Spring 1985 issue of Signs: Journal of Women in Culture and Society. *Blocker maintains that both suffragists and temperance crusaders strove to expand women's role in the public sphere.*

The Women's Temperance Crusade raised two issues, and the relations between Crusaders and suffragists cannot be fully comprehended without understanding the positions of both groups on both issues. The first issue was women's right to participate in public affairs: on this issue a large area of agreement existed, which explains why some suffragists found it possible to cooperate with the Crusaders. The second issue was the way in which use of beverage alcohol was to be subject to public control. For [Elizabeth Cady] Stanton and other suffragists it was essential to employ the law. Their insistence on this point came from their faith in the power of the ballot, which was confirmed for them by the apparent success of black enfranchisement. That success, however, was more symbolic than practical. The Crusaders needed immediate practical results—closing retail liquor outlets to stop the rising tide of alcohol use. For them, the most relevant example was the earlier attempts at prohibition, in which the use of state power proved futile. Because of these disagreements over the use of the law, not because they differed over women's right of access to the public sphere, Crusaders and suffragists traveled separate paths toward protecting the interests of women.

The contradiction between the alternative to familial roles that activity in the public sphere offered and the exclusion of women from such activity was particularly sharp with respect to civil government. In seventeenth-century New England, citizenship was justified on the basis of familial position; the freeholder was at once the head of the household and a citizen. By contrast, nineteenth-century citizenship was posed as a direct relationship between the individual and his government. In other words, patriarchy was no longer the *official* basis of civil government in modern industrial democracy. However, in reality only men were permitted to become citizens. The exclusion of women from participation in political life in the early nineteenth century was so absolute and unchallenged that it did not require explicit proscription. It was simply assumed that political "persons" were male. The U.S. Constitution did not specify the sex of citizens until the Fourteenth Amendment was ratified in 1869, after women had begun actively to demand the vote. Prior to that, the equation between "male" and "person," the term used in the Constitution was implicit. The same by the way was true of the founding charter of the American Anti-Slavery Society. Written in 1833, it defined the society's membership as "persons," but for six years admitted only men into that category.

The doctrine of separate sexual spheres was supreme in the nineteenth century and even suffragists were unable to challenge certain basic aspects of it. Most notably, they accepted the particular suitability of women to domestic activities and therefore their special responsibility for the private sphere, and did not project a reorganization of the division of labor within the home. Antoinette Brown Blackwell, pioneer suffragist and minister, asserted, "The paramount social duties of women are household duties, avocations arising from their relations as wives and mothers. . . . The work nearest and dearest before the eyes of average womanhood is work within family boundaries—work within a sphere which men cannot enter." No suffragist of whom I am aware, including the otherwise iconoclastic Elizabeth Cady Stanton, seriously suggested that men take equal responsibilities with women for domestic activities. "Sharing housework" may be a more uniquely twentieth-century feminist demand than "smashing monogamy." To nineteenth-century feminists, domestic activities seemed as "naturally" female as childbearing, and as little subject to social manipulation.

Demanding a Voice in the Public Sphere

Although suffragists accepted the peculiarly feminine character of the private sphere, their demand for the vote challenged the male monopoly on the public arena. This is what gave suffragism much of its feminist meaning. Suffragists accepted women's "special responsibility" for domestic activity, but refused to concede that it prohibited them from participation in the public sphere. Moreover, unlike the demand that women be admitted to trades, professions, and education, the demand for citizenship applied to all women and it applied to them all of the time—to the housewife as much as to the single, self-supporting woman. By demanding a permanent, public role for all women, suffragists began to demolish the absolute, sexually defined barrier marking the public world of men off from the private world of women. Even though they did not develop a critical analysis of domestic life, the dialectical relationship between public and private spheres transformed their demand for admission to the public sphere into a basic challenge to the entire sexual structure. Thus, although she never criticized women's role in the family, Stanton was still able to write: "One may as well talk of separate spheres for the two ends of the magnet as for man and woman; they may have separate duties in the same sphere, but their true place is together everywhere."

Suffragists' demand for a permanent, public role for all women allowed them to project a vision of female experience and action that went beyond the family and the subordination of women which the family upheld. Citizenship represented a relationship to the larger society that was entirely and explicitly outside the boundaries of women's familial relations. As citizens and voters, women would participate directly in society as individuals, not indirectly through their subordinate positions as wives and mothers. Mary Putnam Jacobi identified this as the revolutionary core of suffragism. The American state, she explained, is based on "individual cells," not households. She went on: "Confessedly, in embracing in this conception of women, we do introduce a change which, though in itself purely ideal, underlies all the practical issues now in dispute. In this essentially modern conception, women also are brought into direct relations with the State, independent of their 'mate' or 'brood.'" Without directly attacking women's position within the private sphere, suffragists touched the nerve of women's subordinate status by contending that women might be something other than wives and mothers. "Womanhood is the great fact in her life," Stanton was fond of saying; "wifehood and motherhood are but incidental relations."

The Key to Women's Liberation

On one level, the logic behind the demand for woman suffrage in a country professing republican principles is obvious, and suffragists made liberal use of the tradition and rhetoric of the Revolution. Yet this is not sufficient to explain why suffrage became the core of a *feminist* program, why enfranchisement was perceived as the key to female liberation. I hypothesize that because enfranchisement involved a way for women to relate to society independent of their familial relations, it was the key demand of nineteenth-century feminists. It was the cornerstone of a social movement that did not simply catalogue and protest women's wrongs in the existing sexual order, but revealed the possibility of an alternate sexual order. Unlike the tradition of female protest, from the moral reformers of the 1830s to the temperance women of the 1880s, which was based in the private sphere and sought to reinterpret women's place within it, suffragism focused squarely on the public sphere.

In part, the feminist, liberating promise of enfranchisement rested on the concrete power that suffragists expected to obtain with the vote. Suffragists expected women to use the ballot to protect themselves and to impose their viewpoint on political issues. They anticipated that by strategic use of their political power women would break open new occupations, raise the level of their wage scales to that of men, win strikes, and force reforms in marriage and family law in order to protect themselves from sexual abuse, the loss of their children, and the unchecked tyranny of their husbands. The demand for suffrage drew together protest against all these abuses in a single demand for the right to shape the social order by way of the public sphere. No longer content either with maternal influence over the future voter's character or an endless series of petitions from women to law makers, suffragists proposed that women participate directly in the political decisions that affected their lives. "Like all disfranchised classes, they began by asking to have certain wrongs redressed," Stanton wrote. But suffragism went beyond what she called "special grievances" to give women's protest "a larger scope."

In evaluating suffragists' expectations of the power that the vote would bring women, it is important to keep in mind the structure of political power in the nineteenth century. Political decisions were less centralized in the federal government and more significant at the local level than they are now. Herbert Gutman's analysis of the assistance which local politicians gave labor activists in nineteenth-century Paterson, New Jersey, suggests that Susan B. Anthony's prediction that woman suffrage would win women's strikes had some basis in reality.

Even granted the greater power of the individual voter over political decisions that would affect her or his life, suffragists did not understand the ballot as merely a weapon with which to protect their interests in the political process. They also expected enfranchisement to transform woman's consciousness, to reanchor her self-image, not in the subordination of her familial role, but in the individuality and self-determination that they saw in citizenship. This was a particularly important aspect of the political thought of Elizabeth Cady Stanton, the chief ideologue of nineteenth-century suffragism. It is developed most fully in "Solitude of Self," the speech she thought her best. She wrote there: "Nothing strengthens the judgment and quickens the conscience like individual responsibility. Nothing adds such dignity to character as the recognition of one's self-sovereignty." Elsewhere, she wrote that, from the "higher stand-point" of enfranchisement, woman would become sensitive to the daily indignities which, without due appreciation for her own individuality, she ignored and accepted. She developed the theme of the impact of enfranchisement on women's self-concept most fully in a speech simply titled, "Self-Government the Best Means of Self-Development."

Given the impact on consciousness that suffragists expected from the vote, they generally refused to redirect their efforts toward such partial enfranchisements as municipal or school suffrage. Although these limited suffrages would give women certain political powers, they were suffrages designed especially for women and justified on the basis of women's maternal responsibilities. Their achievement would not necessarily prove women's right to full and equal participation in the public sphere. Suffragists did not simply want political power; they wanted to be citizens, to stand in the same relation to civil government as men did. As a result, it was primarily clubwomen who worked for school and municipal suffrage, while those who identified themselves as suffragists continued to concentrate on the admission of women to full citizenship.

Antisuffragists Feared a Revolutionary Change

An important index to the nature and degree of suffragism's challenge to the nineteenth-century sexual order was the kind and amount of opposition that it inspired. Antisuffragists focused on the family, its position *vis-à-vis* the state, and the revolutionary impact of female citizenship on that relation. In response to suffragists' demand that modern democracy include women, antisuffragists tried to reinstate a patriarchal theory of society and the state. The family, they contended, was the virtual, if not the official unit of civil government, and men represented and protected the women of their families in political affairs. Antisuffragists regularly charged that the enfranchisement of women would revolutionize the relations of the sexes and, in turn, the character and structure of the home and women's role within it. The 1867 New York Constitutional Convention expressed this fear for the future of the family when it rejected suffrage because it was an innovation "so revolutionary and sweeping, so openly at war with a distribution of duties and functions between the sexes as venerable and pervading as government itself, and involving transformations so radical in social and domestic life."

Most suffragists were much more modest about the implications of enfranchisement for women's position within the family. They expected reform of family law, particularly of the marriage contract, and the abolition of such inequities as the husband's legal right to his wife's sexual services. They also anticipated that the transformation in woman's consciousness which enfranchisement would bring would improve the quality of family relations, particularly between wife and husband. Stanton argued that once women were enfranchised they would demand that democracy be the law of the family, as well as of the state. Her comment suggests that, by introducing women into a form of social organization not based on patriarchal structures, she expected enfranchisement to permit women a much more critical perspective on the family itself. However, suffragists regularly denied the antisuffragists' charge that woman suffrage meant a revolution in the family. Most would have agreed with Jacobi that, if antisuffragists wanted to argue that familial bonds were mere "political contrivances," requiring the disfranchisement of women to sustain them, suffragists had considerably more faith in the family as a "natural institution," able to survive women's entry into the public sphere.

Suffragists worked hard to attract large numbers of women to the demand for the vote. They went beyond the methods of agitational propaganda which they had learned as abolitionists, and beyond the skills of lobbying which they had developed during Radical Reconstruction, to become organizers. As suffragists' efforts at outreach intensified, the family-bound realities of most women's lives forced more and more domestic imagery into their rhetoric and their arguments. Yet suffrage remained a distinctly minority movement in the nineteenth century. The very thing that made suffragism the most radical aspect of nineteenth-century feminism—its focus on the public sphere and on a nonfamilial role for women—was the cause of its failure to establish a mass base. It was not that nineteenth-century women were content, or had no grievances, but that they understood their grievances in the context of the private sphere. The lives of most nineteenth-century women were overwhelmingly limited to the private realities of wifehood and motherhood, and they experienced their discontent in the context of those relations. The enormous success of the Women's Christian Temperance Union, particularly as contrasted with the nineteenth-century suffrage movement, indicates the capacity for protest and activism among nineteenth-century women, and the fact that this mass feminism was based in the private sphere. The WCTU commanded an army in the nineteenth century, while woman suffrage remained a guerrilla force.

Unlike the woman suffrage movement, the WCTU took as its starting point woman's position within the home; it catalogued the abuses she suffered there and it proposed reforms necessary to ameliorate her domestic situation. As the WCTU developed, its concerns went beyond the family to include the quality of community life, but its standard for nonfamilial relations remained the family and the moral values women had developed within it. The WCTU spoke to women in the language of their domestic realities, and they joined in the 1870s and 1880s in enormous numbers. Anchored in the private realm, the WCTU became the mass movement that nineteenth-century suffragism could not.

The WCTU's program reflected the same social reality that lay beyond suffragism—that the family was losing its central place in social organization to nondomestic institutions, from the saloon to the school to the legislature, and that woman's social power was accordingly weakened. Yet the WCTU, Luddite-like, defended the family and women's traditional but fast-fading authority within it. Its mottos reflected this defensive goal: "For God and Home and Native Land"; "Home Protection." In 1883, the WCTU formally endorsed the demand for female enfranchisement, but justified its action as necessary to protect the home and women within it, thus retaining its family-based analysis and its defensive character. The first resolutions introduced by Frances Willard in support of suffrage asked for the vote for women in their roles as wives and mothers, to enable them to protect their homes from the influence of the saloon. This was the woman suffrage movement's approach to female oppression and the problem of spheres stood on its head—women entering the public arena to protect the primacy of the private sphere, and women's position within it. Yet, the very fact that the WCTU had to come to terms with suffrage and eventually supported it indicates that the woman suffrage movement had succeeded in becoming the defining focus of nineteenth-century feminism, with respect to which all organized female protest had to orient itself. Even though the WCTU organized and commanded the forces, the woman suffrage movement had defined the territory.

Changes in Women's Lives

Suffrage became a mass movement in the twentieth century under quite different conditions, when women's position *vis-à-vis* the public and private spheres had shifted considerably. Despite, or perhaps because of, the home-based ideology with which they operated, the WCTU, women's clubs, and other branches of nineteenth-century feminism had introduced significant numbers of women to extradomestic concerns. Charlotte Perkins Gilman noted the change among women in 1903: "The socialising of this hitherto subsocial, wholly domestic class, is a marked and marvellous event, now taking place with astonishing rapidity." Similarly, Susan B. Anthony commented at the 1888 International Council of Women: "Forty years ago women had no place anywhere except in their homes, no pecuniary independence, no purpose in life save that which came through marriage. . . . [I]n later years the way has been opened to every avenue of industry—to every profession. . . . What is true in the world of work is true in education, is true everywhere." At the point that it could attract a mass base, suffragism no longer opened up such revolutionary vistas for women; they were already operating in the public world of work and politics. The scope and meaning of twentieth-century suffragism requires its own analysis, but the achievement of nineteenth-century suffragists was that they identified, however haltingly, a fundamental transformation of the family and the new possibilities for women's emancipation that this revealed.

For Discussion

Chapter One

1. In what way does Abigail Smith Adams's argument in her letter to John Adams differ from that contained in her letter to Mercy Otis Warren? What differences can you find in the arguments John Adams employs in his letter to Abigail Smith Adams and in his letter to James Sullivan? What reasons might account for these differences, in your opinion?

2. What examples of appeals to divine authority do you find in the viewpoints of Catharine E. Beecher and Angelina Emily Grimké? In what ways do these religious references help or hinder their arguments?

3. In the view of Mrs. A.J. Graves, what positive benefits do separate spheres provide to women and society? What misfortunes does she warn will result if women leave their sphere? In Margaret Fuller's opinion, what problems result from women's limitations? What benefits does Fuller believe will occur if women leave the domestic sphere? To what degree do you think each author's assessment accurately reflects reality and to what degree is each author idealizing or exaggerating women's situations? Explain.

Chapter Two

1. What reasons does Henry W. Bellows provide to support his contention that both sexes have equally contributed to discrimination against women? What examples does William Lloyd Garrison use to argue that men bear the greater responsibility for women's oppression? Does the fact that both authors are men affect your assessment of their viewpoints? If so, how?

2. How would alterations in women's dress styles significantly affect women's rights and improve women's lives, according to Gerrit Smith? How would changes in women's status allow women more freedom in dress, in the opinion of Frances D. Gage? On what points, if any, do Garrison and Gage agree about the connection between women's attire and women's rights?

3. List the reforms that Elizabeth Cady Stanton suggests to improve women's lot in marriage. List the marriage reforms proposed by Antoinette Brown Blackwell. Which reforms seem more reasonable or workable to you? Why?

4. Do you feel that including women in the proposed Fifteenth Amendment would have been appropriate, or do you believe such inclusion would have delayed or prevented passage of the amendment? Use examples from the viewpoints of Wendell Phillips and Parker Pillsbury to defend your answer.

Chapter Three

1. Edward H. Clarke and Elizabeth Stuart Phelps both agree that young women often become invalids after finishing college, but they differ on the cause of the problem. What supporting facts do Clarke and Phelps use to bolster their positions? How much of each author's argument is based on conjecture?

2. Julia Ward Howe lists twelve reasons why women should be granted suffrage. Which of these reasons do you find most compelling, and which the least? Explain your answer. Which of Howe's reasons does Emily P. Bissell refute in her viewpoint? What additional antisuffrage arguments does Bissell present, if any?

3. How does Theodore Roosevelt's rhetorical style differ from that of Margaret Sanger? In your opinion, which of the two authors bases his or her argument more on appeals to emotion? Which bases his or her reasoning more on facts? Explain.

Chapter Four

1. Jennifer Colton provides a balance sheet of advantages and disadvantages of leaving her job. How many entries under Colton's "Lost" column are actually arguments in favor of being a full-time housewife? Does Betty Friedan provide any additional disadvantages to being a full-time housewife that Colton does not list? If so, what are they? Comparing the two viewpoints, do you think the advantages of being a full-time housewife and mother are greater or less than the advantages of working outside the home? Why?

2. Marya Mannes makes several points in favor of legalizing abortion. Which of her points pertain to women's rights and which pertain to separate issues? In what situations, if any, does Robert F. Drinan believe that a woman's rights supersede those of a fetus? Do Mannes and Drinan agree on any case in which legal abortion is permissible? If so, in which case? Do they agree on any situations in which abortion should not be allowed? If so, explain the situations.

3. What is the Radicalesbians' definition of "the woman-identified woman"? With which parts of this definition does Anne Koedt take issue? Why?

4. According to Margaret M. Heckler how would the Equal Rights Amendment positively affect working women? In the opinion of Phyllis Schlafly, how would passage of the Equal Rights Amendment adversely affect working women? Which author's argument do you find more convincing? Explain your reasoning.

Chapter Five

1. Ellen Carol DuBois argues that it is misleading to assess the radicalness of the suffragists by today's standards. Do you agree or disagree? Why?

2. Historians still debate the impact of the suffrage movement and the attainment of women's suffrage. On which results do William L. O'Neill and Ellen Carol DuBois agree, if any?

General Questions

1. Based on the viewpoints in this book, list some of the successes and some of the failures of the women's rights movement. Do you believe that the women's rights movement has largely succeeded or failed? Explain. How important do you think these successes or failures have been to the lives of modern Americans, if at all?

2. Which common themes are prevalent in the viewpoints that defend feminist causes? Which are prevalent in the viewpoints that defend traditional female roles? Are any of these arguments still used in the present day? If so, which ones? Which have lost their power to convince, if any?

Chronology

1647	Margaret Brent appears before the Maryland Assembly to request the right to vote in her official capacity as the governor's executrix. Her petition is denied.
1775	Thomas Paine publishes the first article supporting women's rights in America.
1776	Abigail Smith Adams urges her husband, John Adams, to help secure new laws to curb the unlimited power of husbands over wives.
1790	Judith Sargent Murray publishes "On the Equality of the Sexes."
1792	British author Mary Wollstonecraft publishes *A Vindication of the Rights of Women*, which is widely read in American intellectual circles.
1798	Charles B. Brown publishes *Alcuin*, a fictional work that advocates women's rights.
1807	New Jersey withdraws the right of women to vote. Women who met the state's property-owning qualifications had been voting since 1787.
1818	Hannah Mather Crocker publishes *Observations on the Real Rights of Women*.
1821	Emma Willard opens the Troy Female Seminary, which offers a more challenging academic curriculum than other schools for women.
	Connecticut becomes the first state to pass a law against abortion.
1828	Scottish immigrant Frances Wright becomes the first woman in America to lecture publicly to large audiences of men and women.
1832	Maria Stewart becomes the first American-born woman to publicly address mixed audiences.
1833	Oberlin College, the first American college to admit women, is founded.
1834–1848	New York feminists campaign for passage of the state's Married Woman's Property Act, which would give married women more control over their own property.
1838	Angelina Emily Grimké and Sarah Grimké are criticized for giving public lectures to mixed audiences.

June 12–20, 1840	At the World Anti-Slavery Convention in London, women delegates are segregated and not allowed to address the convention. Lucretia Mott and Elizabeth Cady Stanton meet at the convention and vow to work for women's rights.
1841	Alabama passes the first state law to permit abortions to save the life of the mother.
1848	The New York Married Woman's Property Act is passed.
July 19–20, 1848	The first Woman's Rights Convention—organized by Elizabeth Cady Stanton, Lucretia Mott, Maria Coffin Wright, Jane Hunt, and Mary Ann McClintock—is held in Seneca Falls, New York. Sixty-eight women and thirty-two men sign the Declaration of Sentiments.
1849	Elizabeth Blackwell becomes the first woman to receive a medical degree from an American college.
October 23–24, 1850	The First National Woman's Rights Convention is held in Worcester, Massachusetts.
1851	Mary Sharp College becomes the first women's college to require classical languages and a rigorous four-year course of study.
March 1851	Susan B. Anthony and Elizabeth Cady Stanton meet; over the next few years, Stanton persuades Anthony to work for women's rights.
1852	Catharine Beecher founds the American Women's Education Association as part of her campaign to transform teaching into a woman's profession.
1853	Paulina Wright Davis begins publication of the *Una*, the first newspaper of the women's rights movement.
	Antoinette Brown Blackwell becomes the first woman to be ordained in a mainstream religious denomination.
1859	The Indiana state legislature passes a liberalized divorce reform bill.
1865–1887	Thirty-three states and the District of Columbia pass laws giving married women control of their own wages and earnings.
1866	The American Equal Rights Association is formed, with the purpose of working for suffrage for blacks and women.
	Elizabeth Cady Stanton becomes the first woman candidate for Congress.
1867	Kansas becomes the first state to vote on women's suffrage; the referendum is defeated.

1868	Susan B. Anthony, Elizabeth Cady Stanton, and Parker Pillsbury begin publication of the *Revolution*, a feminist periodical.
	The Working Woman's Association is established.
	A federal women's suffrage amendment is first introduced in Congress.
1869	The Roman Catholic Church issues its first pronouncement against abortion.
February 26, 1869	Congress approves the Fifteenth Amendment, which grants black men the right to vote but excludes women.
May 1869	Elizabeth Cady Stanton and Susan B. Anthony establish the National Woman Suffrage Association to work for a national suffrage amendment.
November 1869	Lucy Stone and Henry Blackwell found the American Woman Suffrage Association to obtain suffrage through the amendment of individual state constitutions.
December 10, 1869	The Wyoming Territory becomes the first to grant women the right to vote.
1870	The Utah Territory grants women the right to vote.
March 30, 1870	The Fifteenth Amendment is ratified.
1871	The Anti-Suffrage Party is founded.
January 11, 1871	Victoria Woodhull addresses the House Judiciary Committee, arguing that the Fourteenth Amendment gives women the right to vote.
1872	Victoria Woodhull becomes the first woman to run for president of the United States.
November 28, 1872	Susan B. Anthony is arrested for voting. She subsequently stands trial and is fined $100, which she refuses to pay.
1873	Congress passes the antiobscenity Comstock Law, effectively banning most birth control information from the U. S. mails.
	In *Bradwell v. Illinois*, the U.S. Supreme Court upholds an Illinois state law that prohibits female lawyers from practicing in state courts.
1874	In *Minor v. Happersett*, the U.S. Supreme Court rules that the denial of suffrage to women is constitutional and that the Fourteenth Amendment does not pertain to women.
July 4, 1876	Susan B. Anthony and Matilda Joslyn Gage disrupt the official Centennial program at Independence Hall in Philadelphia in order to present their "Declaration of Rights for Women" to the acting U.S. vice president, Thomas W. Ferry.

1887	The *True Woman*, the first periodical devoted to the antisuffrage cause, begins publication.
1890	The National Woman Suffrage Association and the American Woman Suffrage Association merge to form the National American Woman Suffrage Association. The organization commits itself to working for suffrage state by state.
July 23, 1890	Wyoming is admitted to the Union, thus becoming the first state allowing women's suffrage.
1893	Colorado grants women the vote.
1896	The National Association of Colored Women is established.
	Idaho grants women suffrage.
1907	Harriot Stanton Blatch forms the Equality League of Self-Supporting Women (later the Women's Political Union).
1908	In *Muller v. Oregon*, the Supreme Court upholds Oregon's law mandating a ten-hour maximum workday for women.
1910	The first women's suffrage parade is held in New York City.
	Washington grants women the franchise.
1911	California gives women the vote.
	The National Association Opposed to Woman Suffrage is formed. The organization publishes the *Woman's Protest*, an antisuffrage journal.
1912	Oregon, Kansas, and Arizona grant women the vote.
1913	Alice Paul establishes the National Women's Party to press for a federal suffrage amendment.
	The Alaska Territory gives women suffrage.
1914	Montana and Nevada grant women the vote.
1916	Margaret Sanger opens the nation's first birth control clinic; shortly thereafter she is arrested and jailed for doing so.
	Representative Jeanette Rankin of Montana becomes the first woman to be elected to the U.S. Congress.
1917	Margaret Sanger founds the National Birth Control League.
	New York gives women the right to vote.
1918	Michigan, South Dakota, and Oklahoma grant women the vote.
1919	The National Federation of Business and Professional Women's Clubs is founded.

1920	Congress establishes the Federal Woman's Bureau, an agency within the Department of Labor, to collect information and advocate government action on behalf of wage-earning women.
February 14, 1920	The National American Woman Suffrage Association renames itself the League of Women Voters.
August 26, 1920	The Nineteenth Amendment is signed into law, guaranteeing American women the right to vote.
1923	The Equal Rights Amendment is first introduced in Congress.
1933	Frances Perkins becomes the first woman cabinet member when President-elect Franklin D. Roosevelt chooses her to be secretary of labor.
1942	Planned Parenthood is created out of the Birth Control Federation of America.
1947	Marynia Farnham and Ferdinand Lundberg publish *The Modern Woman: The Lost Sex*, which argues that women should devote themselves to being homemakers and mothers.
1952	The Democratic Party abolishes its Women's Division.
1955	The Daughters of Bilitis, a national lesbian organization, is founded in San Francisco.
1960	The Food and Drug Administration approves the birth control pill.
1961	President John F. Kennedy appoints the Presidential Commission on the Status of Women, chaired by Eleanor Roosevelt.
1963	Betty Friedan publishes *The Feminine Mystique*.
	Congress passes the Equal Pay Act, making it illegal to set different pay scales for men and women who perform the same job.
1964	Congress passes the Civil Rights Act of 1964; the act includes Title VII, which forbids discrimination on the basis of sex.
1965	The Johnson administration creates the Equal Employment Opportunity Commission.
1966	The National Organization for Women (NOW) is founded.
1968	The Women's Equity Action League is established.
1969	Kate Millet publishes *Sexual Politics*.
	Shirley Chisholm becomes the first black woman elected to the U.S. Congress.
1970	The Nixon administration announces that henceforth federal contracts would contain a clause mandating the employment of a certain quota of women.

August 26, 1970	The Women's Strike for Equality, held on the fiftieth anniversary of the passage of the Nineteenth Amendment, becomes the largest demonstration ever held for women's rights.
1971	Betty Friedan, Bella Abzug, and Shirley Chisholm found the National Women's Political Caucus.
	Gloria Steinem begins publication of *Ms.* magazine.
1972	Phyllis Schlafly founds Stop ERA, an organization dedicated to blocking passage of the Equal Rights Amendment.
	Congresswoman Shirley Chisholm becomes the first black woman to run for president.
	Congress passes the Higher Education Act; the act includes Title IX, which bans discrimination in education on the basis of sex.
March 22, 1972	Congress approves the Equal Rights Amendment; by the end of the year twenty-two of the necessary thirty-five states have ratified it.
1973	The National Black Feminist Organization is founded.
January 22, 1973	The U.S. Supreme Court legalizes abortion in *Roe v. Wade*.
1974	The Coalition of Labor Union Women is organized.
1976	Congress prohibits the use of federal funds for abortions.
September 25, 1981	Sandra Day O'Connor is sworn in as the first female Supreme Court justice.
1982	The Equal Rights Amendment, short of ratification by three states, is withdrawn.

Annotated Bibliography

Historical Studies

Lois W. Banner. *Women in Modern America: A Brief History.* New York: Harcourt, Brace, Jovanovich, 1974. A concise and very readable general history.

Beverly Beeton. *Women Vote in the West: The Woman Suffrage Movement, 1869–1896.* New York: Garland Publications, 1986. A history of the state-by-state campaign to win suffrage in the western United States.

Anne M. Benjamin. *A History of the Anti-Suffrage Movement in the United States from 1895 to 1920: Women Against Equality.* Lewiston, NY: Edwin Mellen Press, 1991. Examines the rise of a movement against women's suffrage and its connections to the liquor industry.

Carol Ruth Berkin and Mary Beth Norton, eds. *Women of America: A History.* Boston: Houghton Mifflin, 1979. An anthology of historiographical articles (and a few primary documents) covering selected topics in women's history.

Ruth Bordin. *Woman and Temperance: The Quest for Power and Liberty, 1873–1900.* Philadelphia: Temple University Press, 1981. A history of the Women's Christian Temperance Union (WCTU) that examines the links between the temperance movement and women's rights.

Jane Jerome Camhi. *Women Against Women: American Anti-Suffragism, 1880–1920.* Brooklyn: Carlson Publishing, 1994. This comprehensive survey of nationwide antisuffrage women's organizations concentrates on the movement's attempt to block ratification of the Nineteenth Amendment.

William Chafe. *The American Woman: Her Changing Social, Economic, and Political Roles, 1920–1970.* New York: Oxford University Press, 1972. A thorough overview of events and trends in women's rights following the ratification of the Nineteenth Amendment.

Nancy F. Cott. *The Bonds of Womanhood: "Woman's Sphere" in New England, 1780–1835.* New Haven, CT: Yale University Press, 1977. This study of New England women's lives and experiences argues that the philosophy of woman's sphere contributed to a sense of sisterhood essential to the birth of the women's movement.

Nancy F. Cott. *The Grounding of Modern Feminism.* New Haven, CT: Yale University Press, 1987. A history of women's organizations between

1910 and 1930, specifically concentrating on feminist issues other than suffrage.

Nancy F. Cott, ed. *History of Women in the United States: Historical Articles on Women's Lives and Activities.* 20 vols. New York: K.G. Saur, 1992. An extensive anthology of definitive articles on various aspects of women's history.

Carl Degler. *At Odds: Women and the Family in America from the Revolution to the Present.* New York: Oxford University Press, 1980. A voluminous social history of women with an emphasis on the concerns of nineteenth-century feminism.

John Demos. *A Little Commonwealth: Family Life in Plymouth Colony.* New York: Oxford University Press, 1970. A study of Puritan New England women, families, and communities that makes ingenious use of evidence from the material culture.

Thomas Dublin. *Women at Work: The Transformation of Work and Community in Lowell, Massachusetts, 1826–1860.* New York: Columbia University Press, 1979. Examines the impact of industrialization on working women, in particular the factory workers of the Lowell textile mills.

Ellen Carol DuBois. *Feminism and Suffrage: The Emergence of an Independent Women's Movement in America, 1848–1869.* Ithaca, NY: Cornell University Press, 1978. An analysis of the early women's suffrage movement focusing on the post–Civil War break between the feminists and the abolition movement.

Barbara Leslie Epstein. *The Politics of Domesticity: Women, Evangelism, and Temperance in Nineteenth Century America.* Middleton, CT: Wesleyan University Press, 1981. An account of the development of a distinct women's culture that took root among New England and Midwestern middle-class women.

Sara Evans. *Personal Politics: The Roots of Women's Liberation in the Civil Rights Movement and the New Left.* New York: Knopf, 1979. Traces the beginnings of the 1960s women's liberation movement from the earlier civil rights and radical New Left movements.

Eleanor Flexner. *Century of Struggle: The Woman's Rights Movement in the United States.* Cambridge, MA: Harvard University Press, Belknap Press, 1959. A groundbreaking and still valuable history of the century-long campaign for women's suffrage.

Philip S. Foner. *Women and the American Labor Movement: From Colonial Times to the Eve of World War I.* New York: Free Press, 1979. Traces the efforts of major national unions to organize working women, culminating with the creation of the Women's Trade Union League.

Linda G. Ford. *Iron-Jawed Angels: The Suffrage Militancy of the National Woman's Party, 1912–1920.* Lanham, MD: University Press of America, 1991. A fascinating account of the radical and controversial tactics of suffragist Alice Paul and her National Woman's Party.

David J. Garrow. *Liberty and Sexuality: The Right to Privacy and the Making of* Roe v. Wade. New York: Macmillan, 1994. A comprehensive history of the background of the U.S. Supreme Court's *Roe v. Wade* abortion rights decision as well as a history of the decision itself.

Rochelle Gatlin. *American Women Since 1945.* Jackson: University Press of Mississippi, 1987. A social, political, and cultural overview of the history of women since World War II.

Paula Giddings. *When and Where I Enter: The Impact of Black Women on Race and Sex in America.* New York: William Morrow, 1984. This in-depth exploration of the history of black women in America includes their involvement in the suffrage campaign and their attempts to deal with racism within the women's rights movement.

Linda Gordon. *Woman's Body: Woman's Right: A Social History of Birth Control in America.* New York: Grossman, 1976. A pioneering study, especially valuable for its examination of Margaret Sanger and the struggle for birth control rights.

Susan M. Hartmann. *The Home Front and Beyond: American Women in the 1940s.* Boston: Twayne, 1982. A history of working women during World War II and their impact, both societal and individual, on the immediate postwar period.

Delores Hayden. *The Grand Domestic Revolution.* Cambridge, MA: MIT Press, 1981. A history of radical feminist ideas for rearranging social and family life in the interests of sexual equality.

Joan Hoff-Wilson. *Law, Gender, and Injustice: A Legal History of U.S. Women.* New York: New York University Press, 1991. Takes an extensive look at the laws that have affected American women and argues that women have yet to achieve full legal equality in the United States.

Maureen Honey. *Creating Rosie the Riveter: Class, Gender, and Propaganda During World War II.* Amherst: University of Massachusetts Press, 1984. An examination of the attempts by the federal government and popular culture to redefine women's roles during the war effort and then to convince women to leave the workforce after the war ended.

Thomas J. Jablonsky. *The Home, Heaven, and Mother Party: Female Anti-Suffragists in the United States, 1868–1920.* Brooklyn: Carlson Publishing, 1994. Focuses on the organization history of the antisuffrage movement and disproves the theory that the antisuffragists were merely pawns of male interest groups.

Jacqueline Jones. *Labor of Love, Labor of Sorrow: Black Women, Work, and the Family from Slavery to the Present.* New York: BasicBooks, 1994. A comprehensive portrait of the lives of working black women from slavery to the late twentieth century, drawing on both demographic evidence and personal accounts.

Eugenia Kaledin. *Mothers and More: American Women in the 1950s.* Boston: Twayne, 1984. A thorough survey of women's lives and concerns during a time when the women's rights movement had lost much of its impetus.

Linda K. Kerber. *Women of the Republic: Intellect and Ideology in Revolutionary America*. Chapel Hill: University of North Carolina Press, 1980. An insightful history of the political, legal, and social status of women in the United States during and after the American Revolution.

Linda K. Kerber and Jane DeHart Matthews, eds. *Women's America: Refocusing the Past*. New York: Oxford University Press, 1982. An anthology that contains an effective mixture of historiographical articles and primary documents.

Linda K. Kerber, Alice Kessler-Harris, and Kathryn Kish Sklar, eds. *U.S. History as Women's History: New Feminist Essays*. Chapel Hill: University of North Carolina Press, 1995. A collection of scholarly essays on women's history and the women's rights movement in the United States.

Alice Kessler-Harris. *Out to Work: A History of Wage-Earning Women in the United States*. New York: Oxford University Press, 1982. This study of the relationship between working women and family life argues that most women have entered the labor force because of economic need rather than because of feminist ideals.

Aileen S. Kraditor. *The Ideas of the Women's Suffrage Movement, 1890–1920*. New York: Columbia University Press, 1965. An overview of the suffrage movement that emphasizes its middle-class, essentially bourgeois center.

William Leach. *True Love and Perfect Union: The Feminist Reform of Sex and Society*. New York: Basic Books, 1980. This study of the interrelationships between feminism and other social movements focuses on the years between 1850 and 1880.

J. Stanley Lemons. *The Woman Citizen: Social Feminism in the 1920s*. Urbana: University of Illinois Press, 1973. Argues that the women's rights movement did not die with the ratification of the suffrage amendment and examines the activities of feminists between the Progressive Era and the New Deal.

Gerda Lerner. *The Majority Finds Its Past: Placing Women in History*. New York: Oxford University Press, 1979. A collection of historiographical essays by one of the preeminent scholars of women's history.

Christine A. Lunardini. *From Equal Suffrage to Equal Rights: Alice Paul and the National Woman's Party, 1910–1928*. New York: New York University Press, 1986. Examines the final push to achieving passage of the Nineteenth Amendment and the first campaign for the Equal Rights Amendment.

Joanne Meyerowitz, ed. *Not June Cleaver: Women and Gender in Postwar America, 1945–1960*. Philadelphia: Temple University Press, 1994. An important anthology of scholarly articles and essays pertaining to the social history of women following World War II.

Ruth Milkman. *Gender at Work: The Dynamics of Job Segregation by Sex During World War II*. Urbana: University of Illinois Press, 1987. Examines patterns of sex segregation in the workplace, particularly in the automotive and electrical manufacturing industries, during a time when there was an influx of women workers.

Ruth Milkman, ed. *Women, Work, and Protest: A Century of U.S. Women's Labor History*. New York: Routledge and Kegan Paul, 1985. Scholarly essays on such topics as women's occupations, organizing efforts, and strikes.

James C. Mohr. *Abortion in America: The Origins and Evolution of National Policy, 1800–1900*. New York: Oxford University Press, 1978. An overview of abortion laws of the nineteenth century and the public's reaction to those laws.

Mary Beth Norton. *Liberty's Daughters: The Revolutionary Experience of American Women, 1750–1800*. Boston: Little, Brown, 1980. A history of the positive impact that the American Revolution had on the lives of American women.

William L. O'Neill. *Everyone Was Brave: A History of Feminism in America*. Chicago: Quadrangle Books, 1969. This history of the suffrage movement contends that the struggle for women's rights lost impetus after the ratification of the Nineteenth Amendment.

James Reed. *From Private Vice to Public Virtue: The Birth Control Movement and American Society Since 1830*. New York: Basic Books, 1978. An exhaustive investigation of the movement for birth control rights, especially the effects of such rights on women's lives.

Sheila M. Rothman. *Woman's Proper Place: A History of Changing Ideals and Practices, 1870 to the Present*. New York: Basic Books, 1978. A compelling survey of the changing attitudes about women's roles and the ways in which those attitudes have shaped women's experiences.

Leila J. Rupp and Verta Taylor. *Survival in the Doldrums: The American Women's Rights Movement, 1945 to the 1960s*. New York: Oxford University Press, 1987. A study of women's rights organizations from World War II through the 1960s, focusing on the roots of the modern feminist resurgence.

Marylynn Salmon. *Women and the Law of Property in Early America*. Chapel Hill: University of North Carolina Press, 1986. A detailed investigation of married women's legal rights, North and South, between 1750 and 1830.

Anne Firor Scott. *The Southern Lady: From Pedestal to Politics, 1830–1930*. Chicago: University of Chicago Press, 1970. An analysis of women's reform activities in the South that led to the formation of a prosuffrage constituency.

Carroll Smith-Rosenberg. *Disorderly Conduct: Visions of Gender in Victorian America*. New York: Knopf, 1985. A collection of articles and essays that examine the difference between women's roles and reality in the nineteenth century.

June Sochen. *Movers and Shakers: American Women Thinkers and Activists, 1900–1970*. New York: Quadrangle, 1973. Pays special attention to feminist writers and activists during the time between the ratification of the suffrage amendment and the beginning of the women's liberation movement.

Barbara Miller Solomon. *In the Company of Educated Women: A History of Women and Higher Education in America.* New Haven, CT: Yale University Press, 1985. A history of women's efforts to gain access to higher education and the relationship between education and feminism from the colonial era to the twentieth century.

Julia Cherry Spruill. *Women's Life and Work in the Southern Colonies.* Chapel Hill: University of North Carolina Press, 1938. The first comprehensive study of the daily life and status of women in southern colonial America.

Susan Strasser. *Never Done: A History of American Housework.* New York: Pantheon, 1982. A history of the relationship between housework, new technologies, and women's lives from the early nineteenth century to recent times.

Leslie Woodcock Tentler. *Wage-Earning Women: Industrial Work and Family Life in the United States, 1900–1930.* New York: Oxford University Press, 1979. This general study of working-class women argues that their work experiences often reinforced traditional sex roles.

Laurel Thatcher Ulrich. *Good Wives: Image and Reality in the Lives of Women In Northern New England, 1650–1750.* New York: Knopf, 1982. An examination of Puritan women's status and their contributions to the successful settling of the New England colonies.

Winifred D. Wandersee. *On the Move: American Women in the 1970s.* Boston: Twayne, 1988. This general survey of the women's liberation movement emphasizes such organizations as the National Organization for Women and explores the reasons for the concurrent backlash against feminism.

Winifred D. Wandersee. *Women's Work and Family Values, 1920–1940.* Cambridge, MA: Harvard University Press, 1981. An examination of the impact of the Great Depression on the lives of working women, their economic needs, and their ongoing commitment to family life.

Susan Ware. *Holding Their Own: American Women in the 1930s.* Boston: Twayne, 1982. A short volume covering women's issues and women's rights during the Great Depression.

Lynn Y. Weiner. *From Working Girl to Working Mother: The Female Labor Force in the United States, 1820–1980.* Chapel Hill: University of North Carolina Press, 1985. Explores enduring issues concerning working women, such as child care, equal pay, and society's reaction to women working outside the home.

Barbara Welter. *Dimity Convictions: The American Woman in the Nineteenth Century.* Athens: Ohio University Press, 1976. A diverse collection of essays on a variety of aspects of women's lives in the Victorian era.

Jean Fagan Yellin. *Women and Sisters: Antislavery Feminists in American*

Culture. New Haven, CT: Yale University Press, 1989. A study of the interconnections between the abolitionist movement and the women's rights movement, exploring the way in which abolitionism often led to feminism.

Primary Sources and Document Collections

Rosalyn Baxandall, Linda Gordon, and Susan Reverby, eds. *America's Working Women: A Documentary History—1600 to the Present*. New York: Norton, 1995. This collection includes documents from the colonial era to the late twentieth century, focusing specifically on working-class women.

Susan Groag Bell and Karen M. Offen, eds. *Women, the Family, and Freedom: The Debate in Documents*. Stanford, CA: Stanford University Press, 1983. An intriguing anthology that juxtaposes American writings concerning women's rights with contemporaneous English and European documents.

W. Elliot Brownlee and Mary M. Brownlee, eds. *Women in the American Economy: A Documentary History, 1675–1929*. New Haven, CT: Yale University Press, 1976. Provides a diverse selection of attitudes toward women's participation in the economy as workers, consumers, homemakers, and taxpayers.

Mari Jo Buhle and Paul Buhle, eds. *The Concise History of Woman Suffrage*. Urbana: University of Illinois Press, 1978. This abridgment of the multivolume *History of Woman Suffrage* includes many documents selected from the writings of Elizabeth Cady Stanton, Susan B. Anthony, and other leading feminists of the nineteenth century.

Karlyn Kohrs Campbell, ed. *Man Cannot Speak for Her*. Vol. 2, *Key Texts of the Early Feminists*. Westport, CT: Greenwood Press, 1989. A compilation of early feminist speeches and writings that emphasizes women's use of rhetoric to gain support for their cause.

Mary Cohart, ed. *Unsung Champions of Women*. Albuquerque: University of New Mexico Press, 1975. This sourcebook of primary documents concentrates on pre–twentieth century arguments for the equality of women.

Joanne Cooke, Charlotte Bunch-Weeks, and Robin Morgan, eds. *The New Women: A MOTIVE Anthology on Women's Liberation*. Indianapolis: Bobbs-Merrill, 1970. A collection of primary sources from the magazine *MOTIVE*, published during the early years of the women's liberation movement.

Nancy F. Cott, ed. *Root of Bitterness: Documents of the Social History of American Women*. New York: Dutton, 1972. This thorough collection of primary sources contains traditional and feminist views of women's lives from colonial times to the end of the nineteenth century.

Sylvia R. Frey and Marian J. Morton, eds. *New World, New Roles: A Documentary History of Women in Pre-Industrial America*. Westport, CT: Greenwood Press, 1986. A compilation of primary documents concerning women's experiences and rights from early colonial times to 1815.

Betty Friedan. *The Feminine Mystique.* New York: Dell, 1963. The manifesto of the modern feminist movement. Friedan particularly concentrates on the status of middle-class American women in the years following World War II.

Elizabeth Frost and Kathryn Cullen-DuPont, eds. *Women's Suffrage in America: An Eyewitness History.* New York: Facts On File, 1992. An extensive sourcebook of primary documents that focuses on women's struggle for suffrage from 1800 to the passage of the Nineteenth Amendment.

Michael S. Kimmel and Thomas E. Mosmiller, eds. *Against the Tide: Profeminist Men in the United States, 1776–1990.* Boston: Beacon Press, 1992. Unique primary source collection containing the writings and speeches of men who advocated women's rights.

Aileen S. Kraditor, ed. *Up from the Pedestal: Selected Writings in the History of American Feminism.* Chicago: Quadrangle, 1968. A comprehensive anthology of feminist and antifeminist writings from the 1600s to the 1960s.

Winston E. Langley and Vivian C. Fox, eds. *Women's Rights in the United States: A Documentary History.* Westport, CT: Greenwood Press, 1994. This sourcebook of feminist and antifeminist documents emphasizes women's political and legal rights.

Gerda Lerner, ed. *Black Women in White America: A Documentary History.* New York: Vintage, 1992. An important anthology of historical documents by African-American women that includes their activities in and opinions on different facets of the women's rights movement.

Gerda Lerner, ed. *The Female Experience: An American Documentary.* Indianapolis: Bobbs-Merrill, 1977. This collection highlights women's writings on many aspects—both traditional and nontraditional—of the female life cycle.

Bert James Loewenberg and Ruth Bogin, eds. *Black Women in Nineteenth-Century American Life: Their Words, Their Thoughts, Their Feelings.* University Park: Pennsylvania State University Press, 1976. A collection of primary sources that reveal the experiences of women who struggled with issues of sexism and racism in their own lives.

Shirley Wilson Logan, ed. *With Pen and Voice: A Critical Anthology of Nineteenth Century African-American Women.* Carbondale: Southern Illinois University Press, 1995. A compilation of speeches by seven nineteenth-century African Americans who were among the first women to speak publicly about feminist issues and race relations.

Ferdinand Lundberg and Marynia F. Farnham. *Modern Woman: The Lost Sex.* New York: Harper and Brothers, 1947. This psychological study of American women in the mid–twentieth century argues against feminism and in favor of women's fulfillment through traditional roles.

Wendy Martin, ed. *The American Sisterhood: Writings of the Feminist Movement from Colonial Times to the Present.* New York: Harper and Row, 1972. A collection of primary sources that examine women's political, legal, economic, and social status throughout American history.

Kate Millett. *Sexual Politics*. Garden City, NY: Doubleday, 1970. An expansive discussion of the women's liberation movement's contention that Western society is inherently sexist.

Beth Millstein and Jeanne Bodin, eds. *We, the American Women: A Documentary History*. New York: Jerome S. Ozer, 1977. A documentary overview of women's political and social history in America.

Robin Morgan, ed. *Sisterhood Is Powerful: An Anthology of Writings from the Women's Liberation Movement*. New York: Random House, 1970. This collection of feminist articles from the early years of the women's liberation movement covers such topics as minority women and feminism, lesbianism, nonsexist language, and working women.

Judith Papachristou, ed. *Women Together: A History in Documents of the Women's Movement in the United States*. New York: Knopf, 1976. This thorough compilation contains documents on various aspects of feminism from the 1830s to the 1970s.

Lana Rakow and Cheris Kramarae, eds. *The Revolution in Words: Righting Women, 1868–1871*. New York: Routledge, 1990. A collection of articles first printed in the *Revolution*, a feminist periodical edited by Elizabeth Cady Stanton, Susan B. Anthony, and Parker Pillsbury.

Alice S. Rossi, ed. *The Feminist Papers: From Adams to de Beauvoir*. New York: Columbia University Press, 1973. Gathers the essential documents of the early women's rights movement, including influential British and European writings that were widely read by American feminists.

Phyllis Schlafly. *The Power of the Positive Woman*. New Rochelle, NY: Arlington House, 1977. Presents a devastating critique of modern feminism and argues against such feminist causes as abortion rights and the Equal Rights Amendment.

Miriam Schneir, ed. *Feminism: The Essential Historical Writings*. New York: Random House, 1972. A comprehensive sourcebook that contains American, British, and European feminist documents from the eighteenth century to the post–World War I era.

Elizabeth Cady Stanton, Susan B. Anthony, et al., eds. *History of Woman Suffrage*. Vol. 1. New York: Fowler & Wells, 1881; Vols. 2 and 3. Rochester, NY: Charles Mann, 1881 and 1886; Vol. 4. Indianapolis: Hollenbeck Press, 1902; Vols. 5 and 6. New York: Little and Ives, 1922. An exhaustive collection of documents from the beginnings of the women's rights movement through the ratification of the Nineteenth Amendment.

Nancy Woloch. *Early American Women: A Documentary History, 1600–1900*. Belmont, CA: Wadsworth, 1992. Includes both feminist and antifeminist arguments on a wide variety of women's rights issues.

Index

abolitionist movement, 118
  influence on South
    encourages change, 43-45
    promotes intransigence, 37, 38
  opposition to, 72
  split by Fifteenth Amendment
    debate, 115-16
  successes of, 86, 113
  women's participation in, 34, 55
    is wrong, 37-38
abortion
  illegal, 170, 171
  is necessary for women's health, 175,
    178, 179-80
  is woman's right, 175
  mothers' feelings after, 171, 181
  should be legal, 170-75
    con, 176-82
  for unwed mothers, 180
    need for, 171, 174
    shame of, 181-82
  violates child's right to life, 178-79
  violates sanctity of life, 178, 182
    con, 171, 172-73
  will be used against African
    Americans, 180
    con, 172
  women's need for, 173-74
Abortion (Lader), 175
Adams, Abigail Smith, 26, 28, 30
Adams, John, 26, 28, 30, 32
Addams, Jane, 221
Adolescence (Hall), 124, 129
adoption, 174, 181
African Americans, 31
  attitude toward birth control, 172,
    180
  enslavement of, 60, 72
  need legal abortion, 172, 174
    con, 180
  plight of similar to women's plight,
    60, 79-80, 85, 188
    con, 110
  voting rights for, 146, 218, 219
    must be supported, 108-13
    should include women, 116-18
  see also abolitionist movement
American Anti-Slavery Society, 70, 232
American Law Institute (ALI), 179,
  180
American Woman Suffrage
  Association, 132, 218

Andrews, Stephen Pearl, 218
Anthony, Susan B., 115, 216, 217, 222,
  234, 238
antislavery movement. *See* abolitionist
  movement
Anti-Suffrage: Ten Good Reasons
  (Goodwin), 145
Aries, Phillipe, 230
Australia, 134

Beecher, Catharine E., 34, 39
Beecher, Henry Ward, 218
Bellows, Henry W., 65
Bible
  justifies women's public activism,
    41, 44
    con, 37-38
birth control, 152
  cannot help African Americans, 180
    con, 172
  is essential to women's freedom,
    153-54
  must be primarily woman's
    responsibility, 155-56
  as privacy right for married couples,
    178
bisexuality, 192-94
Bissell, Emily P., 140
Black Panther, 180
Blackwell, Antoinette Brown, 98, 232
Blackwell, Henry, 95
Blocker, Jack S., 231
Bloomer, Amelia, 75, 77
bloomers, 75, 81, 85
Bunch, Charlotte, 193

careers, for women. *See* work, by
  women
Catt, Carrie Chapman, 137
child labor laws, 225, 226
children
  benefit from stay-at-home moms,
    163-64
  public policies harm, 154
  should be wanted, 175
  state's interest in
    promoting bearing of, 149, 150-51
    protecting lives of, 178-79
  suffer from working moms, 143, 144
  of unhappy marriages, 57, 90, 93
  women must choose whether to
    bear, 156

Chisholm, Shirley, 172
chivalry, 78-79
Christianity, 139
  encourages activism, 43
  Stanton's view of, 223
  on women's roles
    allows public action, 40, 41
    limits to gentle influencer, 35-37
Civil Rights Act (1964), 204
Civil War, American, 108, 132, 214,
  218, 219
Claflin, Tennessee Celeste, 217-18
Clarke, Edward H., 122, 127, 128
clothing, women's
  bloomers, 75, 81, 85
  deforms the body, 80
  explains women's oppression, 75-82
    con, 83-87
  imprisons women, 77-78, 130, 214
  less restrictive
    public reaction to, 83, 85
    would destroy myths about
      women's inferiority, 78-79
      con, 86
  miniskirts, 194
Colorado, 133, 134-35, 136, 137, 138,
  146
Colton, Jennifer, 160
Comstock Act (1873), 219
Conference on Abortion and Human
  Rights (1966), 174
Constitution, U.S.
  Amendments to
    Fourteenth, 108, 116, 198, 232
    Fifteenth
      women should support, 108-13
      con, 114-18
    Nineteenth, 198, 226
    proposed
      Child Labor Amendment, 225
      Equal Rights Amendment,
        225-26
        is needed, 197-201
        would be harmful, 202-208
    assumed "person" meant "male,"
      232
Council on the Status of Women, 208

Deakin, Alfred, 134
Declaration of Independence, 30, 66,
  73, 216
Declaration of Sentiments (1848), 68,
  70, 71, 73, 216-17
Democratic Party, 114
Dew, Thomas R., 49
divorce
  increase in, 144, 150
  laws

harm women, 73
  liberalization of
    is needed, 88-97
      con, 98-107
    would encourage marital
      breakups, 104-105
  unnecessary if women had equal
    rights, 106
Douglass, Frederick, 110
dress. See clothing, women's
Drinan, Robert F., 176
DuBois, Ellen Carol, 228

education
  decline in, 50
  group vs. individual, 49
  policy, 134-35
  should be different for boys and
    girls, 123-25
  for women
    college, 199-200
    has been denied, 73
    hurts reproductive function,
      125-26
    is harmful, 122-26
      con, 127-31
    must recess during menstrual
      period, 126
    should teach motherhood, 124
Equal Rights Amendment
  is needed, 197-201
  origins of, 225-26
  would be harmful, 202-208
Equal Rights Association, 115-16, 118
Essay on Slavery and Abolitionism, An
  (Beecher), 34, 39
Fair Labor Standards Act, 199
family
  as agent of women's oppression,
    229, 230, 233
  bad marriages harm, 93
  declining position of, 52-53
  distinction from society, 230-31
  effect of suffrage on, 235-36
  God's intent in establishing, 47, 53
  importance of, 52, 148, 151
  influence of, 51, 53
  men who abuse, 56-58, 93
  size
    women should be able to limit,
      152-56
      con, 147-51
  women must act outside of, 59,
    166-67
  women's role in
    allows exercise of female talents,
      51-52
    differs from men's, 149

duty to create and raise, 150-51
excludes outside work, 143, 144,
163-64
con, 168-69
as prime responsibility, 47, 50-51,
143
see also roles, gender
Farnham, Marynia F., 162
Female Anti-Slavery Society, 39
Feminine Mystique, The (Friedan), 165
feminists
activism of, in social reforms, 220
class issues, 220-21, 225-26
defined, 212-13
must be lesbians, 187, 189
con, 191-92, 194-96
should not be according to sexual
relations, 193-94
as women who defy gender roles,
191
lesbian, 184, 185, 187, 189, 191-92,
194-96
nineteenth-century
conservatism of, 219-20
on housework, 232
radicalism of, 229
see also suffrage movement;
women's rights movement
Fifteenth Amendment
language of, 109, 116
purpose of
to extend franchise, 110
to help Republican Party, 114, 116
women should support, 108-13
con, 114-18
Fourteenth Amendment, 108, 116, 198,
232
Freedman, Blanch, 206
Friedan, Betty, 165
Fuller, Margaret, 54, 57

Gage, Frances D., 83, 112
Garrison, William Lloyd, 70
gay rights movement, 192-93
see also lesbians
General Association of Massachusetts
Congregational Churches, 36
General Federation of Women's Clubs,
223, 224, 225
Geyer, Georgie Anne, 205
Gilman, Charlotte Perkins, 220, 224,
237-38
Goodwin, Alice Duffield, 145
Graves, A. J., 46
Grenfell, Helen L., 134-35, 138
Griffiths, Martha, 203-204
Grimké, Angelina Emily, 39

Grimké, Sarah M., 215-16
Griswold v. Connecticut, 178, 179

Hall, G. Stanley, 124, 129
Harvard College, 122
health, 175, 180, 181
Heckler, Margaret M., 197
Henrie, William, 174
Herbert, Elizabeth Boynton, 221
Hilgers, Thomas W., 178
homemakers, 143, 163-64
see also family; work, by women
Howe, Julia Ward, 132, 222
Hyson, Brenda, 180

Idaho, 135, 136
*Ideas of the Woman Suffrage Movement,
The* (Kraditor), 216
immigrants, 109, 110, 142, 146

Jacobi, Mary Putnam, 233, 236
Johnston, Jill, 187
jury duty, 145

Key, Ellen, 223
Koedt, Anne, 190
Kraditor, Aileen, 216, 229

Lader, Lawrence, 175
Lasch, Christopher, 215
law
abortion, 170, 171, 172-73, 174, 176,
182
divorce, 91, 96
should be liberalized, 88-97
con, 98-107
marriage, 95, 100, 102
must respect individual rights, 90-91
League of Women Voters, 224-25
Lerner, Gerda, 230
Lesbian Nation: The Feminist Solution
(Johnston), 187
lesbians
are only true feminists, 187, 189
con, 191-92, 194-96
attitude toward bisexuality, 192-94
challenge heterosexual women,
186-87, 193
have rejected traditional sex role,
184, 185
not necessarily, 195-96
Letters to Catharine E. Beecher (Grimké),
39
Lewis, A. Lawrence, 136
Lindsay, Judge, 134, 136-37, 138
Lister, Mrs. A. Watson, 134
Long, Margaret, 133

Lundberg, Ferdinand, 162
Lusk, Hugh, 138-39

Mahan, Asa, 68, 70
Mannes, Marya, 170
marriage
affects men and women equally, 101
con, 94, 96
and feminism, 194-95
harms women, 73, 94
men's control of, 97
must be permanent, 99, 100-101,
102-103
radical nineteenth-century ideas of,
217-18
resolutions regarding, 89-90, 99-100
right to privacy in, 179
and separation, 95-96, 100
should be delayed, 105-106
should be viewed as contract, 92, 97
con, 102-103, 105
suffrage movement's effect on, 236
unhappy
harms family life, 93
not made by God, 94-95
women must work to redeem, 102,
103-104
women must maintain
independence in, 101-102, 106-107
see also divorce; family
Martineau, Harriet, 215
Maternal Associations, 53
McDaniel, Naomi, 207
Mecklenburg, Marjory, 178
men
cannot fairly represent women's
interests, 58-60
guilt felt by, 72
have intentionally oppressed
women, 70-74
con, 65-69
to feel superior, 71
opposition to abortion, 172
physical strength of, 49, 67, 203
relations with women
abusive, 56-57, 93
women should work to redeem,
103-104
as enslaving to women, 58
love, 69
women's influence over, 31, 36-37
roles of
as breadwinner, 149
in public sphere, 49, 143-44
as tyrants, 27
should grant women more rights,
26-29

con, 30-33
ways of gaining influence, 36, 40
women must be viewed as equal to,
78-79, 81-82, 223
Miller, Elizabeth Smith, 75
Milton, John, 89
Modern Woman: The Lost Sex
(Lundberg & Farnham), 162
Mormons 146, 217
motherhood
can be combined with career, 169
con, 143
duties of, 102, 149-51
hazards of emphasizing, 221-23
importance of, 53, 97
must be voluntary, 154, 156
women should be educated for, 124
see also children; family
Mott, Lucretia, 85, 225
Mullen, W. E., 137

National American Woman Suffrage
Association, 136, 137, 157
National Birth Control League, 152
National Council of Negro Women,
207
National Organization for Women,
166
National Woman's Suffrage
Association (NWSA), 218, 224-25
Native Americans, 31, 59
Negroes. See African Americans
New York Herald, 85
New York State Association Opposed
to Woman Suffrage, 140
New York Women's Trade Union
League, 206
New Zealand, 133, 138-39
Nineteenth Amendment, 198, 226
Noble, Jean, 207
Noyes, John Humphrey, 217, 219

O'Neill, William L., 212, 229
organizations
distract people from God's will,
48-50
growing influence of, 48-49, 215
overpopulation, 173

Paine, Thomas, 31
Phelps, Elizabeth Stuart, 127
Phillips, Wendell, 101, 108, 117, 118
physicians
errors made by, 128-29
who provide abortions, 174, 177
women, 129-30
Pickens, Francis W., 44

Pillsbury, Parker, 114
Planned Parenthood, 152, 173
politics, 236
 affects women and children, 154
 distinction from personal life, 191,
  194-95
 women are too busy for, 146
 see also suffrage movement
Power of the Positive Woman, The
 (Schlafly), 202
Preston, William Campbell, 43-44
property ownership
 barred to women
  and divorce, 106
  is unjust, 56-57, 73
 as qualification for voting, 33
Purvis, Robert, 117

Quakers, 39, 59
Quest: A Feminist Quarterly, 193

race-suicide, 151, 154
Radcliffe College, 122
Radicalesbians, 183, 194
Rauschenbush, Walter, 223
reform, public, 220
 is piecemeal
  due to bad compromises, 117-18
  by necessity, 111-12, 113
 women should act for, 39-45, 59
  con, 34-38
 see also suffrage movement;
  temperance movement
Republican Party
 betrayal of abolitionists, 118
 founding of, 117
 support for Fifteenth Amendment,
  114, 116
Revolution, American, 26, 27, 30, 31
Riordan, Gayle, 178
Roberts, Mary Helen, 205
Roe v. Wade (1973), 170, 176
roles, gender
 Christian teachings on, 35-37, 40, 41
 female, 191, 196, 213-14
  boredom of causes illness, 130-31
  definition of
   by men, 187-88
   should not be in terms of sex
    partner, 193-94
  and exclusion from public sphere,
   232
  family is primary to, 47, 50-51, 143,
   150-51
  as helpmeet and homemaker,
   149-50
  is subordinate

 due to nature, 35, 67
 due to unfair laws, 85-86
 women's cooperation with,
  77-81, 82, 107
 leads to self-hatred, 188-89
 rejection of
  by heterosexual women, 191,
   194-95
  by lesbians, 184-85
 as sexual object, 185-86
 male, 27, 49, 143-44, 149
Roosevelt, Theodore, 147, 224
Rose, Ernestine, 68, 70, 71, 74
Russell, G. W., 138

Sanger, Margaret, 152
Schlafly, Phyllis, 202, 204
Second Continental Congress
 (1775–1776), 26-27, 30
Sex in Education (Clarke), 122, 127, 128
sexuality, 194
 and abortion, 174-75, 181
 bisexuality, 192-94
 lesbian, 186-87, 195-96
 radical nineteenth-century ideas of,
  217-18, 219
 used to define women, 185-86,
  187-88, 192, 194
Shakers, 217
Shaw, Anna Howard, 154
Sheppard, Mrs. K. A., 133
Sinclair, Andrew, 221
slavery. *See* abolitionist movement
Smith, Daniel Scott, 229
Smith, Elizabeth Oakes, 106
Smith, Gerrit, 75, 83, 84
Smith-Rosenberg, Carroll, 229
social security, 198
Stanton, Elizabeth Cady, 75, 76, 91, 98,
 115, 216
 radical ideas of, 232, 233
 on Christianity, 223
 on divorce, 88, 220
 on marriage and family, 217, 236
 "Solitude of Self" speech, 234-35
Stearns, Jonathan F., 51
Stewart, Maria, 44
Stone, Lucy, 85, 95
Stop ERA, 202
suffrage. *See* vote, right to
suffrage movement
 class issue in, 220-21
 demand for women's citizenship,
  233, 235
 differences with temperance
  crusaders, 231, 237
 opposition to, 235-36

political organizing of, 236
shift to conservatism, 213, 219,
223-24
elevation of motherhood, 221-23
success of
brought women into public
sphere, 230-34, 237-38
did not help feminism, 224-25,
226
was radical, 228-38
con, 212-27
only in early period, 216-19
see also feminists
Sullivan, James, 30

Taylor, William R., 215
teachers, women, 135
temperance movement, 113, 216
differences with suffragists, 231, 237
failures of, 221-22
mass appeal of, 236-37
successes of, 86
Thomas, M. Carey, 129
Thomas, Mary F., 80
Thompson, Vance, 149

Unbought and Unbossed (Chisholm),
172
United States
discriminatory policies against
women, 199
should use women's talents, 201
slavery betrays ideals of, 55
Utah, 135, 146

vote, right to
based on property ownership, 33
cannot be denied to the ignorant,
111, 144
denied to foreigners, 109, 110
extended to African Americans, 109,
110, 112, 113
extended to women
effect on family life, 235-36
is beneficial, 138-39
is harmful, 142-44
improves election process, 138
con, 145-46
male oppression prevents, 73
reasons against, 140-46
enfranchises corrupt women, 145
enfranchises ignorant women,
146
female delicacy, 32
harms national interests, 144-46
too burdensome, 141-42, 145
violates nature, 141

women do not want, 146
reasons for, 132-39
improves laws
on education, 134-35, 138
on public vices, 135-36
improves quality of candidate
nominations, 136-37
increases dignity, 133-34
increases interest in public
affairs, 137
is a right, 137
after Revolutionary War, 32-33
should be part of Fifteenth
Amendment, 115-18
won on state-by-state basis, 113
and right of petition, 38, 45
see also Fifteenth Amendment;
suffrage movement

wage differences, between men and
women
due to discrimination, 199
due to women's home duties, 143
in teaching, 135
see also work, by women
Warren, Mercy Otis, 26, 27
Washington state, 205
Welter, Barbara, 214
Willard, Frances, 221-22, 237
Woman (Thompson), 149
Woman and the New Race (Sanger), 152
Woman in America (Graves), 46
Woman in the Nineteenth Century
(Fuller), 54
Woman's Advocate, 112
Woman's Party, 225
Woman's Rights Convention
First, 73, 88, 216-17
Second, 65, 66-67
Fourth, 68, 70
Tenth, 88, 98, 101
New York City's, 85
skepticism about, 81
women
abused by husbands, 56-58, 93,
103-104
domestic sphere of, 214, 230-231
allows exercise of varied talents,
51-52
is fulfilling, 46-53
is primary responsibility, 47,
143-44
is restrictive, 54-61
suffragists' challenge to, 232-33,
237-38
women must act outside of, 59,
106-107

exclusion from public sphere, 232
freedom for, 60-61
  requires birth control, 153-56
  requires legal abortion, 172, 175
influence over men, 31
  gained by being gentle, 36-37, 49,
    53
  as repugnant belief, 40-43
oppression of
  female role in, 68, 77-81, 82
  is not ill-intentioned, 65-68
  men are responsible for, 70-74
position of
  is privileged, 51
    precariousness of, 76
    women do not desire, 55
  should be active and purposeful,
    106-107, 168-69
poverty among caused by
  men taking earnings, 85
  not working, 79-81
rebellion by
  is possible, 27, 44
  is silly, 29, 31
in religion, 73, 214
  can be leaders, 40, 41, 44
  should play quiet role, 36, 17
should act for public reform, 39-45,
  59
  con, 34-38
should have legal rights, 26-29, 44,
  58
  con, 30-33
views of
  as delicate, 32
    con, 81, 107
  as equal to men, 78-79, 81-82, 89
  need reexamination, 67-69
  Victorian, 213-15, 221, 223
  see also roles, gender; work, by
    women
Women of Industry, 207
Women's Christian Temperance
  Union (WCTU)
  conservatism of, 221-22, 223, 224
  mass appeal of, 236-37
Women's Joint Congressional
  Committee, 225
women's rights movement
  antislavery movement antecedent
    of, 34
  and class issues, 220-21, 225-26
  compromises made by, 216
  divisions in

after Civil War, 218-19
over lesbianism, 183, 190
during 1920s, 225
turn-of-the-century, 212-13
hostile reaction to, 72-73, 74, 113, 216
lesbians in, 183, 190
  are only true feminists, 187, 189
  con, 191-92, 194-96
  straight women can ally with, 193
  straight women's
    uncomfortableness with, 186
program of
  must reform women first, 79-80
  should not judge women's
    personal lives, 194-96
  should not try to reform men, 189
  should reject heterosexuality,
    183-89, 193
    con, 190-96
  will fail, 76
    con, 84, 86-87
and women's clothing
  as imprisoning, 77-78, 79
  as unimportant, 84-86, 194
  see also suffrage movement
Woodhull, Victoria, 217-19
work, by women, 85
  benefits of, 129-30, 161-63
    fulfilling, 165-69
    improves marriage, 168
    improves self-image, 169
  discrimination against, 198-99
  guilt caused by, 161, 168
  harms of, 160-64
    family life suffers, 143, 144, 163-64
    masculinizing effect, 162
    as heads of households, 198
  in home is most important, 47, 50-51,
    143
  labor legislation on
    early disputes over, 225-26
    ERA will eliminate, 204-205
    need for, 203, 206, 207
  must be creative and challenging,
    166-67
  office vs. factory, 205-206
  physical jobs
    harms of, 206-207
    men can do better, 203, 207, 208
  shows women's strength, 59,
    129-30, 214
World Health Organization, 175
World War II, 160, 206
Wyoming, 135, 136, 137, 138